A LITERARY SYMBIOSIS

Contributions to the Study of Science Fiction and Fantasy

Series Editor: Marshall Tymn

The Mechanical God: Machines in Science Fiction
Thomas P. Dunn and Richard D. Erlich, editors

Comic Tones in Science Fiction: The Art of Compromise with Nature
Donald M. Hassler

Formula Fiction? An Anatomy of American Science Fiction, 1930–1940
Frank Cioffi

H. P. Lovecraft: A Critical Study
Donald R. Burleson

A LITERARY SYMBIOSIS

Science Fiction/Fantasy Mystery

HAZEL BEASLEY PIERCE

CONTRIBUTIONS TO THE STUDY OF SCIENCE FICTION
AND FANTASY, NUMBER 6

GREENWOOD PRESS
WESTPORT, CONNECTICUT · LONDON, ENGLAND

Library of Congress Cataloging in Publication Data

Pierce, Hazel.
  A literary symbiosis.

  (Contributions to the study of science fiction and
fantasy, ISSN 0193-6875 ; no. 6)
  Bibliography: p.
  Includes index.
  1. Science fiction—History and criticism. 2. Detec-
tive and mystery stories—History and criticism.
I. Title. II. Series.
PN3433.6.P54 1983   809.3'876   83-1710
ISBN 0-313-23065-X (lib. bdg.)

Library of Congress Catalog Card Number: 83-1710
ISBN: 0-313-23065-X
ISSN: 0193-6875

First published in 1983

Greenwood Press
A division of Congressional Information Service, Inc.
88 Post Road West
Westport, Connecticut 06881

Printed in the United States of America

10 9 8 7 6 5 4 3 2 1

To
Frank H. Beasley
and
Arthur J. Pierce

CONTENTS

viii   *Contents*

PART IV: The Science Fiction/Fantasy Gothic Mystery

ACKNOWLEDGMENTS

I wish to acknowledge the aid given for this project by the Kearney State College Faculty Research Services Council, the generous assistance of Mrs. Anita Norman and Mrs. Gloria Graham of the Kearney State College Library staff, and the collegial support of the Kearney State College English Department. I am grateful to Robert Mittan and Martha Pierce who contributed their typing skills to preparation of the manuscript, and to the members of my family who supported the effort with their tolerance and interest. Very special thanks are due to Dr. Helen Stauffer for her professional advice and encouragement and to Arthur J. Pierce for his practical editorial assistance and moral support.

INTRODUCTION: PARTNERS AS INDIVIDUALS

"It's a Bird! It's a Plane! It's a Superman!" This oft-paraphrased sequence of sentences from a title of a 1950s musical has become so familiar that many people have forgotten the genesis of the Superman character in the 1938 comic strip or its earlier inspiration, Philip Wylie's *Gladiator* (1930). As they evoke the image of a be-caped, muscular man marked with the *S* emblem on his chest, the sentences also celebrate the universal need to identify, categorize, or pigeonhole human experiences according to known criteria. If an object flies, it must be a bird or a plane; to accept a man flying with no artificial means of support requires imagination and a high degree of tolerance.

Classification rests upon time-honored tradition, as witness Aristotle's laws of identity (A equals A), exclusion (X is either A or B), and contradiction (X cannot be both A and B). At times some persons have over-simplified or failed to test these equations against contemporary reality. In some instances ethical judgment has changed the original intentions of the philosopher and substituted A equals *good*, thereby conveying a subtle rebuff to B or X. Fiction is not immune from this need to establish identities and assign value. In the war of classification a small battle swirls around the terms *mainstream* and *popular*. Within the battle minor skirmishes occur as aficionados of the various popular narrative styles stake out claims for westerns, romances, science fiction, fantasy, mysteries, adventure stories, spy thrillers, and so on. They seek special identity by employing definitions, listing conventions, or establishing confining rules for each form.

A thoughtful reader, therefore, recognizes and makes the requisite adjustment in those situations wherein two modes merge or cross over the formal lines.

With this in mind we can turn with interest to the more practical implications of a literary symbiotic relationship such as we find in science fiction/fantasy mystery fictions. Biologists will remind us that symbiosis, while signifying a close relationship, also admits a possibility that the relationship may not necessarily benefit one or both of the partners. In fact, some novels attempting a merging of two modes may succeed more in producing antibiosis, a state in which one partner suffers from the effort. Before arriving at any evaluation of success for specific science fiction/fantasy mystery novels, we must consider three major factors. First, it is well to consider each mode separately, establishing its identity and unique qualities. Then we must determine what common ground, if any, they share. And finally, we must ask the important question: what differences must be reconciled in order for the symbiotic relationship to flourish?

The history of the host mode, science fiction/fantasy, records a continuous effort at definition. Both practitioners and readers feel a need to foster recognition of the uniqueness of the mode and establish its right to exist as a legitimate member of the literary community despite a quondam association with the pulp magazines. Naming is one obvious avenue toward the first goal. Some terms applied to early work now sheltered under the science fiction/fantasy umbrella focused on purpose. Mary Shelley's *Frankenstein* (1818) still retains some of its early reputation as a Gothic horror story, while Karel Čapek's *R. U. R.* (1921) was lauded as social satire. Critic Sam Moskowitz in a 1957 essay, "How Science Fiction Got Its Name," refers to work by Jules Verne as "scientific speculative adventure." [1] Descriptive labels applied to the novels of H. G. Wells have included "scientific" fantasy and scientific romance, the quotation marks in the former indicating a questionable use of science and the word *romance* in the latter denoting extravagance and a lack of realism. Wells himself called *The Time Machine* (1895) "my first scientific fantasia." [2]

In the early 1920s editor Hugo Gernsback adopted the term *scientific fiction* to describe the stories included in *Science and Invention*, even billing the August 1923 issue of that magazine as the "Scientific Fiction Number." Later on Gernsback planned a new magazine to be called *Scientifiction*, a name which did not catch the public fancy.

Both labels were soon supplanted by the more manageable and direct *science fiction*, a term readers came to associate with both the physical sciences and their engineering or technological extensions. These extensions in turn spawned the rather melodramatic *space opera* to denote technological adventure stories bordering on fantasy. Many science fiction readers and writers argue for a sharp division between their product and fantasy. William L. Godshalk, in "Alfred Bester: Science Fiction or Fantasy?" (*Extrapolation*, May 1975), offers an ingenuous system of categorization based on the initial premise that science fiction is a branch of fantasy. He divides fantasy into (1) pure fantasy; (2) philosophic fantasy; (3) critical fantasy; and (4) realistic fantasy. Then he admits science fiction into the fourth category. However, if we admit the critical faculty and the philosophical effort as part of the sum total of human knowledge (*scientia*), all but the first category may well be subsumed by the single term *science fantasy* or by one with more specific denotation, *science fiction/fantasy*.

The mid-twentieth century brought increasing public interest in psychology, sociology, anthropology, linguistics, and similar disciplines dealing more directly with the human phenomenon than with physical or technological phenomena. Writers of science fiction/fantasy responded by incorporating these "soft sciences" into their work. Predictably, additional descriptive labels have come forth to reflect this expanded scope of science: futuristic fiction, extrapolative fiction, speculative fiction. As yet, no one of these has warranted primary acceptance, although all are useful, particularly in critical studies of the genre.

Along with labeling goes expanded definition. Much ink has been spilled in the attempt to fit science fiction into a compact description. Gernsback in explaining his term *scientifiction* allied it with the stories of Verne, Wells, and Poe as "charming romance intermingled with scientific fact and prophetic vision."[3] In his Introduction to *Explorers of the Infinite* (1963), Sam Moskowitz recognized science fiction as "a branch of fantasy" which aids the reader by "utilizing an atmosphere of scientific credibility for its imaginative speculations in physical science, space, time, social science, and philosophy."[4] More concisely, Lester del Rey called science fiction "the myth-making principle of human nature today."[5] Brian Aldiss offered both a philosophical task and a formal conclusion as he defined science fiction as "the search for a definition of man and his status in the universe which will stand in our advanced but confused state of knowledge (science), and is characteristically cast in the Gothic or post-Gothic mould.''[6] Like Moskowitz, Aldiss accepts the close relationship of science fiction with science fantasy or fantasy in general. It is obvious from this sampling of definitions that there are points of agreement but no one unified view.

Despite their differences it is informative to explore the implications of some of the terms used in the sampling. Imaginative speculation, myth-making principle, prophetic vision, search for man's place in the universe—these carry complex connotations. ''Myth-making principle'' and ''prophetic vision'' place science fiction/fantasy in a long and august metaphysical tradition, while ''search for man's place in the universe'' evokes centuries of philosophical effort. ''Charming romance'' we may apply with impunity to tales of fantasy throughout the years. However, as science fiction, all must work from hard facts and systematized knowledge firmly based in the contemporary world to science in the broad sense of *scientia*. They will find concrete embodiment in conventions and themes we have come to expect in science fiction/fantasy: space travel; alien contact and distant worlds; parallel or alternate worlds; utopias and dystopias; robots and their many homeostatic offspring; time travel; hard science and its technology; soft science and its body of findings. Scientific fact and scientific credibility allow myth, fantasy, philosophy, and metaphysics to join their speculative and imaginative strength to the world of reason.

Science fiction/fantasy is idea-based. It asks a question: how will human beings respond to a situation *if* thus and so should happen? The narrative serves the answer, clothing it in technological, sociological, psychological, or futurological detail. Note that these terms all end in *logical*. Science fiction/fantasy demands logical development of the idea within the established parameters. Hard science fiction, based on fact or accepted premise, can extend the fact or premise into a future when technology could conceivably turn fact into machinery and premise could evolve into a real situation. Such logical developments allow authors to describe in detail space ships, posit sentient beings on far planets or moons, work out detailed future societies with the almost certain interplanetary politics and social problems. Such concrete embodiments Brian Stableford has called ''ideative flourishes.''[7] Despite the pejorative connotation of the word *flourishes*, the setting and background of well-written and well-plotted space adventures do grow logically out of the contemporary experience.

Science fiction/fantasy based in the soft sciences often proves more accessible to a general reader. Whether the author uses an alternate, parallel, or future world extrapolated from present time, he makes social comment or delivers psychological prophecy. When developed along the logical lines demanded by the original fact or premise, the society may be utopic, dystopic, or a slightly distorted image of current life, distorted just enough to jolt recognition of the irony or satire directed against the contemporary world. "What if the Axis had won World War II?" asks Philip K. Dick's *The Man in the High Castle* (1962). The novel's answer is an irreal view of the historical world, but one in which national characteristics are recognizable, thereby inviting us to consider life under such circumstances. What if one lived in a society in which technological know-how and sorcery existed compatibly as "science"? The world of Randall Garrett's Lord Darcy, for example, alerts us to a society assigning value to arcane thought as complementary to the rational, logical modes of thought. Inner space also has lured the imagination of the writers of science fiction/fantasy. Twentieth-century questions about behavior modification, manipulation of choice by external conditioning, personality, and semantic influences on mind and behavior have found their way into modern science fiction/fantasy, demanding their own unique logic.

Futurological informs many of the plots used by science fiction/fantasy. Whether the root of the narrative is embedded in technology, sociology, psychology, or general science, the development of the narrative may extend into a time out of the here and now. Perhaps the logic of the extension provokes action in a near future, 1999 or 2099. Perhaps it operates in a far future, 20099 or more. Whatever that future may be, the responsible author gains our willing suspension of disbelief or sense of wonder by the logic of his or her extension. Wild and wonderful events may happen in space opera or sword and sorcery tales; chilling ends may be served in psychological and sociological futures. Once we accept the basic scientific premise, the logic of the extrapolation will continue to assure acceptance of the narrative, and especially its basic idea.

What of the other partner in the symbiotic relationship we consider here? What of mystery fiction? One can argue that all fiction employs mystery until the final page. After all, the author invites the reader from the beginning to read on to answer the question: how does it come out in the end? In some cases the mystery may be slight. By formula modern romances require that everything come out all right in the end and everyone live happily ever after. What mystery there is lies in the author's teasing the reader with false obstacles in the path of true happiness. The contemporary literature of exhaustion or the absurdist novels offer a mystery inherent in any situation deviating from the expected flow of events, whether this be deviation from traditional form, language patterns, ethical criteria, or human patterns of action.

But these are mystery stories only in a very loose sense of the word. What is a conventional mystery story? To ask the simple question is to elicit a simple answer: it is a story about a problem, usually originating in an act of violence, a problem which must be solved so that life may resume its even tenor. Before conventional order reasserts itself, events tend to assume a perverse life of their own, an order dictated by secrecy and intrigue. The unexpected becomes the expected; the unknown becomes the real. The unexplained or seemingly inexplicable is the norm. We must answer certain stock questions: What happened? Who is responsible for the act? (Whodunit?—to use the well-known cliché.) Why? Who can or will solve the problem?

The specific answer to the last question depends upon which variety of mystery story we speak of. Sensational literature covers the detective story, the police procedural, spy stories, thrillers, as well as the story of terror and horror commonly referred to as Gothic tales. If the problem or puzzle involves a local crime, the question finds an easy answer. Obviously the local authorities will be called in; their efforts may be aided or supplanted by a detective, either official or private, professional or amateur. When the problem spreads from the local society into the broader reaches of national or international intrigue, we often find a solution impossible. Unlike local problems, political intrigue does not wear black or white; right and wrong become relative against a backdrop of clashing social and moral criteria. In these thrillers we find spy versus counterspy; agent versus double agent; the "moles" digging underground versus the "beavers" busily constructing aboveground. The reader watches as counterforces are marshalled and put into action. The scoreboard at the end of the mystery thriller does not read win or lose but rather checkmate or stalemate. In the Gothic tale the puzzle to be solved usually arises from very personal sources: a family secret; the campaign of evil against a fragile and innocent psyche; intrigue involving supranatural forces. The solution must lie in a stronger force than the disruptive or threatening one: the force of logic and reason, a vital personality, or even à counterforce existing on the suprahuman level.

In the above forms of the mystery mode the answers to Who? and Why? usually must await the denouement, usually in the last chapter. One might argue with good reason that little real mystery exists in any of these stories, since mystery fiction runs to formula. Nonetheless, there is mystery. It lies in the details, the interplay of bits of information and misinformation, gradually being sorted out up to the moment of discovery. These activities operate untarnished by our awareness of the formula in which they are operating.

Mystery fiction obviously is situation-oriented. A character may find himself in a seemingly untenable situation. Unidentified forces menace peace of mind and even life itself. Secrecy urges fear and wonder. The rational mind, usually in the person of the detective or spy, pits itself against the unexplained, yet is ever conscious of the possibility of ultimate defeat by the irrational. In turn, a reader must deal with "a riddle wrapped in a mystery inside an enigma," if we may here adopt and apply Winston Churchill's well-known 1939 description of Russian action. While most mystery stories do resolve the problem or puzzle in favor of the rational explanation, they also celebrate the strength of the irrational part of human behavior in the person of the murderer, the thief, the terrorist, the anarchist, the Other.

When we align the basic imperatives of science fiction/fantasy and mystery fiction, one must admit some problems in merging the two. Science fiction/fantasy is idea-oriented; mystery fiction, situation-oriented. Science fiction/fantasy leans heavily on futurological speculation and extrapolation involving inner and outer space and firmly based at the starting point on scientific theory or credible scientific possibilities. Mystery fiction operates primarily in the here-and-now, occasionally in the world of the occult. The world of the detective story, the police procedural, and the spy thriller is easily recognizable from everyday experiences, direct or secondhand through the mass media. The characters of mystery fiction we may meet over the back fence, at a cocktail party, or via the television screening of the evening news. The characters of science fiction/fantasy pose a different problem. While the humans may act and talk as we do, they must deal with worlds as yet foreign to our experience, albeit becoming more familiar with each succeeding orbital flight or space walk. Some who appear human may betray our recognition, as does the grandmotherly person who in Ray

Bradbury's *Martian Chronicles* (1950) turns out to be a Martian assuming human form in an attempt to effect human demise. The perfect housemate, beautiful Helen O'Loy in Lester del Rey's 1938 short story of that title, is as yet unobtainable in stores selling androids. Despite the speed with which the space shuttle orbits our world, we have yet to wait for those special trips through hyperspace, even for the special gates which will teleport us via matter transmission from New York to Paris or London in microseconds.

These differences in the two modes appear insurmountable obstacles to anyone attempting symbiosis. Can the resultant synthesis be an acceptable piece of fiction, free of absurdities which may render the story a travesty of either form? Remarks of early science fiction/fantasy writers and editors reflected this very concern. In his introduction to *Asimov's Mysteries* (1968) Isaac Asimov recalls being told in the late 1940s that "science fiction would not play fair with the reader," [8] since the author could confuse the reader with esoteric clues and devices unknown in the reader's experience. Larry Niven in the Afterword to *The Long ARM of Gil Hamilton* (1976) reminds us again that the omnipresent *they* "said it couldn't be done." One major voice in this chorus was editor John Campbell who, according to Niven, gained "intense satisfaction" when Hal Clement proved him wrong with *Needle* in 1949. [9] In 1952 James Blish, writing as critic under the pseudonym of William Atheling, Jr., bemoaned the "leaking over into science fiction" of certain conventions of the mystery story, especially those from the private-eye stories. These conventions he rated (or rather *berated*) as "the clichés of another and now completely fossilized idiom." [10] Damon Knight, while lauding Asimov's *The Caves of Steel* (1954) for its mixture of murder and detective, referred to other efforts as "miscegenations." [11]

Such negativity may be attributable to several causes. Having served its apprenticeship in the early pulp magazines, science fiction/fantasy had acquired a devoted following of fans, or "addicts" in the view of some other readers. Many of these early fans became writers in the mode, later moving on to editorial positions and even later speaking as critics. Men such as these recognized the popular appeal of science fiction/fantasy, the pleasure it gave its fans. But they also recognized its literary weaknesses to be overcome before the mode would receive wider acclaim and acceptance. Fan-writer-critic James Blish specifically listed primary considerations: the standards of competence common to all good literature, especially technical competence in narrative practice and characterization. In addition to these basic skills he emphasized the importance of "freshness of idea, acuity of observation, depth of emotional penetration" [12] and other factors.

The Roman critic Horace in *Ars Poetica* (c. 8 B.C.) emphasized the dictum that writing should delight and instruct. Science fiction had fulfilled the first requirement for its small group of avid readers. With the late 1960s and 1970s readers began to claim the second task for their field. Following Gernsback's early strictures emphasizing the scientific base for the stories and Campbell's insistence on style and content, others began to make claims for the educative value of the mode. In a society increasingly aware of its reliance on technology and also painfully aware of the gaps in understanding of both the operation and future effect of that technology, some readers saw in science fiction/fantasy a way to gain some mental control of their machine-bound environment. Alvin Toffler in *Future Shock* (1970) went so far as to suggest that we look at science fiction not as literature but as a "kind of sociology of the future," providing an "imaginative exploration of the jungle of political, social, psychological, and ethical issues" which all, but more especially the children, would have to confront in the future. [13] Such a suggestion takes Horace very much at his word.

With such effort being directed toward honing the art of writing science fiction/fantasy and toward directing it to serious tasks such as Toffler proposes, it is small wonder there should be serious objections to drawing upon the conventions of other literary fields. One can easily understand the reluctance to consider any merit in utilizing conventions from the more established and equally popular mystery fiction. After the several decades of work to change the status of science fiction/fantasy and to improve its quality, any move to utilize the "fossilized idiom" might appear as a step backward. Priding itself on its freedom to speculate imaginatively about the future and people's place in it, science fiction/fantasy drew back temporarily from the mystery mode, at the same time encouraging the sense of wonder in its own special mysteries.

However, the two modes do have much in common. Authors who have succeeded in drawing the conventions of mystery fiction under the science fiction/fantasy themes have done so not by giving up that vaunted freedom but in exerting a disciplined freedom. Take, as one example, the common use of society with its social, political, and ethical criteria. Both modes are firmly based on human reactions to disruptions of the status quo, be it confrontation with alien mentality or criminal mentality. In the subsequent solution of the problem the narrative can sensitize a reader to analogous problems in the contemporary society. The two modes also share an interest in the logical process of the human mind, especially the mind as it focuses on details, be it to deduce answers from clues at hand or to build up a credible extrapolation from a known scientific fact. Most important, both science fiction/fantasy and mystery fictions deal with human nature in all its complexity. One strand of that complexity is people's wont to satisfy their darker side. In the freedom of planning a future world how does an author accommodate the bent toward violence, destruction, betrayal? What will constitute crime in the near or far future? How do the futuristic characters impose punishment? What system of ethics pervades human action in the process of apprehending, trying, and sentencing the disorderly members of the group? As science fiction/fantasy addresses such questions, it runs in tandem with the mystery story.

Science fiction/fantasy has suffered severe criticism on the point of weak characterization. It has answered by pointing to its idea-centered orientation. In a story of a parallel or alternate society the social imperatives take precedence over the individual; they in turn represent the body social. However, when social systems clash in principle, heads of state meet, wars are mounted, and information is needed for victory to be assured. At this point a stock figure comes into play—the spy or undercover agent, that lonely, oft-romanticized figure whose exploits save or doom the entire social group. Here science fiction/fantasy, especially the sub-mode of space opera, finds a kindred theme in spy thrillers.

Finally, apologists for science fiction/fantasy homogeneity inevitably fall back on the word *science* in the label. Science, they maintain, is what makes this mode unique. Usually this word translates into technology with the vivid and detailed descriptions of futuristic machines: machines for transportation into time and space, machines to replicate human beings, machines which produce a plethora of tools or playthings for the futuristic experience. *Science* also shelters another image—the men in a laboratory struggling to solve a small puzzle of the universe, perhaps finding a solution but effecting little or no change in the larger operation of the universe, only a small change in our awareness of it. Here we find another common ground. Since the early days of the Munsey magazines mystery fiction has opened a door to science. Primitive as they seem now, these early scientific detective stories utilized technology—the lie detector, fingerprinting materials, and other mechanical aids. The worker in the laboratory seeking a clue to a physical puzzle has his mirror image in the worker on a criminal case fitting clues together to find an answer to a social puzzle.

Mystery fiction's emphasis on situations can reinforce science fiction/fantasy's presentation of an idea. Idea-oriented fiction falls of its own weight unless buoyed by human beings interacting and then acting out ramifications of those ideas. Robert Scholes has said, "We need suspense with intellectual consequences." [14] One of the firmest points upon which we may rest the argument for the literary symbiosis of these two popular literatures rests on that need. A skillful author can use the techniques of suspense afforded by the mystery conventions to the advantage of his speculative idea. Obviously with a field as prolific as science fiction/fantasy one cannot hope to consider every example of a novel or short story using the mystery conventions to its benefit. Also, not every practitioner of such a synthesis has been completely successful. Even so, the literary symbiosis of science fiction/fantasy and mystery fiction is worth critical attention.

NOTES

1. Sam Moskowitz, *Explorers of the Infinite: Shapers of Science Fiction* (Cleveland, Ohio: World Publ. Co., 1960), p. 314.

2. H. G. Wells, *Experiment in Autobiography* (New York: Macmillan, 1934), p. 172.

3. As quoted by Moskowitz, p. 226.

4. Moskowitz, *Explorers of the Infinite*, p. 11.

5. As quoted by Thomas D. Clareson, "The Other Side of Realism," in *SF: The Other Side of Realism*, Thomas D. Clareson, ed. (Bowling Green, Ohio: Bowling Green Univ. Popular Press, 1971), p. 1.

6. Brian W. Aldiss, *Billion Year Spree* (New York: Schocken Books, 1974), p. 8.

7. Brian Stableford, "Space Opera," in *The Science Fiction Encyclopedia*, Peter Nicholls, ed. (Garden City, N.Y.: Doubleday, 1979), p. 561.

8. Isaac Asimov, *Asimov's Mysteries* (1968; rpt. New York: Dell, 1974), p. 14.

9. Larry Niven, *The Long ARM of Gil Hamilton* (New York: Ballantine, 1976), p. 177.

10. William Atheling, Jr., *The Issue at Hand* (Chicago: Advent, 1964), p. 18.

11. Damon Knight, *In Search of Wonder* (Chicago: Advent, 1967), p. 93.

12. Atheling, p. 12.

13. Alvin Toffler, *Future Shock* (New York: Bantam, 1972), p. 425.

14. Robert Scholes, *Structural Fabulation* (Notre Dame, Ind.: Univ. of Notre Dame Press, 1975), p. 41.

PART I

THE SCIENCE FICTION/FANTASY DETECTIVE STORY

CHAPTER 1

FROM POE TO THE SCIENTIFIC DETECTIVE

Before any merger takes place, the interested parties should take a careful look at the respective properties involved. Of special interest is the property being acquired by the major stockholder. Identical concerns inform a literary merger as well as a business one. In this case when science fiction decides to utilize or acquire the conventions of the detective story, it is incumbent on all interested parties to know what is acquired, how they originated, how used in the original form, and how reliable they proved to be.

With many genre or modes of literature both critics and practitioners take great pains to establish a lineage; the older and more classical the ties, the more honorific the effort in some eyes. Some historians of the detective story trace its ancestry to writings dated before the birth of Christ. Dorothy Sayers in the *Omnibus of Crime* (1929) offers four examples of primitive tales of detection: the stories of Bel and of Susanna from the Apocryphal Scriptures; King Evander's story of Hercules and Cacus from the *Aeneid*, and Herodotus' reference to King Rhampsitus in his chapter on the history of Egypt. Ellery Queen in *Queen's Quorum* (1969) adds other ancient sources: Cicero's *De Divinatione*, the *Gesta Romanorum*, tales in Boccaccio's *Decameron* and Chaucer's *Canterbury Tales*, parts of *The Arabian Nights' Entertainments*, and of the adventures of Till Eulenspiegel (Tyll Owlglass).

True, in each of these there is a deception and/or crime. In the four anthologized by Sayers theft predominates (counting theft of good name and reputation in the story of Susanna and the elders). Cicero concerns himself with arrogant, high-handed theft as exercised by the governor Verres; in his speech he presents the legal procedure of amassing facts, evidence, and witnesses, all model procedure for contemporary detective work. The tales from the *Decameron* and *Canterbury Tales* contain examples of deception, theft, murder, and crimes against the social mores of the time. Many subordinate characteristics of the different works here mentioned do foreshadow techniques now used as standard conventions in contemporary tales of detection: disguise, false witness, false clues, locked rooms, analysis, and disposal of the criminal by rational methods.

However, the anecdotes or complete stories included in the above group exist for purposes other than highlighting the detection process. In the stories of Bel and Susanna, Daniel does study the clues, analyze the situations, and uncover and rectify the misdeeds, but in the context of the original pieces the emphasis falls on the moral actions of Daniel in correction of the false beliefs. Herodotus proposes to record history; Cicero speaks as the champion of honest administration. The storytellers of the *Decameron* are less interested in the process of detection than in entertaining their listeners with vicarious thrills or amorous intrigue. In some of these early examples the culprit gains honor, as does the thief of the treasure of King Rhampsitus have honor accorded to him by the King himself for the thief's bold ingenuity in outwitting all of the official traps set for him. Rhampsitus' thief may better serve as a progenitor for a later *picaro* or the more modern Raffles of mystery fiction than as the criminal in a drama of detection.

Other historians make more modest claims of lineage. "The Haycraft-Queen Definitive Library of Detective-Crime-Mystery Fiction," a list purporting to cover the "cornerstones" of the mode from 1748– 1948, characterizes Voltaire's *Zadig* (1748), the *Mémoires de Vidocq* (1828–29), and Edgar Allan Poe as great grandfather, grandfather, and father respectively of the modern detective story. Julian Symons in *Mortal Consequences* (1972), while acknowledging the earlier possibilities, does give space to *Zadig*, then goes on to nominate William Godwin's *Caleb Williams* (1794) as a solid contender for initiator of the general mode of crime literature, followed by Vidocq and Edgar Allan Poe as later major influences.

The claim made for *Zadig* rests upon two brief experiences of the hero as related in chapter 3. Zadig, a young Babylonian gentleman, while walking in a wood one day is approached by a party of the

Queen's eunuchs and other officials of the court; they inquire whether he has seen the Queen's dog. He disclaims having seen the dog, although he had accurately described it as a spaniel bitch, a small dog with long ears and a lame foot, one which had newly whelped. A few minutes later another official search party comes upon Zadig, inquiring of him whether he has seen the King's horse. Again disclaiming actual sight of the animal he describes its physical appearance and its accouterments in such detail as to cast grave suspicion upon himself. Accused of the theft, Zadig stands before a magistrate to receive a sentence of a beating and subsequent exile. Before execution of the sentence, the two animals are found, thus assuring Zadig's freedom. The magistrate demands explanation for Zadig's detailed description of both animals. Point by point, Zadig spells out his close observations of traces in the sand, impressions on the ground, disarrangement of dust on the leaves, marks on stones, all which gave him clues to their appearance. The explanation shows a keen mind operating on a problem demanding powers of deduction. Excellent as the episode is in exemplifying deductive reasoning, it represents but a minor part of the novel and serves more to alert a reader to the social injustices of the time and the arbitrary nature of human existence.

Caleb Williams serves a similar purpose. In the 1794 preface (withdrawn in the original edition because of possible inflammatory consequences) William Godwin proposed his story as "a study and delineation of things passing in the moral world . . . a general review of the modes of domestic and unrecorded despotism, by which man becomes the destroyer of man." [1] Despite the avowed moral and social purpose, Godwin's novel can better be read today as a mystery story, a notable ancestor of modern detective-crime literature. It contains two major crimes plus the possibility for a third: a murder; a coldly plotted miscarriage of justice; and the insane chase and harassment with intent to destroy the title character. It has a "detective," although in 1794 that label had yet to be invented for this special use.

Caleb acts as detective at two different times. At first he merely collects data to satisfy his own curiosity about his employer's paradoxical behavior. Mr. Falkland, a man of impeccable reputation and status, of great magnanimity and compassion, bears a personal weight of sorrow. When his naive curiosity discovers Falkland's secret, Caleb finds himself the unwilling focus of Falkland's vengeful attention. Falkland hounds Caleb. Caleb's life is blighted; normal conduct, thwarted; every human contact, soured by Falkland. Now Caleb turns his detectival concern to search out the cause for this harassment. When he succeeds in collecting the data to save himself, he finds to his dismay that a court of law will not determine guilt or innocence on intuitive data when hard evidence is lacking. In supplementary remarks to an 1832 edition of the novel William Godwin discussed the writing of his "mighty trifle," saying that he especially reveled in "the analysis of the private and internal operations of the mind," and in the work at "tracing and laying bare the involutions of motive . . . in exploring the entrails of mind and motive." [2] Godwin is echoed over a century later by Philip Trent in E. C. Bentley's *Trent's Last Case* when he writes to his editor of the Manderson murder, speaking of the "treachery and perverted cleverness" which intimates "the deeper puzzle of motive underlying the puzzle of the crime itself." [3]

Caleb Williams anticipates two stock characters of more modern detective-crime mysteries: the criminal as heroic figure and the criminal turned law-enforcer. Despite the trouble and anguish Falkland has visited upon Caleb, the latter views his former master as a heroic figure, a tragic hero whose downfall comes of his own *hubris*, his overweening self-pride. The second stock characterization affords not only the meeting with Gines the thief but also a moral view of how thieves see themselves. During his flight from Falkland's vengeance Caleb becomes an unexpected guest of Captain Raymond's gang of thieves. During a conversation Raymond describes them to Caleb as "thieves without a licence . . . at open war with another set of men, who are thieves according to law." [4] Upon expulsion from the gang, Gines, a self-avowed enemy of Caleb, becomes a "bankrupt thief turned thief-taker in despair" (to borrow a phrase from Godwin's son-in-law Percy Bysshe Shelley). Even as Godwin ironically describes Gines as one joining the "honourable fraternity of thief-takers," he has Caleb note that Gines "was intimately persuaded that there was no comparison between the liberal and manly profession of a robber, . . . and the sordid and mechanical occupation of a blood-hunter." [5]

This stock character took on more romantic proportions and authority from the real-life career of François Eugène Vidocq (1775–1857), French chief of detectives in Paris from 1809 to 1827 and again for a short period in the early 1830s. An ex-convict with direct experience gained from local jails and maximum-security prisons as well as from association with highwaymen and the criminal underground, Vidocq brought a wealth of expertise to his first official position as police spy in 1809 and later in 1812 as first chief of the bureau, now better known as the Sûreté. Vidocq operated on the premise that one sets a thief to catch a thief; a criminal of any kind knew best the way another criminal would operate. A second premise, less dramatic but just as worthy, was that a criminal at work this way stood a chance at rehabilitation. Following his retirement from the Sûreté, Vidocq went into business, not the least notable for our subject here being his private detective agency established in 1834, predating the prestigious Pinkerton agency.

Vidocq's exploits, later recorded and possibly inflated in his *Mémoires* (1828), made him a legendary figure. His reputation gained reinforcement from literary friends, such as Balzac, Hugo, Dumas, who drew upon his exploits for their novels. He became the model for Balzac's Vautrin and later for Emile Gaboriau's police detective Lecoq. Eugène Sue's *Les Mystères de Paris* (1842–43) took details of the Parisian underworld and criminal element from Vidocq's career. Not only was he known in France, but his fame spread world-wide. While a criminal, his ability to concoct successful escapes and later as an official his success with the use of disguises, criminal informers, new methods of detection (many of them now commonplace) set him apart from other police officials.

To an extent Vidocq's fame helped to foster the attitude of disdain which more contemporary literary detectives accord the officials with whom they must work. It is ironic that Vidocq's personal "official" methods fell victim to the very disdain he seemed to have for the regular police methods he replaced. One expression of this reverse prejudice came from a literary detective destined to claim great fame in literary crime circles. At one point in Edgar Allan Poe's "The Murders in the Rue Morgue" (1841) the narrator declares himself in general agreement with public sentiment that the murders of the L'Espanaye women are insoluble. C. Auguste Dupin, Poe's very logical amateur detective, calmly puts the affair in his perspective:

The Parisian police, so much extolled for *acumen*, are cunning, but no more. There is no method in their proceedings, beyond the method of the moment. . . . Vidocq, for example, was a good guesser, and a persevering man. But, without educated thought, he erred continually by the very intensity of his investigations. He impaired his vision by holding the object too close. He might see, perhaps, one or two points with unusual clearness, but in so doing he, necessarily, lost sight of the matter as a whole. Thus there is such a thing as being too profound. [6]

Few would accuse Dupin of failing to use method or educated thought or clarity of vision in his work detailed in Poe's analytical tales: the aforementioned "Murders," "The Mystery of Marie Roget" (1842), and "The Purloined Letter" (1845). In these tales Edgar Allan Poe introduced patterns and techniques now revered as conventions; for his success historians of the detective mystery mode have designated him the "father of the modern detective story." To review these conventions here will alert us to their later use in both mystery fiction and science fiction/fantasy stories.

Predating Sherlock Holmes and his faithful Watson by more than forty years, Poe's tales established the amateur detective of superior mental endowment and his close associate of less acute mental powers as stock characters. Poe's plots are deceptively simple: establish a puzzle, have the detective solve it, and then explain the steps in the solution clearly and logically. During the process Poe introduced suspense, often with the aid of the confidant-narrator whose befuddlement mirrors our own. With him we are amazed at the seeming simplicity of the solution. In addition to being the recipient of the explanation the narrator-friend also serves as the focus of the many mini-lectures Dupin administers on the finer points of his investigation, the details which make up the necessary data for solution.

Edgar Allan Poe also introduced in "The Murders in the Rue Morgue," the original fictional locked-room mystery, if we discount the story of Bel as fiction. The puzzling aspect of a brutal double-murder lies in the condition of the room in which it took place. Although it is in great disarray, nothing valuable is missing; all windows and doors are securely locked from the inside. Official depositions establish such "facts" as the narrowness of the chimney, the security of the locks, the loneliness of the couple, the secluded area in which they live. However, Dupin considers other depositions which report an exchange of shrill and gruff voices; these "facts," in conjunction with his findings based on his dedication to all details no matter how slight, lead him to the solution.

Subsequent authors have proved the viability of Poe's locked-room technique by using and elaborating on it. Among these we can count

Israel Zangwill, *The Big Bow Mystery* (1892); Arthur Conan Doyle, "The Adventure of the Speckled Band" (1892); Jacques Futrelle, "The Problem of Cell 13" (1907); Melville Davisson Post, "The Doomdorf Mystery" (1918); S. S. Van Dine, *The Canary Murder Case* (1927); and several of John Dickson Carr's novels. In fact, Carr included an entire chapter on the technique in *The Three Coffins* (1935). In "The Locked-Room Lecture" Carr's amateur detective Dr. Gideon Fell delivers a most complete explanation of the technique by classifying the various crimes and the obvious methods of committing them and then discussing technical means by which the perpetrator effected his escape or seeming absence from the premises. True to his expansive personality and verbosity, Fell prefers to call the technique "the hermetically sealed chamber." [7]

Two tales not using Dupin as the main character also add to the stock of techniques Poe contributed to the mystery story. In "The Gold Bug" (1843) William Legrand deciphers a message presumably giving the position of a buried treasure. The cipher uses symbols and numbers to stand for letters of the alphabet; the major key to the solution of the cipher lies in the fact that the letter *e* is the most prevalent letter used in the English language. Legrand's detailed explanation to his friend also illustrates what Poe in the introductory discourse to "The Murders in the Rue Morgue" termed *attention*. Attention assures that it is "the more concentrative rather than the more acute player who conquers." [8] Legrand working at the cipher demonstrates concentration at its best.

In "Thou Art the Man" (1844), a mixture of the macabre and the mysterious, Poe presents a murder and a trail of false clues, one of which is based on an elementary ballistics test. Then he uses a melodramatic scene in which the corpse rises up to accuse the real murderer, thereby eliciting instant confession. Such a denouement with the least likely person as the criminal has spawned its own host of followers and variations on the theme, one of the most famous being Agatha Christie's *The Murder of Roger Ackroyd* (1926).

There is little dissent to Poe's status as a major influence on the development of detective mystery conventions. The detective and confidant-friend stock relationship, the locked-room pattern, the least-likely person as criminal, the cipher—all buttress his position in that process. Poe also anticipated science fiction/fantasy mystery by his use of some scientific theories of his day, such as Cuvier's studies of animals and the theory of probability.[9] While persons interested in the symbiosis of science fiction/fantasy and the detective story will find these urtypical conventions of use, perhaps what is more pressing is justification for the melding of idea- and situation-oriented material. Poe's introductory exposition to "The Murders in the Rue Morgue" addresses this problem in a philosophical way.

In this exposition Poe addresses the complexity of the analytical process, noting the impossibility of analyzing that special mind which "glories" in the "moral activity which *disentangles*."[10] Poe italicizes the last word, thus emphasizing the importance of the action of the situation. But let us also italicize the term *moral activity*. *Moral* intimates a concern for principles, an ethical standard dictating choice, social relationships, and political purpose. It also moves the purpose of the analysis from the strictly mechanical or procedural to one animated by criteria. From Poe's outline of the analytical process also emerges an important adjunct to the procedural tactics. He begins with the expected advice: identify the problem; then concentrate on details, excluding nothing relevant, be it ever so ordinary or seemingly coincidental. Know what to observe, for much depends on the quality of that observation. One of the most important observations must be of the opponent, in order to gain an accurate measurement of the other's intellect. This mixture of reason and imagination, of the practical and the psychological, provides a fertile seed-bed for situation and idea to grow together.

In the years between the two major amateur detectives, Poe's Dupin and Doyle's Sherlock Holmes, a more sympathetic attitude existed toward the authorities than in the pre-Poe days. Some historians of the detective mode attribute the change in public attitude to the growth of regular police forces both in England and on the Continent. In England the Bow Street Runners, a quasi-official force established by Henry Fielding in 1750, had operated until the early nineteenth century but had acquired a dubious reputation. Writing in *Household Words* (July 27, 1850) Charles Dickens censured them with "To say the truth, we think there was a vast amount of humbug about those worthies."[11] In 1829 Sir Robert Peel gradually replaced the Bow Street Runners by a Metropolitan Police Force; in 1842 a detective arm of the force came into existence. It is this force that Dickens lauds in the *Household Words* articles: "The Modern Science of Thief-taking," "A Detective Police Party," and "Three 'Detective' Anecdotes." It is also upon the members of this force that Dickens drew for the characterization of his Inspector Bucket of the Detective who plays a minor though memorable part in *Bleak House*.

Poe had pointed the way toward executing in fiction the "moral activity that disentangles"; Dickens had raised the reputation of the character of the official detective. To extend the formula and character to novel length, especially the length demanded by the serial publication of the nineteenth century, demanded additional techniques. To the painstaking detailed analysis of the Poe tales, these later authors added more complication, necessitating drawing upon adventure, romance, and sensationalism.

Noteworthy is the expanded interest in characterization, individuation of the stock character within the formula. Emile Gaboriau, dubbed "the father of the detective novel," [12] modeled his Lecoq upon the famous Vidocq, but Lecoq assumes a personality of his own, as he moves into more responsible positions from aide-de-camp to a superintendent of police in *L'Affaire Lerouge* (1863) to being the man in charge in *Monsieur Lecoq* (1869). "An old offender, reconciled to the law,—a jolly fellow, cunning, quick, and useful in his way, but secretly jealous of his chief, whose abilities he held in light estimation" is our introduction to Lecoq in the first novel. [13] In later ones he becomes the master of disguise, the possessor of a computer-like mind, and one who in *Le Crime d'Orcival* (1867) can quietly boast: "Monsieur has only to inquire at the prefecture and he will learn that I know my profession." [14]

English and American writers of this period offered solid detective-operatives with less shady origins and less flamboyant operations. There was the memorable Hawkshaw in Tom Taylor's melodrama, *The Ticket-of-Leave Man* (1863), a commonplace person but master of disguise and dogged attention to the job. In *The Moonstone* (1868) Wilkie Collins contributed the "celebrated" Sergeant Cuff, summoned from London to aid an inept local superintendent recover the stolen gem. Elderly, lean, melancholy, he is the antithesis of a heroic figure. As described, "he might have been a parson, or an undertaker, or anything else you like, except what he really was." [15] But Cuff does have strength in his steely grey eyes and indulges in one eccentricity. He fancies roses, thus anticipating the orchid-loving Nero Wolfe by many years. Ebenezer Gryce, Anna Katharine Green's detective in *The Leavenworth Case* (1878), shares similar characteristics: elderly and competent. But where Cuff is lean, Gryce is well padded; where Cuff is called a "less comforting officer to look at for a family in distress," [16] Gryce invites confidence in distress. While Gryce does not have a personal eccentricity, he also foreshadows a Nero Wolfe characteristic by using a subordinate to do his more arduous legwork as does Wolfe use Archie Goodwin.

Notwithstanding their additions to the detective novel, the foregoing contributions pale slightly in the light of the Sherlock Holmes canon. Ask almost any person casually to name a famous detective, and the predictable answer in most cases will be "Sherlock Holmes." Even though detective Holmes flatly criticizes Dupin as "a very inferior fellow" [17] and Lecoq, "a miserable bungler," [18] his creator, Conan Doyle, obviously drew on the techniques provided by these predecessors. Like Dupin, Holmes has a confidant-friend, a little more obtuse perhaps, but more voluble in his record of the Great Detective's exploits. Like Lecoq, Holmes fancied and was adept at disguise and pursued his quarry with like energy. While Cuff and Lecoq and other literary minions of the law are referred to in their respective novels as "celebrated" before they have opportunity to demonstrate their right to that epithet, Dr. Watson's record will show that Holmes holds an undisputed claim to the term. Master of both the analytical process and the moral activity which disentangles, Holmes has received ample testimony for his celebrity by the many imitators that have followed him, not only in mainstream detective stories but in the several pastiches and parodies featuring such detectives as Solar Pons, Picklock Holes, Shamrock Jolnes, Hemlock Jones, Schlock Homes, and others.

Conan Doyle also influenced the novel in another significant way. Where Collins and Dickens had fleshed out the detective figure and put it in a novel-length story, they had in so doing subordinated it to other concerns. Doyle, on the other hand, used the extra length to build up setting, manipulate minor characters, and create the necessary atmosphere of suspense so as to give the detective a more credible time in which to work out the problem. That he was eminently successful is evident in such locales as Helen Stoner's bedroom in "The Adventure of the Speckled Band" (1892), the Great Alkali Plain in *A Study in Scarlet* (1887), the cellar in "The Red-Headed League" (1892), as well as others in which Doyle added many details of Victorian London, thus giving the stories a period atmosphere to complement the unraveling of the puzzle. Equally important is Doyle's use of arresting minor characters who add not only complexity but also color to the narrative. To name but a few, there are the ragged street urchins Holmes euphemistically calls "the Baker Street division of the detective police force"; Detective Gregson and Inspector Lestrade; the ubiquitous Dr. Watson; and the unforgettable Napoleon of Crime, Professor Moriarty. These and others who enter only in their respective cases testify to the strength of the characterization of Holmes himself, a strength reinforced rather than challenged by the strong minor characters.

To compare the eccentric brilliance of a Dupin or Holmes to the plodding efficiency of a Bucket or Cuff is to become aware of a growing division in the ranks of detectives to follow. Julian Symons divides these later characters into "the Supermen and the Plain Men." [19] The Plain Men are eminently forgettable as people, retiring, commonplace, albeit efficient in solving their cases, as one notes in Martin Hewitt's career. By contrast, the Supermen might well boast, each in his own way, as does Holmes in *The Sign of Four* (1890) that he is "the only one in the world." [20] Despite Holmes' following criticism of Watson's reportage as being tinged with romanticism, the Supermen detectives do function as romantic characters. Set apart by their intellectual prowess, their lack of family or financial woes, and their unalloyed appreciation of their own abilities, these detectives enjoy not only the mental exercise but also the drama of the untangling process. The Supermen usually boast some unique characteristic. One remembers Max Carrados' blindness; Father Brown's affiliation with the Church; Prof. S. F. X. Van Dusen's extraordinary name with the equally extraordinary epithet as The Thinking Machine; the religious fervor of Uncle Abner. Later Supermen detectives include Hercule Poirot, proud of his "little grey cells"; the aristocratic Lord Peter Wimsey; the very ethnic Charlie Chan; hardboiled and headstrong Sam Spade; and others often more memorable for their personality than for the situations they resolve.

While the twentieth century found the detective formula well established and the mode a popular one, some disparate attitudes toward it manifested themselves. One reflected the urge to assure respectability by formulating rules for its production. In 1928 S. S. Van Dine listed twenty rules which he labelled as "very definite laws—unwritten, perhaps, but none the less binding; and every respectable and self-respecting concocter of literary mysteries lives up to them." [21] Like Aristotle describing tragic drama of his time in the *Poetics*, Van Dine attempted to isolate the conventional practices which in the best sense make detective fiction work. In the same year Monsignor Ronald A. Knox offered a similar service in his "Ten Commandments of Detection." Both sets of rules are strongly couched in the negative: thou shalt not do this or that in a detective story. Again in the same year the Detection Club was founded in London; its oath, among other services, subtly pledges its members to an acceptable level of performance.

The twentieth century also saw a heightening critical response to the detective story. These responses run the gamut of opinion from outright defense as indicated by the title of G. K. Chesterton's 1902 "A Defence of Detective Stories" to outright attack in Edmund Wilson's 1945 "Who Cares Who Killed Roger Ackroyd?" Others took more moderate but nonetheless searching views of the mode such as R. Austin Freeman's balanced assessment in "The Art of the Detective Story" (1924) and Raymond Chandler's brief for the realistic detective story over the classic detective story in "The Simple Art of Murder" (1944). Interest in the roots and growth of the mode initiated historical accounts as compressed as Dorothy Sayers' Introduction to the first *Omnibus of Crime* (1928) and as comprehensive as Julian Symons' *Mortal Consequences* (1972). That the critical sense has not died down in more contemporary times is evidenced by the healthy critical response in journals such as *The Armchair Detective* and *Clues*.

Concomitant with this movement toward critical attention there arose a pessimistic trend. A strong vein of doomsaying had been an integral part of commentary on the detective story, for as early as 1905 an unsigned article in the London *Academy* had proclaimed the decay and ultimate demise of the literary detective.[22] Although the detective did not decay and leave the literary scene, the question continued to be asked: what is the future of the detective story? In a letter to A. D. Peters serving as a preface to *The Second Shot* (1930) Anthony Berkeley faced that question head-on. He quotes an unnamed reviewer who had suggested two ways detective fiction could go: the writer could experiment with narrative movement or he could develop character and atmosphere. Berkeley favored the latter, seeing future readers as being attracted to psychological problems with the puzzle being one of "character rather than a puzzle of time, place, motive, and opportunity," as he puts it. Berkeley poses Why? rather than Who? as the primary question, one necessitating exploration of the mind of the deceiver in the story rather than a search for his identity. H. Douglas Thomson in a 1931 study claimed stasis for the detective story because of its level of perfection, one which foreshadowed no future, "no process of natural growth."[23]

As so often happens to doomsayers, later developments arise to refute their worst fears. For the detective story these changes added to the flexibility of the mode, proving it adaptable to changing times as well as amenable to enrichment of tried and true conventions. In 1907 R. Austin Freeman had introduced his Dr. John Thorndyke, expert in forensic pathology and the scientific methods then available for analysis of clues. In the above-mentioned "The Art of the Detective Story" Freeman described his use of a new narrative pattern, one he designated as an "experiment, an inverted detective story in two parts." This allows the author to reveal full knowledge of both crime and criminal at the beginning of the story, while devoting the last half to explanation of the detective's art. Freeman assured recognition of the pattern in "The Case of Oscar Brodski" (1912), for example, by entitling the first part as "The Mechanism of Crime" and the second as "The Mechanism of Detection." In "A Case of Premeditation" (1912) the subtitles are more dramatic with Part I as "The Elimination of Pratt" and II as "Rival Sleuthhounds," *sleuthhounds* here referring both to the human detective and to the bloodhounds whose "detecting" Thorndyke derogates.[24]

The appeal of the inverted pattern lies in the intellectual pleasure generated by watching the detective bring the known criminal to justice. In the prefatory essay to *The Singing Bone* (1912) Freeman suggested a substitution for the question "How was the discovery achieved?" for the more usual one of "Who did it?" (or "whodunit?" if you prefer the more colloquial phrasing). "Who did it?" admits room for sensationalism upon which Freeman cast a most critical eye. Instead, he opted for a return to the more satisfying pleasures of the mind, recognizing that the mode was primarily a work of ratiocination although that works hand-in-glove with the imagination. The suggestion is strong here that the detective story would benefit by a return to Poe's moral activity that disentangles away from the more romantic sense of astonishment favored by some contemporaries of popular detective fiction.

A second major change in the detective story occurred with the advent of the American "hard-boiled school." The character of the tough-guy private investigator developed out of the detective story pulps, notably *Black Mask*, in the 1920s and 1930s. From Carroll John Daly's Race Williams through well-known characters as Dashiell Hammett's Continental Op and Sam Spade, Raymond Chandler's Philip Marlowe, Ross Macdonald's Lew Archer, and John D. MacDonald's Tracy McGee the character has followed a fairly predictable pattern. Yet, each creator has given his hero a uniqueness to enrich the common expectations. In so doing the crime and mystery writers have achieved a vitality that can complement the general tone of adventure permeating much of science fiction.

The stock character of the private investigator parades under several labels, depending on his personality or method of operation. He may be termed the hard-boiled detective (or *dick*), the tough-guy private eye (or only *private eye*), the gumshoe, the shamus, and in a more dignified strain, the P.I. or private investigator. Some aficionados of the mode trace the term *private eye* back to the trademark of the Pinkerton's National Detective Agency. The Pinkerton sign featured a large staring eye topped by a strongly drawn eyebrow and complemented by the motto, "We Never Sleep." Others prefer to attribute the term to a bastardization of the more dignified *private investigator* or a mispronunciation of its initialled form. Along with labeling, the private eye has endured the inevitable comparisons any popular mode invites. He has been variously compared to the knight of chivalric romance or to the horseman of the Old West riding down the dusty road of a lawless frontier town or to Robin Hood. While these claims may burden a Continental Op or Sam Spade individually, they allow them collectively to stake their claim in the general classification of hero of romance.

Finding their audience in popular magazines such as *Black Mask*, this group of authors created a unique detectival style. First, the detective as a realized character suffered a radical sea-change. No amateur motivated by social magnanimity or by need of intellectual excitement, the hard-boiled detective worked for his livelihood as a private investigator. No close associates conferred such complimentary epithets as Thinking Machine or Celebrated Detective upon him; any labels other than proper names were purely functional, such as Dashiell Hammett's Continental Op. No admiring Watson mirrored his every move or recorded his every word. Without this stock confidant-friend this new detective had no need to engage in lengthy exposition of clues or detailed psychological dissection of the criminal mind. The words which replaced the long discussions now came as terse, colloquial dialogue, short passages describing rapid action, or ironic internal conversations by which the reader came to understand the detective's inner compulsions. Ross Macdonald in his chapbook, *On Crime Writing* (1973), designates this new detective as "the classless, restless man of American democracy, who spoke the language of the street."[25]

While his motivation was purely functional, this new man went about his professional work in quite a different style from a Dupin or Holmes. Instead of enjoying the moral activity which disentangles, this new breed untangled their puzzles with activity often verging on the illegal and immoral. Even so, there comes through a strong sense of a private moral code, one resting on the rough philosophy of to thine own self be true because you can trust no one else—not the police, not the crooks, not even the woman you love or the seemingly innocent bystander. Physical force often replaced intellectual dynamics. Where Holmesian clones or imitators rested on their intellectual powers, the hard-boiled detective had to be ready to act out of gut instinct, shooting first and questioning later.

But there are trade-offs. For each strength he fights against a weakness. This man pays the price of all solitary souls—loneliness. With no friend on the "mean streets" in which he works, even those who would engage his sympathy may and often do betray him. He expects and receives violence from unexpected quarters, fully ready to return in kind. Since his usual milieu is urban with an occasional foray into suburbia, the private detective is awash in humanity, most frequently the backwash of human corruption and weakness. This detective has little traffic with the intimate, elite groups of an English country house or luxury hotel, even with the fairly sedate metropolitan environment in which a Sherlock Holmes worked. The hard-boiled detective's "Baker Street Irregulars," if any at all, wear the label *informers*, aides never to be trusted wholly, always wary of exploitation and therefore quite willing to exploit this solitary inquirer. While the private eye's situation does not admit sympathy for either his luckless informers or more luckless victims per se, the moral man behind the professional facade feels sympathy for the individual as a symbol for the entire human community.

In more contemporary times this restless man has tended to mirror social disorder sharply despite his seeming classlessness. In some novels the detective functions less as a hero or protagonist than he does as the antagonist. In Ross Macdonald's words, the private investigator of today serves as "a consciousness in which the meanings of other lives emerge."[26] He may lose his purpose completely as the clarifier of a situation of deception and move toward being a more aggressive corrector of the ills of society, a less benevolent form of the traditional Robin Hood figure. Since moral issues in contemporary society do not appear as black and white as in former eras, the late twentieth-century literary detective can see himself as the sole arbiter of the moral decision.

This complex and multi-faceted literary mode has much to offer an author with imagination to engage the physical, mental, and moral activity which disentangles. Despite the shifts in emphasis throughout the years certain conventions remain well-tested, available for a symbiotic relationship. The three major stock characters—the superior intellect of the amateur; the lonely, tough private investigator; and the self-ordained corrector of social ills—all maintain their beings in modern detective fiction. The former will carry the double burden of solving the case and educating a less acute companion; the hard-boiled detective will work Raymond Chandler's "mean streets" in dogged pursuit of an answer; the latter will put his frustrations to work in aggression against the ills of society around him.

The technical formula of plotting includes the locked room mystery, the inverted pattern, the importance of material clues balanced with psychological maneuvering of the opponent. The oft-suggested pact between writer and reader still remains an accepted state of affairs: the reader should be privy to information available to the detective even though he does not reveal the details of his solution until the end. If the detective story plays the game fairly, it should offer a reader the opportunity to pit his own intellectual power against the character's mind. In addition, modern readers expect some depth of meaning; the puzzle for its own sake satisfies less than the combination of puzzle and the social and ethical implications behind each affront to person, property, or ideals. In this last expectation idea merges with situation.

In the 1940s debate on the merging of the detective story formula with the conventions of science fiction, one key issue hinged on the major dictum: the detective story must play fair with the reader. Both Van Dine's "rules" and Knox's decalogue had stressed situations to be avoided: accident, coincidence, supernatural agencies or gimmickry, undiscovered poisons, special technology or scientific theories demanding special explanations for the reader. By extension, could a detective of a future society arrive at rational, logical deductions without use of mechanical or scientific aids unknown to the twentieth-century reader? To use Isaac Asimov's well-known term, could a science fiction detective solve his case without resorting to use of his "pocket-frannistan," thus taking unfair advantage of the readers?

If such doubts assailed the writers of a generation earlier, we have no record of them. These men, often too melodramatically for our taste today, drew upon chemistry, physics, psychology, and other sciences for the popular scientific detective story, a form which Sam Moskowitz termed as "frequently science fiction by courtesy."[27] To some readers mention of inventions such as the wireless or machines such as gyroscopes and portable seismographs may well have seemed like "pocket-frannistans," but that did not detract from the popularity of scientific detectives such as Luther Trant, Craig Kennedy, Dr. John Thorndyke, Dr. Henry Poggioli, and others. Instead, the use of science injected a note of realism and contemporaneity that served them well. Here was science not extrapolated, but interpolated.

To Sir Arthur Conan Doyle again must go credit for producing the ur-scientific detective in Sherlock Holmes. As a medical student in Edinburgh Doyle had studied under Dr. Joseph Bell, whose personal appearance, personality, and methods of diagnosis and analysis later influenced Doyle's characterization of Holmes. But Holmes is not Bell translated. Holmes we see mainly through Watson's eyes, with a brief introduction from Watson's friend Stamford. In *A Study in Scarlet* (1887) Stamford describes Watson's possible future roommate as "a little queer in his ideas—an enthusiast in some branches of science . . . well up in anatomy, and he is a first-class chemist . . . whose studies are very desultory and eccentric."[28] Early in their own association Watson rates Holmes's scientific qualifications, awarding him a "profound" knowledge of chemistry augmented by "variable" and "practical" knowledge of botany and geology respectively. With anatomy he is "accurate but unsystematic"; in astronomy he receives an unqualified "nil." In "The Five Orange Pips" (1892) the two men with some amusement recall this report card, and Holmes makes a point that it has always been his wont to acquire as much knowledge as possible on as many subjects as possible, stocking his "little brain-attic" and storing the rest in "the lumber-room of his library."[29]

Primarily a man of thought rather than of action, in the laboratory

Holmes did value the empirical approach and the specialized dedication of the scientific method. As witness to the first, Watson makes a point of mentioning Holmes's monographs on specialized technical problems of detection: distinguishing ashes of various tobaccos and evidence of occupation left upon the human body. In *The Sign of Four* (1894) Holmes himself discusses his self-created profession of "the only unofficial consulting detective" in the world. One additional comment is pointed: "Detection is, or ought to be, an exact science and should be treated in the same cold and unemotional manner."[30]

During the same decade L. T. Meade (Mrs. Elizabeth Thomasina Meade Smith) and her collaborators produced a series of short mystery stories, based either on scientific fact or involving a scientific or pseudo-scientific discovery. In "A Race with the Sun" (1897), written with Clifford Halifax, scientist-inventor Gilchrist is working on a smokeless and odorless explosive of great potential military value. As an altruistic and patriotic gesture he plans to give the weapon to England when he has perfected it. One day he is approached by a trio of persons who claim to be working along identical lines; they, however, hope to sell the explosive to Germany for a prodigious sum. Applying subtle professional pressure, they ease Gilchrist into sharing his data with them, but when time comes for the reciprocal sharing, they double-cross him. Rousing from the drugged state to which they have reduced him, Gilchrist finds himself bound beneath a balloon sweeping up into a storm. Tied beneath him are two containers, the glass one with hydrogen and chlorine and a tin canister with nitroglycerin. When the sun's rays hit the glass jar, it will explode, in turn setting off the nitro and killing him. The fact that Gilchrist saves himself is of secondary importance to the authors' literary use of the three chemicals.

Stories from the Diary of a Doctor (1894), the first collection of Meade and Halifax stories, focused entirely on medical mystery. In later collaborations with Robert Eustace, Meade continued to use medical and scientific explanations in the solutions to the crimes, as in "Where the Air Quivered" (1898). Young Archie Forbes fears for his life. While on a visit in Mecca he and a friend had thoughtlessly violated the sacred Kaaba. As a consequence they received threats of revenge, and the friend did meet his death. After Archie receives a parchment scroll containing the clue to the hour of his own death, he calls off his engagement. His fiancé and her father consult a Dr. Khan, a non-practicing physician now doing chemical research and forensic medicine as a hobby. After interpreting the message on the parchment Dr. Khan prescribes a plan to forestall the projected murder, the weapon being a modified dart gun which projects a "vortex ring" of concentrated anhydrous hydrogen cyanide in the victim's face.

"The Face in the Dark" (1903) and "Madame Sara" (1903) both illustrate the lengths to which early writers of mystery could push their scientific explanations. In the first one Laurence Hyne, an amateur photographer who prides himself on "a fair knowledge of science," becomes the *ex officio* guardian of Granby Manners, a rather naive young man saddled with enormous debt at the death of his father. Upon either his failure to pay the interest or his own death Granby's estate will revert immediately to his creditor. To ensure this outcome, the villain hangs Granby up by his feet, thinking to cause death by congestion of blood in the head. This method, the attending physician explains, would leave no trace once the body was cut down.

Madame Sara, also known as the Sorceress of the Strand, appears in a series of crime stories. In the one which bears her name Meade and Eustace cast a private investigator and also a local police surgeon to solve one murder and prevent a second. While tracking down an heir to an estate soon to be settled, the investigator comes to know Madame Sara, a beauty consultant, who seems to have undue influence over two of the female heirs. When one of the sisters dies under strange circumstances, the investigator calls in the local police toxicologist to aid him. The murder investigation proceeds in tandem with the search for other heirs; the two join in one track when an earlier connection is made between Madame Sara and a newly found male heir who is dying and who has signed away all rights to the estate to a cohort of Madame. The third death is aborted when the doctor traces the poison to a "tooth-stopping" or a temporary filling recommended by Madame Sara and installed by the same cohort who had cheated the male heir. By her cleverness Madame Sara escaped conviction, going on to become one of the first female super-criminals in five other stories in *The Sorceress of the Strand (1903)*.

In *The Red Thumb Mark* (1907) Dr. John Evelyn Thorndyke, doctor, legal expert, and walking encyclopedia of esoteric information, joined the parade of scientific detectives. His creator, R. Austin Freeman, however considered him "an investigator of crime . . . not a detective."[31] In some of the eleven Thorndyke novels and series of short stories Freeman made Dr. Thorndyke well-known for appearing at the scene of the crime carrying his portable laboratory, a small, green, canvas-covered case containing miniaturized spirit lamp, microscope, test tubes, and sundry instruments for his research. The concrete presence of the case spotlights Dr. Thorndyke's unique method. In addition to the specialized medical and legal knowledge he possessed, he emphasized the importance of acting instantly to preserve clues both on the person and the place of the crime; of investigating systematically and scientifically each clue no matter how insignificant it seemed to be; and of having a trained scientist aid the police.

The value of this method showed up well in "The Case of Oscar Brodski." En route to an inquest in the service of an insurance company, Dr. Thorndyke and his friend Jervis find themselves temporarily delayed at a junction where a man ostensibly has been run over by a train. The man is identified as Oscar Brodski, a diamond merchant. With the reluctant permission of the local police inspector Dr. Thorndyke goes to work. He makes slides of items such as a crumb of food from the coat of the dead man and a tuft of fabric from between two teeth of the decapitated head. At the scene of death he picks up fragments of glass to be studied under the microscope from his handy case; and even later as the trail leads them to a nearby house, he tests residue from the fireplace in a "little flask, fitted for Marsh's arsenic test." The results of his on-the-spot laboratory tests enable the police to identify the death as murder instead of suicide.

During the same decade that Freeman's Dr. Thorndyke captured an audience with his medico-legal specialties two American collaborators, Edwin Balmer and William MacHarg, added another dimension to the scientific detective. In *The Achievements of Luther Trant* (1910) the title character, a "Practical Psychologist," as the sign on his office door in Chicago proclaimed, used the "necromancy" of the then new psychology of Freud, Jung, Munsterberg, and others in his investigative work. "The Private Bank Puzzle" illustrates these special techniques at work. The young acting president of an old and reputable Chicago banking house engages Luther Trant to investigate incidents involving the aging cashier. Papers have disappeared from his waste basket; his coat disappeared, then reappeared for no logical reason; his blotters were stolen from his desk. For the elderly man, already distraught by a recent and unjust accusation of theft leveled at his son, these insignificant but aggravating occurrences threaten to push him over a mental brink. In his disturbed state he keeps predicting a second robbery at the bank.

Trant puts his scientific psychology to work in the case. First, he gives the old cashier three tests, one for memory and the other two for attention. Then he asks the entire force of bank clerks and tellers to take a test of association. The first three reveal the cashier's failing faculties. This condition caused him to mishandle some sums of money; the money is easily located and the son is then exonerated. Through the fourth test Trant is able to pinpoint the employee who is planning the second robbery, hoping to pin it on the cashier's son.

Early scientific detectives increasingly showed their awareness not only of scientific theory and laboratory work but of the new technology resulting from it. Edwin Balmer in his own 1909 novel, *Waylaid by Wireless*, had used Marconi's relatively new invention of the radio-telegraph in the con job perpetrated by his rogue-hero on a naive young mark. Balmer and William MacHarg's Luther Trant is no stranger to similar machines. Trant backs up his psychological methods with an impressive array of devices such as a chronoscope, kymograph, plethysmograph, galvanometer, and other now equally anachronistic equipment. "The Eleventh Hour" (1910) features one of these. Trant receives a dramatic call for help from a Walter Newberry, who fears he will be beyond help after the hour of eleven that evening. Unfortunately Trant, enjoying a day off, fails to receive the message in time, arriving at the Newberry home just in time to hear the shot that kills Newberry. He remains at the Newberry home to aid the police. In the ensuing investigation Trant traps the killer by testing the suspects with a machine he calls an electric psychometer, a device for testing emotional responses to questions. During the test he notes that the psychometer is a more refined piece of equipment than the galvanometer he had used in a prior case to identical ends. With such a device here and in "The Man Higher Up" (1909) Luther Trant gained the honor in detective story history of being the first fictional character to use a lie detector, primitive though it be, in the process of detection.

Luther Trant's surefire combination of hard science, psychology, and technology adapted for crime detection soon had its emulators. Probably the best known at the time was a professor of chemistry living half a continent away from the Chicago territory of Luther Trant. Arthur B. Reeve's Craig Kennedy first appeared in 1910 and continued in popularity for well over two decades in stories, novels, and films. Some Craig Kennedy devotees pinned the label "the American Sherlock Holmes" on the Reeve character, a label partially merited by the omnipresence of Walter Jameson, a reporter for the *Star* and the detective's companion and chronicler. A major difference, however, is that Jameson operates less as a confidant-friend than as a press agent-reporter. Throughout Jameson's narratives the reader receives constant reminders of Kennedy's wont to keep up on scientific developments in fields other than his own. It is to Jameson that Kennedy sets forth his theories on academia's place in crime detection. In "Craig Kennedy's Theories" introducing the collection, *The Silent Bullet* (1912), Kennedy suggests to Jameson that there should be a professorship of criminal science in the universities so that crime detection might benefit by "the same sort of methods by which you trace out the presence of a chemical, or run an unknown germ to earth." [32]

Professor Kennedy's methods reflect his habit of keeping up with all fields as well as his own, for he uses not only chemistry but also bacteriology, psychology, pharmacology, physics, and other sciences in his detectival activities. Sam Moskowitz in *Science Fiction by Gaslight* has remarked on the notably close approximation of the psychological methods and technical devices used by Kennedy in "The Case of Helen Bond" (1910) to those used by Luther Trant in "The Man in the Room" (1909). According to Moskowitz, Reeve continued this practice, verging on paraphrase, through other stories, but more subtly. [33] The debt to Trant can be seen in comparison of this first Kennedy story (later retitled "The Scientific Cracksman") with Balmer and MacHarg's "The Private Bank Puzzle" mentioned above. In Reeve's story Professor Kennedy cracks the case by information gained from a simple word association test, much as did Luther Trant in the bank case. Kennedy goes a step further to reinforce his psychological data with the physical record of the testee's blood pressure as taken by a "plethysmograph," a device also appearing in a list of Trant's equipment in "The Eleventh Hour."

Professor Kennedy's method includes quite a bagful of devices to aid in crime detection, some of which foreshadowed future use but others which were of dubious scientific validity. In "The Scientific Cracksman" (1910) there is the "dynamometer" to measure the pressure necessary to mark a safe; this device he styles his "mechanical detective," adding that it was devised by Bertillon who had allowed Kennedy to copy it for his own use. In "The Bacteriological Detective" (1911) not only does he utilize his knowledge of medical science to track down the typhoid carrier but also the "sphygmograph" to identify the person with the irregular heartbeat which had in turn modified that person's handwriting. In "The Black Hand" (1911) Kennedy installs a "dictograph," serving as a "bug" and a transmitting device. Since Professor Kennedy can always tap his knowledge of the hard sciences, he is able to test invisible ink in "The Poisoned Pen" (1912) or recognize the use of x-ray to destroy the victim's sight in "The Invisible Ray" (1912) or classify paper prints in "The Silent Bullet" (1911). In addition, Reeve's detective makes use of relatively new inventions and procedures such as the weapon silencer, the wireless telegraph, airplane gyroscopes, and electrical resuscitation.

While Luther Trant and Craig Kennedy dominated the scientific detective scene in the pulp magazines during these early years of the twentieth century, others should receive credit for reinforcing the trend of merging science and crime detection. From 1911 to 1913 Michael White published stories featuring two separate detectives: Proteus Raymond, chemical expert in criminology, and Charles Dagett of Dagett's Chemical Institute. From 1911 to 1915 a series entitled "The Strange Cases of Dr. Xavier Wycherly" ran first in an English magazine and later in *The Blue Book Magazine*. Written by Australian-born Max Rittenberg, the series featured the psychological techniques of Dr. Wycherly, especially in his ability to pick up the thought waves of persons who had lived in the area in a past time. Stoddard Goodhue's Dr. Goodrich, Harvey J. O'Higgins' Detective Duff, Charles Wolfe's Joe Fenner, and David H. Keller's Taine of San Francisco, master of disguise, are but a few of the scientific detectives created to meet the growing demand for science blended with imaginative mystery plots.

In *Science Fiction by Gaslight* Sam Moskowitz includes "In Re State vs. Forbes," a one-shot story by Warren Earle published in *The Black Cat* in July 1906. Earle's story demonstrates the degree to which these earlier imaginations drew upon the then-modern technology and blended it with the unbelievable. The brother of a murdered girl kills one of her suitors in cold blood on the street. The ensuing story is the man's "confession" to a lawyer, excusing his actions on the basis of revenge on his sister's murderer. His identification of the murderer is not supported by factual clues, but he explains that his family uses telegraphy for intercommunication. One night upon receiving an urgent summons via telegraphic sounds he rushed to her only to find her dead. Upon taking her body to his laboratory, he found by x-ray that the corpuscles of her blood were so arranged that they spelled out the name of the murderer in Morse code. This name was that of the man he shot. Earle's story certainly must stand either as a bridge to science fiction/fantasy mystery or as a verbal monument to Sherlock Holmes' oft-quoted query: "How often have I said to you that when you have eliminated the impossible, whatever remains, *however improbable*, must be the truth?"

One other early scientific detective merits attention. T. S. Stribling identifies his Dr. Henry Poggioli variously as a professor of psychology, as a professor of criminology, as a professor of criminal psychology at Ohio State University, as an ex-university professor, and as a criminologist per se. These shifts in identity are consistent with the length of time the Poggioli stories appeared in print during the mid-twenties to mid-fifties. Poggioli's science is psychology, although his writer-companion credits the professor also with considerable prescience. Poggioli's *modus operandi* differs considerably from those of his predecessors. Unlike Luther Trant he does not consider psychology in terms of necromancy, even when his auditors give him credit for some magical conclusions. He does not depend on technology, as does Craig Kennedy. His forte is informed knowledge of how and why human beings act as they do. The narrator terms Poggioli's talent as "analytical divination."

In the adventures of Henry Poggioli, Ph.D., T. S. Stribling comes closer to writing what we consider science fiction/fantasy than his predecessors or contemporaries. For one thing his settings impress us as more "alien" than the English locale of L. T. Meade's heroes or the Chicago milieu of a Luther Trant. The stories invite the standard question: "what if" a professor from Ohio State University must investigate a crime in a voodoo society or in a modern Mexican community living under the shadow of Aztec superstitions or in a Hindu enclave in Trinidad? These answers and others come in the five adventures collected in *Clues of the Caribbees* (1929) and the 1945 series of Poggioli stories collected in *Best Dr. Poggioli Detective Stories* (1975). A closer look at two stories, one from each period, reveals the science fiction/fantasy aspects of Stribling's plots, ones which may warrant application of the term out of more than "courtesy."

In "A Passage to Benares," the last story in the 1929 collection, Poggioli experiences multiple existences: the "real" world, a dream world in which he merged as one with Krishna, and an alternate world of the living dead. His real world is that of a curious psychologist who cannot resist breaking a taboo by sleeping one night in a Hindu temple in order to experience firsthand the "psychologic influence of architecture.'' When a thirteen-year-old bride of one day is found decapitated in the temple on the following morning, Dr. Poggioli finds himself cast in the dual role of investigator and criminal. His own arrest forces him to investigate mentally his night's experience, most particularly the nightmare he had experienced then. In the process of self-analysis he mesmerizes himself to the point that he re-experiences union with Krishna, a union which promises loss of entity in infinity and eternity, or what for Poggioli is ''to be lost in this terrible trance of the universal.'' [34] Realizing that his dream is but a variation on a theme running through dreams of five other suspects and also in the ruminations of the wealthy but unhappy father-in-law of the murdered girl, Poggioli spots the common thread which leads him to the true murderer. The discovery instead reveals his current existence in a world where he exists only as the hanged murderer. In the process Stribling leads the reader from psychology to parapsychology with the suggestion of thought transference and manipulation of others by force of will.

A similar combination of sciences turns up in "The Mystery of the 81st Kilometer Stone," of the 1975 collection of stories from the 1940s and 1950s. Professor Poggioli is drawn by chance into a mini-drama featuring the conflict of Western philosophy and lingering Aztec beliefs. The sparking incident occurs when he witnesses an old peon fatally cut by the gyves attached to the legs of a fighting cock. No one in the crowd offers aid. They seem to have been anticipating the tragedy and almost exude a sense of relief at its end. The event throws Poggioli into the company of two brothers, educated by their father in diametrically opposed ways. One is Oxford-educated, therefore molded by Western philosophy and perceptions; the other, native-educated by an old wise man of the area. Conversations with the two revolve around esoterica such as the ''power of the suggestion of death,'' ''soul energy,'' and the creation of energy by destruction by the atom bomb as compared to creation of energy by the destruction of a human being. A second death occurs, again with no rational explanation. Poggioli's companion recalls a possibility once suggested by the psychologist: ''*psychic murder*—the control of matter at a distance through the human will.'' [35] Considering the speculative nature of the situations, T. S. Stribling leaves the reader with some sense of wonder but with a greater sense of having lost a mental contest with his psychologist-detective who in an afterword declares that the ending of the episode of the eighty-first kilometer stone did not in the least surprise him.

By contrast, Austin Hall and Homer Eon Flint did evoke a strong sense of wonder, sensation, and surprise with *The Blind Spot* (1921).[36] Like many serialized novels, *The Blind Spot* does suffer awkwardness in plotting, necessitated by the custom of ending each installment on a note of additional mystery. The first section holds special interest for devotees of the straight detective story, as it features ferry detective Albert Jerome dealing in the traditional logical way with an illogical situation, a puzzle with too many facets.[37] On the San Francisco ferry en route to Berkeley, a cigar clerk draws Jerome's attention to the singular behavior of a passenger. This man is strangely young, yet old, of imposing mien and with impelling eyes that suggest "latent and potent vision" to the detective. Going off duty, Jerome directs the stranger to the home of Professor Holcomb. This worthy academic has received local notoriety with a promised lecture, "The Blind Spot," in which he proposes to disclose concrete, scientific information about the occult. Holcomb's subsequent disappearance causing cancellation of the well-publicized lecture creates a *cause célèbre*. Jerome assigns himself the duty of plumbing the mystery to the end. To this point the Hall-Flint novel offers mystery and detection with only a slight suggestion of scientific extrapolation.

In chapter 5 of the novel, however, when several of Holcomb's students and his daughter enter the plot, the focus of the problem shifts from the single question, "What happened to Dr. Holcomb?" to two more dominating ones: "What is the Blind Spot?" and "How do inhabitants of one time line function amicably with those of another?" With successive shifts of focus from the original question to the latter ones *The Blind Spot* moves further from detection, although detectives Albert Jerome, and in the sequel Samuel J. Flanning, do continue to play important roles in the action. As it moves from straight detection, the novel moves closer to traditional science fiction/fantasy adventure in the interface of parallel universes, human-alien contact, and the emphasis on a need for science to explore the imaginable. On the other hand, *The Blind Spot* offers an exercise in the pitfalls of merging detective conventions with the speculative imperative of science fiction/fantasy.

Although Hall and Flint were writing for another editor, it is surely authors such as they whom Hugo Gernsback had in mind in "How to Write 'Science' Stories."[38] Gernsback offered advice of solid common sense, useful for any writer of fiction. The product, Gernsback emphasized, is *story*. As such it must be interesting, the author making a balanced and integrated use of action, dialogue, and description. Especially he cautioned against over-use of superlatives to create the atmosphere of sensation. More important for the scientific detective story, the author must keep in mind that it is a *science* fiction story and as such must have scientific accuracy, must be "reasonable and logical and must be based upon known scientific principles."[39] Upon this strong and accurate foundation the creative imagination can then erect the plot. In a scientific detective story all fields of science open themselves to the writer; they offer specialized technology and mechanical devices as aids to the detection—or to the commission—of crime. Scientific knowledge contains no inherent moral or ethical sense, hence it is available for use to those outside as well as inside the law. Within the confines of his definition of science fiction as the "exposition of a scientific theme" in the form of a story, he foresaw no conflict with the conventions of the detective story, as long as the author paid scrupulous attention to the rational and logical demands of the scientific knowledge or apparatus used.

Although the *Writer's Digest* article identifies Gernsback as the editor of the newly formed (but unfortunately short-lived) *Scientific Detective Monthly*, his advice represented the 1930 version of his established opinion on science fiction/fantasy. For at least two decades Gernsback had been encouraging the writing of science fiction. As early as 1911 he had published one of his own stories, "Ralph 124C 41+," a story which illustrates Gernsback's bias for detailed description and lists of devices. "Ralph 124C 41+" appeared in *Modern Electrics*, a magazine he edited under several changes of title. As *Science and Invention* it featured several Charles S. Wolfe stories about his scientific detective, Joe Fenner. In 1930 the scientific detective stories found a brief home in the *Scientific Detective Monthly* for which Arthur Reeve served both as consultant and a major contributor of Craig Kennedy stories. The magazine lasted but ten months, some of the issues during that time under the name of *Amazing Detective Tales*.

The demise of the *Scientific Detective Monthly* is understandable if one but considers the date 1930. The world was entering the Great Depression with a general loss of optimism. Business collapse and economic doldrums do not lend themselves to easy solutions. Unlike the scientific detective, the public at large could not rely on a logical and rational analysis of the problem aided by a technical marvel or device to solve that problem immediately.

The readership turned to stories of escapism, what Brian Aldiss labeled the "Gosh-Wow"[40] brand of science fiction, perhaps better la-

beled science fantasy or science adventure. The scientific detective lost
out temporarily to the space captain or the space police. The scientific
intellectual gave way to the brave adventurer; the scene of a crime, to
the cosmic scene of societies or alien cultures in conflict. Even titles
of the new pulp magazines suggest the trend: *Astounding, Future Fiction, Cosmic Stories, Planet Stories*. A full decade hence writers would
again with success amalgamate science fiction/fantasy with detective
fiction, but with a notable shift of emphasis. The conventions of the
detective story would now serve to enrich the host of the symbiotic
relationship, science fiction/fantasy.

NOTES

1. William Godwin, *The Adventures of Caleb Williams or Things as They
Are* (New York: Holt, Rinehart, Winston, 1965), p. xxiii.
2. Ibid., pp. xxx, xxviii, xxix.
3. E. C. Bentley, *Trent's Last Case* (1913; rpt. Del Mar, Calif.: University Extension, Univ. of Calif., San Diego, and Publisher's Inc., 1977), p.
135.
4. Godwin, p. 251.
5. Ibid., pp. 302, 303.
6. *The Complete Works of Edgar Allan Poe*, ed. James A. Harrison (1902;
rpt. New York: AMS Press, 1965), IV (*Tales*, III), pp. 165, 166.
7. John Dickson Carr, *The Three Coffins* (1935; rpt. Boston: Gregg Press,
1979), p. 220. The lecture of this chapter is recapitulated in shorter form in
chapter 13 of *Death from a Top Hat* (1938) by Clayton Rawson.
8. Poe, *Complete Works*, p. 147.
9. References to both of these can be found in Poe's "Murders in the Rue
Morgue." See p. 182 (Cuvier) and p. 179 (theory of probability) of *Complete
Works*, IV.
10. Poe, *Complete Works*, p. 146.
11. Charles Dickens, "A Detective Police Party," *Household Words*, July
27, 1850, p. 409. This article can be located on reel 18 issued by University
Microfilms, Ann Arbor, Michigan 48106.
12. The various familial relationships attributed to these early authors have
been conferred upon them in a formal manner in "The Haycraft-Queen Definitive Library of Detective-Crime-Mystery Fiction" (1951). First published in
Ellery Queen's Mystery Magazine, it has been republished in the 1974 enlarged edition of Howard Haycraft's *Murder for Pleasure* (New York: Biblo

and Tannen, 1974) and in Dilys Winn's *Murder Ink* (New York: Workman, 1977).

13. Emile Gaboriau, *The Widow Lerouge* (1873; rpt. New York: Scribner's Sons, 1901), p. 10. Translated from the French of Emile Gaboriau, but with no credit given to a specific translator.

14. Emile Gaboriau, *The Mystery of Orcival* (Chicago: Bedford, Clark, n.d.), p. 40. No credit given to a specific translator.

15. Wilkie Collins, *The Moonstone* (New York: Pyramid Books, 1961), p. 88.

16. Ibid., p. 88.

17. Sir Arthur Conan Doyle, "A Study in Scarlet" in *The Complete Sherlock Holmes* (1905; rpt. Garden City, N.Y.: Doubleday, 1930), I, 24.

18. Ibid., p. 25.

19. Julian Symons, *Mortal Consequences* (New York: Schocken Books, 1973), p. 87.

20. Doyle, p. 90.

21. S. S. Van Dine's "Twenty Rules for Writing Detective Stories," along with Monsignor Knox's "A Detective Story Decalogue" and "The Detection Club Oath" are collected in *The Art of the Mystery Story*, ed. Howard Haycraft (New York: Biblo and Tannen, 1976), pp. 189–99. This volume also contains the critical articles referred to in the following paragraph of text.

22. Haycraft, *Murder for Pleasure*, p. 276, quotes the reviewer as retiring the detective "to limbo with the dodo."

23. H. Douglas Thomson, *Masters of Mystery: A Study of the Detective Story* (London, 1931; rpt. New York: Dover, 1978), p. 274.

24. The word *sleuth* as now used is a clipped form of *sleuthhound*. Its first use as such is attributed to an 1885 dime-novel detective story by Harland Page Halsey, *Old Sleuth, The Detective*.

25. Ross Macdonald, *On Crime Writing* (Santa Barbara, Calif.: Capra Press, 1973), p. 15.

26. Ibid., p. 24.

27. Sam Moskowitz, *Science Fiction by Gaslight* (1968; rpt. Westport, Conn.: Hyperion, 1974), p. 36.

28. Doyle, p. 16.

29. Ibid., p. 225.

30. Ibid., p. 90.

31. As quoted by Ellery Queen in *Queen's Quorum* (1948; rpt. New York: Biblo and Tannen, 1969), p. 56n. This edition includes supplements through 1967.

32. Arthur B. Reeve, *The Silent Bullet* (New York: Harper and Bros., 1910), p. 3. There exists a discrepancy in dates for this collection, 1912 being the most usual date assigned. *Queen's Quorum*, p. 61, lists a 1912 Dodd, Mead edition as "the first of his books."

33. Moskowitz, p. 45.

34. T. S. Stribling, *Clues of the Caribbees, Being Certain Criminal Investigations of Henry Poggioli, Ph.D.* (1929; rpt. New York: Dover, 1977), p. 311.

35. T. S. Stribling, *Best Dr. Poggioli Detective Stories* (New York: Dover, 1975), p. 91.

36. *The Blind Spot* was first published as a six-installment serial in the May-June 1921 *Argosy-All-Story Weekly*, later put into book form in 1951.

37. In *The Spot of Life* by Austin Hall, also serialized in *Argosy* in 1932, detective Samuel J. Flanning, serving a similar function as that of Jerome, picks up the recurrent mystery of the Blind Spot.

38. Hugo Gernsback, "How to Write 'Science' Stories," *Writer's Digest*, Feb. 1930, pp. 27–29.

39. Ibid., p. 27.

40. Brian Aldiss, *Billion Year Spree: The True History of Science Fiction* (New York: Schocken Books, 1974), p. 211.

CHAPTER 2

THE Abcs OF SCIENCE
FICTION/FANTASY MYSTERY

From recurring remarks by both science fiction authors and science fiction historians one must recognize that it was commonplace to argue in the 1930s and 1940s that science fiction as being written could not marry detective fiction with any degree of success. A writer building a future society or organizing interplanetary forays or using alien life forms as major characters would not or could not play fair with the reader, as dictated by the conventions of the detective story. In a far future, for example, the detective might have access to detecting devices not yet in existence. Since the detective operated in a social milieu born of the writer's imagination and not a fictional representation of the reader's own world, details serving as clues could escape a reader. Value systems of alien cultures, if diametrically opposed to human values, would necessitate a re-definition of crime and criminal activities.

Even as we gaze with nostalgia at the reproductions of the covers and illustrations of those early pulps, such as *Amazing Stories* and *Astounding Science-Fiction* or *Astonishing Stories*, questions arise. Where in those flaming, football-shaped spaceships would a Dupin find the darkness which nourished his genius? Could a cerebral Sherlock Holmes reduce a stalk-eyed, forked-tail, flying creature to a logical, rational, explainable phenomenon? How comfortable would a Dr. Thorndyke carrying his personal laboratory in its green case feel working alongside the be-turbined, be-dialled gadgetry so omnipresent in many of the pictures? While these are facetious comparisons, they do spotlight a basic problem. How could an author couple the vaunted "sense of wonder" with the tidy, rational explanations of a detective mystery? The mysteries of the universe, of space and time, did not lend themselves gracefully to a localized puzzle of crime detection and to a single human brain untangling it. The pessimistic outlook needed only one word to sum it up: *impossible*. Even so, writers tackled the impossible, efforts later to be classified as the aforementioned "miscegenations" by Damon Knight. Three authors, however, disproved the naysayers with notable success: Isaac Asimov, Alfred Bester, and Hal Clement. Their work opened up new avenues not only for science fiction writers but also for the detective mode which some critics had begun to consider a dinosaur in popular literature.

Science teacher Hal Clement (pseudonym of Harry Clement Stubbs) brought to his writing not only a solid background in the hard sciences but also the scientist's method of attention to details. The disciplined marshalling of details to support the feasibility of his human-alien relationships gave credibility to the situations in which his characters find themselves. In *Needle* (1950)[1] these efforts allowed him to produce a science fiction/fantasy detective story in which the reader becomes so familiar with the unfamiliar that the charge of unfairness cannot be laid at the author's door. *Needle* is the story of an alien detective, an alien criminal, and their very ordinary human helpers. Since it is a variation of Freeman's inverted pattern of the detective story, we know the crime and the criminal from the beginning of the story. The major question for Clement remains: how will the detective catch the criminal?

With such a question a reader might expect a fairly simple chase-adventure story, but Clement does not choose the easy way. His aliens face more than the usual complications of such a situation. For one, they come from a distant part of the universe. We meet them in mid-pursuit, just before their cylindrical two-feet by twenty-inch-sized spaceships crash-land in the ocean near Tahiti. For a second, they must make more than expected adjustments to a new environment, for · these two are symbiotic creatures, able to exist only in a congenial host. Their requirements are simple but stringent: oxygen for life, vision and a nervous system for data-gathering, and a host with intelligence. This last is most valuable, for an intelligent host can not only aid in evaluating the gathered data but also can tolerate both the idea and required activity of a symbiotic relationship.

The beginning of *Needle* illustrates how Clement builds credibility through use of subtle details. He introduces the alien detective by function only, naming him "The Hunter," later "The Detective." In this contest between law and outlaw the opponent's label denotes only his role; he is the "fugitive" and the "quarry." At no time does Clement attempt to anthropomorphize either alien by individualizing them with names. Here are two life forms but with one focus each: one to hunt and the other to escape. Later in the course of events the Hunter once thinks of himself as a policeman "hopelessly isolated" from his own world and its assistance. As the hunt progresses, he refers to the fugitive as "our friend," a term then laden with irony made more pointed at the moment of the face-down when the fugitive becomes "Killer."

Even more essential, Clement had to convince readers of a true collegial relationship between alien and human. Most human beings react with revulsion at the mere thought of any uninvited foreign object entering the body, be it a bullet, germs, or virus, or even a tiny sliver of wood in a finger. Society passes laws to prohibit such invasions; medicine marshals great preventive or curative forces; the body itself possesses an array of defensive mechanisms to defeat the intruder. Clement must prepare the reader for an easy acceptance of that against which his being instinctively revolts.

First, Clement made the intruding alien a sentient one, a rational being with a purpose. Before we ever imagine the physical container, we know the mind contained. It resembles our own in that it reasons, fights doggedly for survival, and has a moral imperative governing its actions. *Do nothing that can harm your host.* Repeatedly this statement rings throughout the first few chapters. In fact, it is the breaking of this moral law that has made the Hunter's quarry a fugitive from his own kind, has set him outside the brotherhood of his own race. In the minutes immediately following the crash of the spaceship the Hunter demonstrates the positive side of this dictum when he attempts to save the life of the perit, the creature which has harbored him with mutual benefit to this point.

In addition to the above mental and moral coincidence, Clement made his alien life-form physically similar to one we recognize as part of our natural environment, the amoeba. Even though the Hunter weighs four pounds, quite the antithesis in size to the amoeba we view through a microscope, the alien does bear resemblance to the amoeba. For example, the Hunter can form extensions of itself for various tasks, such as pseudopods for locomotion, much as does an amoeba extrude parts of its body from the greater protoplasmic mass. The Hunter can feed upon minute organisms or microbes in the host's blood stream much as does an amoeba absorbing such organisms in its environment. At one point during the Hunter's "education" of Robert Kinnaird, his human host, he makes the analogy with the amoeba, an analogy which must be modified by an explanation of the more complex structure of the Hunter's species, making it more akin to a benign virus.

Although Clement does not anthropomorphize the alien, we do recognize in the Hunter other characteristics common with our own. The Hunter allows impatience to rule reason at times. He makes mistakes. Despite his patient months-long period of self-education in the nature of his host he errs in pushing the first direct contact. He has misread the level of sophistication of Robert Kinnaird. In attempting to establish initial communication by his usual methods of muscle control and direction, he succeeds only in frightening the young boy to whom the spasms signal only a physical dysfunction. Also, the Hunter is not omniscient. Despite the close identity afforded by physical interstition with his host, the Hunter can no more read Robert's mind than can a human being read the mind of one with whom he has shared many years of closeness by emotional interstition. While he has a purpose he understands well, he also recognizes his own limitations, relying on the intelligence of his host to aid him in the search for and disposal of the criminal he hunts. Once established in trust and understanding, this partnership has little in common with the classical Sherlock Holmes-Watson relationship. In *Needle* the Hunter and Robert Kinnaird both contribute their share of expertise in the planning and execution of the search.

In the search proper the partners engage in that moral activity which disentangles, starting by defining the problem and by asking the proper questions. Where did the alien spaceships land? Near one of a group of islands in the Pacific. Where are we now? At a boarding school in Massachusetts. Where might the fugitive be hiding? In another intelligent life form living on the island, most possibly another human being. Why should Robert help his "guest" in the search? Because the other alien does not observe the primal law of "do no harm to your host" and thus could injure the person now harboring him. How many possibilities for a host exist on the island? One hundred and sixty people. How can Robert return to the island before the expected return for the summer vacation? After ruling out homesickness or accident or running away, Robert suggests some change in his physical condition requiring rest at home, a change which the symbiote could effect by his mere presence and some slight interference with Robert's health. The problem is solved without their efforts when the school authorities, noticing increasing inattention and listlessness on Robert's part, decide to send him home for a few months to straighten out.

Once he brings host and Hunter back to the island, Clement attends to the details of the search and capture. Robert and Hunter must first determine logically where the fugitive came to earth, who might have been in the vicinity at that time, and what procedure to follow in the precise identification of the fugitive's host. Coming from an advanced culture, the Hunter had brought along his specialized instruments for detection; unfortunately they were lost in the crash of the spaceship. The only alternative left to him is to use the human being not only as his instrument of locomotion, sight, and sensitivity but also as a major clue-gatherer. Robert receives unexpected aid from the broad-minded, intelligent local doctor who extracted Bob's strange story after questioning the abnormally fast healing of Bob's leg wound. Systematic suspicion, investigation, and clearing of selected islanders eliminate the workmen under Bob's engineer-father and his own friends who frequent the reef where the quarry had crashed. As Robert's own investigations come to dead ends, the detective picks up details unnoticed by Bob since they concern someone so familiar to him. Hunter notes certain anomalies in the father's behavior. The father takes unwonted chances of injury as if he subconsciously knows he is being protected. Whenever he does sustain a small injury, it heals more quickly than normal, indicating some unnatural agent at work. From this evidence the alien detective deduces that the fugitive lodges in the father, temporarily paying for his lodging with minor protective measures.

When the two aliens meet at the initiative of the detective, he suffers a temporary setback. The fugitive reminds him that there is no ethical way the detective can dislodge his prey from the host without harming the host in direct infraction of his moral code. On the other hand, the fugitive, now addressed as Killer, has no such scruples. The only alternative is to make the present host inhospitable, force the quarry into the open and destroy him, a plan which Robert executes with dispatch. His own compatible symbiote, being stranded with no means of returning to his home galaxy, receives an invitation to remain with Robert in the rather innocuous ending to the novel.

Because of the meticulous detail and the logical explanations Clement used throughout *Needle* he ably defused most of the arguments of his time against the merging of detective fiction with science fiction. He asked but one major concession from his readers: believe that there are elsewhere in the universe intelligent, moral life-forms that can establish adequate lines of communication with human beings and can work cooperatively with them. Once that premise was accepted, Clement could avoid traps such as giving the detective access to devices not available to the reader or laying a trail of clues undecipherable to the reader. In *Needle* alien and human intelligence merged in such a way as to allow the reader to know everything the detective knew and to offer him the fair chance of solving the problem alongside the detective.

Four years later Alfred Bester in *The Demolished Man* (1953) reinforced Clement's accomplishment by re-proving that a very successful merger could be made of the detective mode with science fiction, so successful in fact that *The Demolished Man* received the Hugo Award in 1953 and was runner-up for the Second International Fantasy Award the following year. Clement's *Needle* and Bester's *The Demolished Man* have two common factors: the authors use the inverted pattern for the crime story and they each feature a police detective. There the similarity stops, except for the fact that Bester like Clement has to predispose the reader to accept certain elements in both the detective-criminal relationship and in the societal values. It is to our benefit to look at both the similarities and the differences in their approaches to the problem of merging the two modes of fiction.

The inverted detective story, as originally devised by R. Austin Freeman, appeared in two parts, the first one devoted to a detailed presentation of the crime, the second to the investigation of the crime by a person who did not have all of the knowledge of it that the reader possessed—or it would seem. In that possibility lay the main attraction for the reader. Clement in *Needle* diverted attention from the crime and the investigation in the first part of his novel in order to assure acceptance of the speculative situation. In order to gain this willing suspension of disbelief in the existence of an intelligent alien symbiote, Clement needed the space ordinarily assigned in this pattern to a full introduction of the crime and criminal. As the story boiled down to a search-and-destroy mission, Clement sacrificed some of the drama of the events in order to gain attention to the logical methodology employed in the hunt.

In *The Demolished Man* Bester follows Freeman's pattern more closely. With the first word in the novel he throws us without warning into Ben Reich's nightmare, one sometimes recurring even in a wakeful state. If any one person should feel secure and unthreatened in this world of 2301, it is Reich, wealthy and powerful tycoon, head of Monarch Utilities & Resources, Inc., an interplanetary corporation. But even as he plans the economic domination of the entire solar system, emotional security eludes him. The nightmare follows a disturbing sequence: extreme dissipation of explosive energy; secured areas blown open to a wild kind of freedom; then the forbidding appearance of the Man With No Face, an ominous figure foreboding in its very inaction. Aided by his personal expert doctor, Reich searches for a logical explanation of the dream and willfully selects from the doctor's superficial tests the signs he finds most palatable to his need for a culprit outside himself. He fastens all blame on Craye D'Courtney, his most formidable business rival. A recent coded offer of merger from Reich to D'Courtney had come back with the answer "WWHG" ("accept offer"); in his distraught state Reich reads the code as "offer refused." Always a man of immediate, violent action, a law unto himself, Reich decides to rid himself of both the pesky opposition and the disquieting dream with one decisive action. He will kill D'Courtney.

Reich must solve a series of problems best stated in questions. Where can I find D'Courtney? How can I get past his guard? What means shall I choose for his destruction? For someone with such wideflung power and connections all three problems find easy solutions. Through his network of spies he discovers D'Courtney's residence. During a brief visit to the New York area, he will live at the home of Maria Beaumont, the "Gilded Corpse." At this point Reich complicates the plan by taking over the details for the murder himself. Playing upon the vanity and jaded tastes of the lady, Reich wangles an invitation to a party in her home, also sending her a gift, an old book with directions for a titillating game, Sardine. These allow him, first, access to D'Courtney's vicinity and, most important, time under the cover of darkness demanded by the game, time to locate and kill. Knowing that D'Courtney will be well guarded, Reich steals special eye-drops from the research laboratory of his own company. Shot into the eyes of the guards, these will render them ineffective for at least an hour. Once face-to-face with his victim, Reich can use a fairly untraceable tool for the murder. This ancient weapon from the twentieth century, a pistol with cartridges loaded with special water-filled gel pellets, carries enough impact to kill but leaves no trace except bits of gel in the mouth. It would appear that all bases are covered at this point.

One major obstacle remains. The society of 2301 values extra-sensory perception (esp) to the point that it tests for esp latency and trains those with the slightest bent for esp, grading them according to the degree of proficiency. A Class I esper (a "deep-peeper") can plumb the psyche to the depths of the id; a Class II works with both the conscious and preconscious levels of the mind; a Class III reads minds only on the level of immediate thought. In twentieth-century society this activity is anathema, suggesting invasion of privacy and thought control, but not in 2301. Since the Espers Guild demands a strict code of conduct governing use of the skill, society at large encourages its utility in all areas. Class IIIs, for example, serve as secretaries and memory files. Class IIs work as professionals, doctors, lawyers, teachers. Class Is reserve their talent for the more analytical areas as criminology or for consultative needs, a counseling service to the higher echelons of business, government, and diplomacy. Since the Esper pledge binds the talent to the benefit of mankind, they consider all they "peep" as privileged information.

Obviously, being human, some espers do fault their pledge, selling out to amoral operators such as Reich. In turn, he recognizes he may become vulnerable to espers of his competition, so Reich maintains a staff to protect him. For the murder he knows he can not rely solely on the purchased protection, in case their moral pledge, now broken for his pay, reasserts itself. As a special personal protection he visits Psych-Songs, Inc., to use one of the blocking jingles they sell as a design to foil all but a Class I peeper.

The plan seems foolproof. Chances are that Reich will complete the murder as efficiently as he planned for it. But even a high-level operator can not control the law of probability; Reich has not counted on D'Courtney's friendly reception, based on the latter's assumption that Reich has come to cement the merger. His warm welcome demolishes what self-control Reich has. As D'Courtney's daughter hears Reich's tirade and comes to her father's rescue, she operates as a completely unforeseen and unpredictable factor, bursting in, witnessing the murder, and then escaping to lose herself in the larger populace. Gaining control, Reich completes the murder plan, returns to the party, and takes part in the initial phase of the investigation by the police. He feels secure in the mental protection of the jingle, the loss of perception of the guards, and his own esper phalanx. Nothing should connect him with the murder.

Up to this point Bester fulfilled the requirements of the plot pattern he chose: the reader knows the criminal, has been present both in the planning and execution stages of the criminal act. The author played fair with the readers by explaining thoroughly the function esp serves in this society and suggesting the part it must play in the detecting process. Although in modern society such a talent as extra-sensory perception in the hands of a detective could work to unfair advantage, the author emphasizes that in this 2301 society the telepath operates under moral and social constraints. Bester also assures the reader-detective full knowledge of all the esper-detective discovers. By use of different type styles to differentiate "peeper conversation" from normal verbal interchange Bester opens up the world of telepathic exchange and telepathic delving so that a reader is privy to all clues picked up in that fashion.

As mentioned before, *The Demolished Man* shares yet another element in common with *Needle*: a police detective. Again the similarity stops with this general identification. Where *Needle*'s Hunter is alien, Lincoln Powell is very human. The official description of the Hunter labels him as "companion of Jenver the Second of Police" with no explanation of the specialness of this connection. Lincoln Powell, on the other hand, sports an impressive array of titles: Ph.D. I, Police Prefect of the Psychotic Division, Esper I or "Deep Peeper." The Hunter works alone, acting as detective and as executioner. Powell, responsible for a city of 17.5 million people, draws on the expertise of many well-trained people, especially telepaths of all three classes. But he has limits to his action. He must collect and offer objective data in the form of strong, unshakeable facts establishing motive, method, and opportunity to the judge, "Old Man Mose," the Mosaic Multiplex Prosecution Computer who then passes sentence. The crimes they solve differ. The alien criminal has breached a basic moral dictum by abusing its symbiote host in some unspecified way; Powell's quarry has done cold, calculated murder. Murder in most societies carries heavy moral freight; in 2301 it also affronts the collective consciousness. Here it is a social given that murder is now impossible because the trained police telepaths can detect the criminal impulse before commission. As one character marvels, there has been no such occurrence for decades.

The society of 2301 holds a view of punishment vastly different from the prevalent view in the twentieth century. For centuries traditional punishment has entailed deprivation of freedom or of life, forfeit of property, repayment of the social debt with physical or mental pain. Reclamation, being a difficult procedure, falls low in our list of priorities. Rehabilitation, a most soothing word to use, falls short in practice. In 2301 reclamation is practiced, although masquerading under the grim term "demolition." The process, a psychological one, involves destruction of the socially unacceptable psyche by eradication of established patterns of behavior and embedded memories. Upon arrival at complete disassociation, the process reverses, and rebuilding begins with rebirth of a new ego.

During the preliminary investigation held in Maria Beaumont's home Powell catches a verbal slip which pinpoints Reich as the culprit, but this subjective evidence will not convince the computer judge, which demands facts, particularly in support of a motive of passion rather than the economic motive more evident at this point. Outside pressures complicate Powell's task. Bureaucracy requires adherence to certain rules; the Esper Pledge restrains his use of his most efficient tool, his ability to deep-peep. He must tread lightly in some political quarters, for Powell's superior owes Reich a vaguely defined political debt. More personal pressures cloud the investigation as Powell falls in love with Barbara D'Courtney and begins to have ambivalent regard for Reich.

The developing relationship of Ben Reich and Lincoln Powell demonstrates Bester's commendable use of characterization to enrich the process of detection. When the two men meet, they know each other only as formidable opponents, respectful of the other's professional expertise and command of power. As they progress in the cat-and-mouse game, each learns to know the other man as an individual, in fact, to recognize in the other some of his own attributes. In a surrealistic fashion they are double images: men of power but also men of split personalities. Lincoln Powell recognizes his less admirable side, calling it his Dishonest Abe person. He loves to lie upon occasion, a habit openly acknowledged by both Powell and his close associates. Dishonest Abe, however, is controlled by the ethical Lincoln, that side guided by honor and ethics. While Powell knows and accommodates his two sides, Ben Reich suffers from his divided self. In the world he acts with full energy and control of his farflung interests, but in his private mental world fear and dread consume him, diverting his power to destructive ends. The positive side of self has lost control over the negative one.

From the first nightmare until the end of the novel Bester made Reich's psychological dis-ease a major thread in the plot. The reader is well aware of the corrosive nature of his fear, a fact which the police prefect establishes by degrees during the investigation long before he knows aught of the nightmare. Although Powell is forbidden by law and his Esper Pledge to "deep-peep" Reich, he can use other psychological means to gather information about him. One vital point comes to his attention during a test of Barbara D'Courtney's memory of the murder scene. Under Powell's supervision Barbara goes through a regression to a childlike state; at one point she reveals a mental Siamese-twin image of her and Reich. This intimates a sibling connection, thus opening up the possibility of a quasi-Oedipal relationship with D'Courtney himself. Is Reich a rejected son seeking to wound the loved-lost-now hated father? The answer to the question finds reinforcement in a series of attempts upon Reich's life which investigation uncovers as of Reich's own doing, a subconscious desire to punish himself out of guilt.

Despite the case being built up in Powell's mind Old Man Mose, the computer-judge, requires facts which Powell can not deliver. Only if Reich confesses to the killing can Powell hope for demolition and for Reich that second chance to exist in society as a contributing member instead of a canker sore debilitating it. Powell's admiration for Reich moves him to try a drastic ploy—Mass Cathexis. Using his persuasive powers on the members of the Esper Guild he engages their aid in the project. During this exercise all espers channel their psychic energy into one container—Lincoln Powell—who then concentrates it upon Reich in order to isolate him totally from the universe. The effect is terrifying. Bit by bit, Reich's familiar universe disappears—the stars, the sun, the planets, D'Courtney Cartel—and when he tries to run away and seek refuge in Paris—no Paris. In panic he runs to Powell to confess to the murder and more important, to face his nightmare and see in The Man With No Face a composite of all his fears, the father-son inter-relationship which has so warped his life.

In *The Demolished Man* Alfred Bester succeeded in balancing the science-fictional elements with the detective story conventions. From science fiction comes the setting in a future society. This one, near enough to allow realistic details from our era, has the remoteness necessary to admit development and sophisticated acceptance of telepathic talents. The extrapolation of contemporary psychology rings true, especially as supported by the specific use of Freudian notions. Even the 2301 use of benevolent "brain-washing" and personality reconstruction has seeds in contemporary speculation. Mass Cathexis may produce a highly unlikely effect until we study twentieth-century phenomena such as mass persuasion directed to the individual by different commercial and religious interests. The necessary detective conventions fit easily into the world of *The Demolished Man*. Fully aware that his science-fiction readership might not be as aware of basic techniques of criminal investigation as devotees of straight mystery fiction, Bester included a necessary exposition of motive, method, and opportunity. Sidestepping the trap of pedantry, he put this explanation in the speeches of Lincoln Powell, thus weaving information tightly to detectival action, as well as affording a vehicle for the necessary analytical exercise so vital a part of the detective mode.

While the nineteenth-century originators of the detective mystery worked best in the medium of the short story, twentieth-century science fiction/mystery writers find the extended form of the short novel or novella well suited to their efforts. Both Clement and Bester demonstrated this. Whether the length is dictated by publishing or marketing policies or by authorial need for the exposition necessary to establish a science-fictional atmosphere is matter for debate best carried on elsewhere. It does stand to reason, however, that a length exceeding that of Poe or Doyle does afford the writer the necessary space for scientific extrapolation or detailed description of a future society we cannot know from direct experience.

Isaac Asimov, the third member of our triad of science fiction/mystery trailblazers, worked well in both lengths, as his three sets of series stories indicate. Writing as Paul French, he produced a six-volume series of juvenile books, featuring David "Lucky" Starr, space ranger. With the third volume Lucky Starr begins a shift from space ranger to space detective with his loyal companion, Bigman, following suit. In *The Caves of Steel* (1954) Asimov introduced Elijah Baley of the New York Police in an uneasy alliance with R. Daneel Olivaw, robot detective. In 1957 he extended their adventures in *The Naked Sun* and much later in "Mirror Image" (written to appease popular appeal for a Baley-Olivaw reappearance). During 1955 Asimov's third detective, Wendell Urth, extraterrologist, joined forces with H. Seton Davenport to unravel extraterrestrial puzzles in several short stories linked solely by the main characters.

Asimov is noted not only for the sheer weight of his literary output but also for the fecundity of his imagination. His characters range the universe from earth to moon to planets and to the asteroid belt at will. Time yields to his experiments as he builds future societies, far advanced or far degenerated depending upon the contemporary criterion used for measurement. Asimov adapts with ease the available patterns of the detective mode and the conventional characterizations of the detectives; but by not imitating these patterns slavishly he enlarges their utility. Drawing upon his fund of scientific knowledge, Asimov gave the science-fictional part of his stories a realism which allows the detectival problem to flourish in a situation utterly logical and reasonable.

Asimov had foreshadowed an interest in mystery fiction in a lightly humorous fantasy entitled "Author! Author!" written for *Unknown* in 1943 but unpublished until 1964. Title character Graham Dorn suffers from the overblown popularity of his fictional hero, a detective with the romanticized name of Reginald de Meister. Dorn's readers consider de Meister to be a real person much as do many devotees of soap operas today. They harangue Dorn about his character's future to the point that Dorn decides to terminate the de Meister series. In the course of his decision he has a fantasy encounter with de Meister. In a peremptory manner de Meister informs Dorn that if the readers think he exists, then in truth he does. He has no intention of joining Holmes, LeCoq, and Dupin in any fictional Limbo. To resolve this dilemma, Dorn wreaks vengeance on his pesky character by writing a harridan wife into de Meister's life, thus destroying de Meister's fascination for all female readers and relieving the male readers who could not match de Meister's charisma.

But "Author! Author!" is not science fiction. In 1949 Asimov published "The Red Queen's Race" in *Astounding*. Here he edges closer to the supreme blending remarked on by Sam Moskowitz in *Seekers of Tomorrow*.[2] The police, the political establishment, and later the scientific community face a baffling situation when someone drains the nation's greatest atomic power plant of all its power. In the midst of the devastation police find the body of a Dr. Tywood, nuclear physicist. Is this a case of murder or of sabotage with possible international ramifications? The unnamed narrator-investigator operates alone, acting as a decoy to attract vital information possibly denied a full-scale hue-and-cry. He adopts a quasi-hard-boiled approach, making thinly veiled threats when needed and assuming ignorance of physics to allay suspicions of the academics he interviews. As a result of the thorough combing of the dead physicist's published work and detailed interviews of his colleagues, the investigator notes a bizarre picture emerging.

Motivated by idealism, the physicist had planned to use his time-travel research ("micro-temporal-translation") to introduce twentieth-century scientific data into the libraries of ancient Greece, thereby hoping to head off the centuries-long drift toward atomic destruction. To send the few sheets of data (translated into archaic Greek by a colleague), the professor needed an immense supply of power, hence the drain of the atomic plant. Ironically he is successful, but not in the intended way. The translator, a professor of philosophy, adds the crucial information to explaining the case. As a philosopher he knows the classical atomic theory as advanced by Democritus, Leucippus, and Lucretius, a theory which today can still amaze us with its modernity. In its own day, however, that theory did not seem indigenous to the thought of the day. The translator, recognizing the pitfalls inherent in the physicist's original plan, carefully deleted in his translation all data except that which would account for the basic ideas which the ancients had put forth. As a result no change could be introduced into ancient theory and no subsequent change in the course of world events. Likewise, the authorities have no "crime" and no "criminal," only a drained power plant, a dead body, and a case marked "?".

According to Joseph Patrouch, Asimov himself did not consider "The Red Queen's Race" as a mystery, hence did not include it in *Asimov's Mysteries*.[3] Asimov, most readers, and critics count *The Caves of Steel* (1954) as his first major foray into science fiction/fantasy mystery, indeed perhaps his best production in that mode. According to his own account in the Introduction to *Asimov's Mysteries*, he wrote *The Caves of Steel* to disprove all the negative beliefs about merging science fiction with mystery; then three years later he produced its sequel, *The Naked Sun*, to assure readers that the first one "wasn't an accident."

The Caves of Steel introduces plainclothesman Elijah Baley of the New York Police Department. His New York is not our New York; in fact, we would barely recognize it could we visit it outside of our imagination. Twenty million people live in one building, completely self-contained and closed off from the natural elements. Living space being sharply limited, some hitherto private activities become communal: community kitchens and dining areas, public "personals" instead of private bathrooms. Privacy is a prized possession. Unattainable through physical, spatial arrangement, it is assured only through cultural habits. One never looks or talks to another person in the "personal"; it is the height of bad manners to watch another chewing his food in the community kitchens. Privacy in the name of public decency exists only in that psychic space people maintain around themselves. The City does offer some amenities. Natural food being scarce, the City maintains huge yeast farms for extracting yeast from raw wood and cellulose, and then molding it into different forms to suggest variety for the palate. Transportation is efficient. A system of expressways with graduated accelerations runs continuously, while underground roadways from an earlier era still exist, used only in emergency.

The world of Lije Baley, like that of most human cultures, faces the threat of change. Philosophers since Heraclitus have taught us that all is flux, nothing is constant but change. Poets like Spenser have made us see the "ever-whirling wheel of Change, the which all mortal things doth sway."[4] But we reject the truth, preferring to dispute the inevitable in our own futile ways. The men of Asimov's far future are no different. Their reminder of inexorable change is a steadily rising population, a diminishing food and energy supply, and the complete lack of self-sufficiency in the wake of any major disaster. The citizens of this future New York refuse to face the inevitable. Even Lije Baley working the beat closes his mind to the situation, but he is forced to face it when his superior, Commissioner Enderby, assigns him to investigate the murder of a Dr. Sarton, eminent Spacetown scientist killed by a blaster.

Spacetown represents one facet of this threat of change. Centuries before, humans had traveled in space and colonized the planets able to sustain life. While retaining the physical appearance of men, they developed psychologically in a disparate way. They control their population growth, use robot technology to sustain them in the extensive physical space each can command. Their civilization, termed C/Fe from the chemical symbols for carbon and iron, rests upon cooperation between human and robot. It stresses values diametrically opposed to those of "civism," the term given to the city-based civilization Lije Baley knows. Spacers now maintain an enclave adjacent to New York; their purpose is to proselytize for their C/Fe organization. The earth population resists all their efforts because in C/Fe robots displace human beings in all areas of meaningful activity. Without them people can hope to attain some status and thereby some additional personal space and "luxury" in this society in which status depends upon performance. While the great majority merely fear the invasion of robotry, a small group of Medievalists work underground to subvert any attempt to foist robots on their society. If change is to come, they prefer reversion. The Commissioner of Police, for example, shows Medievalist leanings with his insistence on wearing old-fashioned rimmed glasses. Also he maintains a window in his office, allowing him a view of the outside, the sun and rain, the extent of the earth, sights which set up great psychological stress in most citizens.

Into this complex situation of inter-cultural tension Baley must step to solve the Spacer murder. Since the Spacers themselves requested an earth policeman, it is evident they believe the murderer is not one of their own. To the Earthmen it seems equally evident that the criminal could not be one of theirs because all who enter the Spacer enclave are closely screened. The Spacers, not immune to the many Earth organisms, fear contamination, so they require each entrant to strip, shower, and put on clothes they have cleaned thoroughly. There is no way a man could smuggle a blaster into their compound. While a man could sneak in by other entrances, that also is unlikely given the extreme revulsion experienced by any earth citizen upon being in the open, feeling a breeze on his skin, or smelling the pungency of fresh air. The citizens of New York are all far advanced in their brand of agoraphobia.

Baley must work with R. Daneel Olivaw, a Spacer detective and, as one expects from the C/Fe society, a robot. Here Asimov has provided not one puzzle but at least three, all of which will necessitate moral activity to disentangle. Who murdered Dr. Sarton? Does the murder have interplanetary ramifications with the attendant possibility of invasion and war? Can a human work with a robot on an "equal but parallel basis"? Asimov interweaves the three "mysteries" so that they strengthen each other by lending suspense. The cultural shock of spacer-terran societies on the large scale finds its mirror image in the Baley-Olivaw combination. If Asimov can make us believe that the accommodation of one man to the robot challenge works for the betterment of the relationship at large, then he can more easily move us to the inter-social dilemma and make us believe that accommodation can be accomplished on the larger scale. This philosophical identification of the microcosmic and the macrocosmic problem moves the latter away from the derring-do adventures of the more conventional space opera of the time. It puts the action of the novel on the level of human emotions and human reason, a plane on which the detective story finds its traditional home.

Asimov's detective duo traces a pattern closer to that of the then-embryonic police procedural than of the detective and companion convention of the classical mystery.[5] Unlike Bester's Lincoln Powell, who with wry humor says "I Sherlock for the cops" and whose logical powers do remind us of Holmes, Lije Baley is an ordinary man. He makes mistakes in his deductions and must reassess evidence. He worries about keeping his position, at the same time hoping for upward mobility. He is conscious of his limitations, among them his age of forty-six. Caring for his family and his city, he fears great social change. Despite all, he works this future New York's equivalent of the "mean streets" with little to rely on but doggedness and a sense of loyalty to the job. R. Daneel Olivaw is no Watson, bound to Baley by admiration and a lesser intellect. Instead he is a true thinking machine. Machine in fact, but thinker? It is when Baley comes to realize that Olivaw, too, has his limitations that the partnership begins to work. It is in their second professional liaison in *The Naked Sun* that Baley puts it into words: Daneel Olivaw is "logical only, not reasonable."[6]

In *The Naked Sun* (1957) Asimov redefines the role of the detective in such a way as to facilitate that desired blending of mystery and science fiction more realistically. Elijah Baley, again working with R. Daneel Olivaw, receives an assignment to investigate another murder, this one on one of the Outer Worlds populated by Spacers. The Spacers themselves have requested his services because of their respect for his performance in solving the murder described in *The Caves of Steel*. Underscoring the interplanetary importance of the request, it is the Undersecretary of the Justice Department who delivers the assignment to Baley and speeds his departure. In addition, the Undersecretary orders him to gather sociological data about the Spacers, especially information about their weaknesses. As we know from *The Caves of Steel*, the Spacers had carefully nurtured the general impression that they were all superior physically and mentally to Earthmen. As expected, Baley demurs. He cites his age, his family responsibilities, his lack of qualification for such a job which he calls *spying*, but the Undersecretary insists it is merely data-gathering. He wonders aloud why they do not send along a sociologist, one trained in what to notice and to evaluate as important. The Undersecretary waves all these objections aside with the re-definition of purpose: "a detective is a sociologist, too; a rule-of-thumb practicing sociologist." [7]

A major area appropriated by science fiction is futurism, especially that part of futuristic thought concerned with human society. Some authors prefer working in the honored literary tradition of the utopia while others reflect a more modern pessimistic attitude and build dystopias in their stories. And what if there is other intelligent life in the universe? What kind of society might these alien creatures have? Whether they be placed in a near or a far future, the building of these societies affords an opportunity for authorial imagination and reason to work hand in hand. More important, they allow an end product which may range in effect from fantasy to satire with subtle gradations of intermediate responses.

Keeping the above in mind one can recognize the benefit Asimov gains by assigning his detective a role as sociologist, even a rule-of-thumb one. In Baley's own world on Earth we recognize the end results of many tendencies already detectable in twentieth-century life: the overpopulation and crowding in cities, use of food substitutes, limitation of natural resources, and the persistent Luddite reaction to machinery. While we may feel uncomfortable about Baley's New York, we do experience familiarity when faced with it. But Asimov also presents in this second Baley-Olivaw story an alien culture. Even though the Spacers are human beings, descendants of Earthmen, they have lived in Space for so many generations that their mode of existence, values, and customs are alien to us as well as to Baley. He becomes our surrogate. When he is puzzled by something, we share that puzzlement. When he gains understanding, we do likewise. He solves not only the murder puzzle, his raison d'être in the Outer Worlds, but also the puzzle of societal differences. It is through his understanding that we realize the Solarian society is just another alternative society toward which our own could move.

In both *The Naked Sun* and *The Caves of Steel* a murder and its investigation with subsequent solution and apprehension of the murderer is the primary story line. It is embedded, not grafted, in the science-fictional story line. One could easily lift out the murder with the attendant emphasis on motive, method, and opportunity; what remains would be a solid story about the clash of cultures, terran and extraterrestrial. One could also read it as a social satire focusing attention on the man's relationship with the machine. Asimov's robots range in appearance from the awkward Adam Link types to the very sophisticated humanoid, R. Daneel Olivaw, thinking machine *par excellence* and worthy balance for that universal weakness displayed by humans with emotional sensitivity. At the end of each of the novels Asimov has answered his original questions. Who is the murderer? Does the murder have cross-cultural implications? Can people, or rather, should people learn to work with intelligent machines without fear? The answers all combine at the close of each novel with the characters exchanging some rather didactic observations about the future of humanity and the need for foresight rather than the yearning for the past like the Medievalists in *The Caves of Steel* and the Traditionalists in *The Naked Sun*. Robot technology is here to stay, the characters would finally have us know. The solved murder, the bettered cultural relationships, and one man's accommodation all contribute to this thesis.

Asimov's fascination with robots (we all know his contribution of the Three Laws of Robotics as a science fiction convention)[8] overshadows the mystery, such as it is, in the short story he wrote on request of readers who wanted a Baley-Olivaw comeback. "Mirror Image" poses a less serious crime than murder, although Olivaw explains that a demolished reputation rates as intellectual murder. Two famous Spacer mathematicians en route to an important conference create a potentially dangerous situation when they both file identical reports on a revolutionary theory concerning analysis of neural pathways. Before the filing time they had discussed the method together; then each submitted a paper claiming credit for formulation of the theory and method. They toss strong accusations of professional charlatanry at each other. Except for their ages they are mirror images of each other: same background, same papers, similar accusations; even the two robots they use as personal servants are identical in age and model. Baley searches for a discordant note in this all-too-perfect congruence, relying not on clue-gathering but on his knowledge of human nature. Even Spacers are not immune to professional jealousy. Since the Spacers will not submit to direct questioning, Baley questions their robot-servants. Using his knowledge of the Three Laws of Robotics, he so phrases his questions that one of the robots is faced with an asymmetry in its programming, thus throwing it into stasis and giving weight to Baley's accusation against one of the humans.

As the stories in *Asimov's Mysteries* testify, Asimov continued to demonstrate ability with science fiction/fantasy mysteries well into the late 1960s. In these particular mystery stories, while different sciences add suspense, the solutions to crimes often rely on the human ability to cut through the scientific "fog" to recognize a vital clue arising out of human error. Organic chemistry provides the scientific basis for "What's In A Name?" and "A Dust of Death." In the former a university librarian dies of cyanide poisoning after drinking a cup of tea in the chemistry library office. The senior faculty member, a chemist, aids the police by naming her look-alike colleague as the culprit and the motive as jealousy. He cannot prove her guilt until he challenges her alibi. She claims she was busy checking out a book to a student during the crucial time, but she fails to react at all to an amazing coincidence, one any person familiar with scholarship in organic chemistry would notice. The name of the student tallies exactly with that of the author of the well-known and often-used encyclopedia being checked out. When the librarian is faced with this fact, she confesses to the murder.

In "The Dust of Death" a famous but universally disliked organic chemist is killed in a laboratory explosion. When H. Seton Davenport of the Terrestrial Bureau of Investigation comes on the case, he calls upon the assistance of Llewes' assistants. These men freely admit dislike of Llewes, particularly because of his credit-stealing of their scientific achievements; this supplies motive. Opportunity presents itself daily in the easy availability of explosive materials and also in the known regularity of Llewes' work habits. The police laboratory establishes method when traces of powdered platinum are found on two cylinders of gas, one exploded and the other intact. Only the scientist-helper can explain it to Davenport, for the evidence points to a scientist lately come from a different part of the galaxy where explosive combinations differ because of Earth's atmosphere.

As one might expect from science fiction/fantasy, the science of space travel and space experiments figure in some stories. In "Anniversary," a sequel to "Marooned Off Vesta," three survivors of a space accident become intrigued by the semi-secret activities of the insurance company who after a decade is still collecting pieces of the wreckage floating around in space. The puzzle in this story is not of a crime, unless it be that of society forgetting people after their heroic effort to survive. Using the advanced computer technology of their far-future society, the three sift through information such as the passenger list and the contents of the non-human cargo. The investigation results in their recognition of the reputation of one passenger and the rumored advance in his particular field of optics. The three locate a device after realizing it could be one of the two souvenirs one of them carried from the wreck when they were rescued. Then they must discover what it is. This discovery turns on recognition of a slight distortion of language: *an optikon* being heard instead of the more descriptive *anoptikon*.

Asimov plays with language clues in several stories, playfulness which also denotes his ease with the mode in which he is working. In "A Loint of Paw," one of the short-short stories for which Asimov is well known, an embezzler uses a time-travel machine to outwit the law on the statute of limitations. This is less a mystery story in the sense that motive, means, and opportunity are all well known both to reader and to the legal authorities in the story. Only one puzzle remains: will this clever thief evade the law? He does in a twist of the language it would not be fair to any future readers to divulge here. In a much longer and more complex story, "The Key," Asimov again turns the solution on a pun, in this case a bilingual one. Two men on the moon discover a non-terran device that responds to the flow of emotions from the body. Upon recognizing this as a potential mind-tampering weapon valuable for influencing an ideological struggle on earth, one of the men claims it. The other refuses to give it up, insisting that it go to properly constituted authority. In the consequent struggle the Device triggered by one man's emotions destroys the mind of the other. Before the latter dies, he hides the Device and leaves a clue in a cryptogrammatic message directed to a Dr. Wendell Urth. Urth's acquaintance with both men, who had been his students, aids him in deciphering the message that resolves itself upon a pun.

Wendell Urth, armchair detective *par excellence*, first appeared in an adventure, "The Singing Bell" (1955). In the next ten years he solved three other puzzles, duly reported by author Isaac Asimov in

"The Talking Stone" (1955), "The Dying Night" (1956), and "The Key" (1966). Dr. Wendell Urth, an eminent extraterrologist, never stirs out of his study except to walk across campus to his classes. Despite his aversion to space travel he is the repository of an immense store of data about the galaxy and its secrets. Rotund in appearance, ensconced behind a desk in a room filled with artifacts from the Moon, Venus, Mars, and places represented on his enormous Galactic Lens, Wendell Urth is the ultimate eccentric. He is a true descendent of the Baroness Orczy's Old Man in the Corner[9] with a major exception: unlike The Old Man, whose feeling tends to favor the criminal, Urth is more logically dispassionate.

"The Singing Bell" is a straightforward inverted pattern. Louis Peyton flaunts the law with impunity, knowing that his wit and brains can outstretch the abilities of any police force on earth. Worse than that, the police know it, too. In all of his escapades he has gone scot-free, despite the threat of the psychoprobe, the ultimate weapon used to confirm guilt in this far-future society. The first half of the story details Peyton's pre-planning and execution of a daring robbery of a cache of Singing Bells from the moon. This particular artifact is protected by law, a fact of little moment to Peyton's desire for the quick profit, even if it means killing his small-time accomplice in the process. Peyton's success rests on his use of the established pattern of his life, especially a month-long period of complete seclusion in the mountains. Urth breaks this ironclad alibi when he stages an incident during which Peyton betrays the maladjustment of his muscles to Earth's gravity after his month on the Moon instead of at his earth hideaway.

In "The Talking Stone" Asimov describes a life-form utterly without equal in our contemporary world, a silicony or rock-burrowing, half-stone but talking creature out of the asteroid belt. It subsists on gamma energy. When a space mechanic spots an extra-large silicony on an asteroid miner's space ship, he does something to the ship which will make it stop in space at a place where authorities can then arrest the crew as uranium smugglers. However, a chance asteroid demolishes the space craft first. The mechanics board the damaged ship, find all humans dead, but rescue the silicony to question it about the location of its uranium-rich home. They can make no sense of its answer, "on the asteroid." Naturally such a problem comes to the attention first of H. Seton Davenport who in turn consults Wendell Urth. In a space adventure version of Poe's purloined letter Urth reasons that the coordinates of the silicony's home asteroid would be recorded but hidden in the most open, most obvious place. Because the silicony would identify any place where he rested as an asteroid, the numbers must be on the space ship proper. There they are, combined with the registration number of the ship itself.

The efforts of Hal Clement, Alfred Bester, and Isaac Asimov proved beyond a doubt that in the hands of careful writers a future-society detective or one operating in outer space with alien cultures or robots could be a believable character. The author could play fair with the reader, first by a convincing presentation of the society or world in which the detective would operate; second, by making the crime one of importance to merit the efforts of detection; and, third, building the case in such a way as to allow the reader of sufficient wit to solve the case along with the detective or offer the one of less interest in logical puzzles to enjoy the detective's efforts to use the science of his day in the solution. Their success encouraged both contemporaries and later writers to expand the hybrid mode more imaginatively.

NOTES

1. First published in *Astounding Science-Fiction* in 1949, *Needle* was later expanded into a novel (Garden City, N.Y.: Doubleday, 1950) with a variant title, *From Outer Space*, given to a 1957 edition. A sequel, *Through the Eye of the Needle* (New York: Ballantine, 1978), followed.

2. Sam Moskowitz, *Seekers of Tomorrow* (1966; rpt. Westport, Conn.: Hyperion, 1974), p. 250.

3. Joseph P. Patrouch, Jr., *The Science Fiction of Isaac Asimov* (Garden City, N. Y.: Doubleday, 1974), p. 192.

4. Edmund Spenser, *The Fairie Queene*, Book VII, Canto VI, Stanza 1.

5. Lawrence Treat's *V as in Victim*, generally credited with being the first police procedural setting major conventions for the mode, was published in 1945, nine years before *The Caves of Steel*.

6. Isaac Asimov, *The Naked Sun* (1956; rpt. Greenwich, Conn.: Fawcett, 1972), p. 108.

7. Ibid., p. 18.

8. Asimov includes these laws in several robot stories; they have become a science fiction/fantasy convention in their own right. In the introductory material to *I, Robot* they are given in this full form:

THE THREE LAWS OF ROBOTICS

1. A robot may not injure a human being, or, through inaction, allow a human being to come to harm.
2. A robot must obey the orders given it by human beings except where such orders would conflict with the First Law.
3. A robot must protect its own existence as long as such protection does not conflict with the First or Second Law.

Handbook of Robotics
56th Edition, 2058 A.D.

9. The title character of *The Old Man in the Corner* (1909) sits all day in a London tea shop, listens to the information brought to him by a young reporter, and then brings forth the solution, a true armchair detective.

CHAPTER 3

AND ON TO Z

Writing to Will H. Low in the Epilogue to *The Wreckers* (1892), Robert Louis Stevenson voiced misgivings with the form of the police novel or mystery story current in his day. He described it as that which "consists in beginning your yarn anywhere but at the beginning, and finishing it anywhere but at the end." He found himself "attracted by its peculiar interest when done, and the peculiar difficulties that attend its execution; repelled by that appearance of insincerity and shallowness of tone, which seems its inevitable drawback." In particular, he worried at the "airless, elaborate mechanism" which erased any "impression of reality or life."[1] Had Stevenson lived to read the science fiction/fantasy mysteries of the next century, he would have been moved to comment on the unique impressions of reality and life offered by these writers. The reality and life might be the stern reality of existence faced by an alien life-form as in Clement, or the inner reality of a tortured soul as in Bester, or the reality of a necessary adjustment of human to machine as in Asimov. Whatever the situation, these writers infused new life into Stevenson's "airless, elaborate mechanism."

While taking away nothing from the critical acclaim well deserved by the three authors above, we must not ignore the larger context in which they belong. They were not the first writers to challenge the impossible nor the last to do so. Not all of these others produced stories as noteworthy from a historical standpoint, but they do entertain by illustrating the variety of ways science fiction/fantasy can utilize and expand the formulaic requirements of detective fiction. Given the large output of science fiction/fantasy since the 1930s, it is impossible to mention every short story and novel using the detective mode. A generous sampling from successive decades, however, shows the authors not only responding to the challenge of the merger but also adapting it to a readership becoming sceptical of easy solutions to any human problem.

One might expect one bridge between the two modes to be built on a mystery, say a murder, occurring at a science fiction gathering.[2] The mystery invites questions: Is the murderer alien or human? Can a murder be solved by a detective or the official police not yet converted to acceptance of extraterrestrial life? If solved, what recourse to justice exists? Did the alien, if found to be the murderer, act under altruistic standards of his race's ethical imperatives? The questions multiply. Four novels using this setting at a science fiction meeting illustrate the imaginative directions available. Anthony Boucher's 1942 *Rocket to the Morgue*, written under the pseudonym of H. H. Holmes, involves the Manana Society and features several fictional characters easily identifiable as contemporary science fiction authors. William Marshall's *Sci-Fi* (1981) moves the action to a more exotic setting, Hong Kong during the All-Asia Science Fiction and Horror Movie Festival. Mack Reynolds in *The Case of the Little Green Men* (1951) uses fandom to provide the context for his mystery. Richard Purtill's *Murdercon* (1982) also places his murder at a science fiction convention.

A closer look at *The Case of the Little Green Men* reveals how Mack Reynolds disposed of most of the above questions at the same time ''educating'' a reader into the current jargon and special interests of science fiction fandom. Three members of the Scylla Club hire Jed Knight of Lee and Knight, Private Investigations, to explore the possibility that aliens have infiltrated life on earth, more particularly their organization. These science fiction fen (they patiently explain to Knight that *fen* is the plural of *fan*, modeled after the common transformation of *man* into *men*) show umbrage when he refers to the suspected aliens as ''little green men,'' but insist on his taking the case despite his ignorance. A series of disturbing occurrences change his attitude. One of the men who hired him is killed during a club meeting, the condition of his body suggesting a fall from a great height (a space ship?). A second client awakens to find his room marred by burning (a heat-ray carried by aliens?). Still later, another fan knowledgeable in the subject of extraterrestrials dies from burns during the fan convention (more heat-rays?).

Knight, whose reputation is at an all-time low with the authorities (in the person of Lt. Davis) receives no aid from that quarter. His own ineptitude discredits him with all concerned except the survivors of his original clients. He follows false leads, such as the theft of a fanzine, the ditto master of which gives no clues as to its importance; he can find no one who admits to knowing much about the man murdered at the convention. At last he stumbles on the solution: one of his clients, motivated either by jealousy or fear of discovery of financial misappropriations, has engineered the whole affair by acts of misdirection. He had pushed his cohort from a high place to suggest Martian action; he simulated the heat-ray burn both on the wall of the fanzine writer's room and in the electrocution of the innocent convention manager. The whole affair ends up tidily with the suicide of Knight's client, once he is faced with Knight's deductions.

Although not totally convincing in the case for alien intruders or in the pat resolution of the case, Mack Reynolds has entertained us with his version of that stock character, the inept private investigator, an anti-Philip Marlowe in all respects. Knight is driven by financial needs to take on a highly improbable case, one he cannot take too seriously until the first murder. He carries doggedly on despite discouragement from the police and at times from those for whom he is working. By so doing, he does gain the sympathy of the reader who sees in Knight both a target for our scorn of his gullibility and a vessel for our sympathy as we recognize in him our own potential for that gullibility.

A most difficult combination, if we can judge by the sparse use of it, is that of alien and detective. Hal Clement gained credibility by devoting a sizable part of his novel to the logical explanation of the alien's adaptation and use of his symbiotic environment to forward his investigation. Other authors have treated the alien-detective as subject for parody shading into melodrama. Robert Sheckley's *Mindswap* (1966) and Gardner Dozois and George Effinger's collaborative effort in *Nightmare Blue* (1975) exemplify this trend.

Robert Sheckley's protagonist in *Mindswap* is one Marvin Flynn, thirty-one, a tester of plastic toys, an occupation promising little adventure. Flynn decides that life is passing him by; travel to faraway places will spice up life. An advertisement for a body exchange with a "Martian gentleman" (a futuristic version of the modern house exchanges for vacations) lures him into a body-brokerage company. After signing the requisite papers, he finds himself in due course in a comfortable home on Mars, occupying himself by getting used to the body of one Ze Kraggash. But Marvin Flynn is doomed to a succession of adventures unlike those he had bargained for. Almost immediately Martian authorities arrest him for occupying a body previously "rented" to another alien. Since authorities on Earth cannot locate Ze Kraggash, criminal, con man, villain, Flynn must undergo dispossession and become a bodiless mind. To forestall his fate, Flynn seeks aid at the Bureau of Detection and Apprehension, Interstellar Division; to the lone man on duty he states his problem—"I lost my body."

The case is assigned to middle-aged Martian Detective Urf Urdorf. Detective Urdorf's record is less than comforting, 158 cases, none yet solved. With Flynn he hopes to break the jinx but succeeds only in transferring it. In Urdorf's initial interview with Flynn and the subsequent investigation, author Scheckley succeeds in satirizing bureaucratic inefficiency, tunnel-visioned officialdom, and the self-imposed blindness of persons refusing to consider alternative explanations or even facts. Even when Urdorf, aided by the Northwest Galactic Interstellar Constabulary and the Cassem City Traffic Patrolmen, corners Kraggash to charge him with "illegal Mindswapping, attempted murder, and grand larceny," he suffers the ultimate disgrace by being outwitted at the height of his big scene of triumph.[3]

While Sheckley's parody serves the stern purpose of satire as well as humor, Gardner Dozois and George Effinger in *Nightmare Blue* place their detectives, alien and human, in a hybrid detective story-spy thriller. Earthman Karl Jaeger, billed as the "only individual private investigator on Earth"[4] in this twenty-second-century world, is hired by a wealthy recluse to take pictures in an alien stronghold located in mid-Germany. Finding himself the target not only of the alien Aensas but also of his employer's hired thugs, Jaeger switches employers, going to work for the International Congress. They send him on a search-and-destroy mission involving a special drug believed to originate in the Aensa stronghold. There he meets up with Corcail Sendijer, a lobster-clawed life-form working for the Galactic authorities who are equally fearful of the drug's potential threat. Alien and terran join forces, destroy the plant, and kill off the Aensas in a thriller denouement that reveals plots within plots. Their work done, Sendijer and Jaeger part. Corcail Sendijer has a physical form that Earth is not ready to accept as an equal, no matter how intelligent or helpful he might be to human welfare.

Robots have done little better to expand their turf in science fiction/fantasy mystery stories, despite the model set by Asimov in the Lije Baley-R. Daneel Olivaw novels. The writers who have used robots have run the gamut of artificial intelligences: robot, android, cyborg, computer, all constructs with speech, intelligence, ego, and an ethical sense. These modern constructs still have much in common with the robots in Karel Čapek's *R. U. R.* (1921), a play that coined the word *robot* from the Czech *robata*, or labor. In Čapek's play Rossum's Universal Robots manufacturing complex produces robots to serve as slave labor for humans. Although they resemble humans, they differ in a basic way. The general manager quotes the inventor: "A man is something that feels happy, plays the piano, likes going for a walk, and in fact, wants to do a whole lot of things that are really unnecessary." [5] Of the robots he says: "Mechanically they are more perfect than we are, they have an enormously developed intelligence, but they have no soul." [6] Decades later, Lije Baley in *The Naked Sun* (1957) would recognize his robot-partner's efficiency, bow to his logical grasp of a problem, but recognize that he had no reason, one element needed for soul.

Coming halfway between Čapek's robots and Asimov's Olivaw is Eando Binder's Adam Link, at one time in his existence forced into the role of amateur detective. During 1939–1942 Eando Binder (pseudonym of Otto Oscar Binder and Earl Andrew Binder) produced the Adam Link series, later brought together in the book *Adam Link-Robot* (1965). Adam Link is a machine, a "man" of metal with one crucial addition, a pseudo-brain. With this brain his creator Dr. Link foresees that the robot can be "trained to think, to reason, to perform" in ways helpful to people. [7] Unfortunately Dr. Link has discounted irrational human reactions to the unknown. During his existence Adam runs the gamut of science-fictional melodrama. He is falsely accused of the murder of his creator but is exonerated. He finds a job to support himself, becomes a local hero when he foils a bank holdup, is drafted by the U.S. Secret Service, fights aliens in the battle for earth, then receives the Congressional Medal of Honor. When he realizes his extreme isolation, with the aid of retired Dr. Hillory he creates a mate for himself. Even after receiving status as a U.S. citizen he questions his and Eve's true place on Earth, and they leave to establish their home on the Moon.

The episodes of Adam Link's career of special interest here are "Sherlock of Steel," "The Big Clue," "Robot Rescue," and "Human Monster" (chapters 11 to 14 in the collected stories). Before Dr. Link died, he had programmed Adam with the secret of his own creation, a secret coveted by Dr. Hillory so that he may control the world. Using the knowledge he already has, Hillory can adapt the robots' trans-mind helmets so as to manipulate them by remote control. With this power he directs them first to rob a bank, then plans more nefarious deeds for them. During Adam's fight with Hillory for the couple's freedom Dr. Hillory falls from a cliff to his death, reminiscent of the final struggle of Sherlock Holmes and Professor Moriarty at the Reichenbach Falls. But Hillory's death does not end their troubles, for they are arrested for bank robbery and three murders. Jack Hall, a human friend, convinces authorities to try Eve for the crimes, thereby acquiring legal status for her along with Adam.

To discover the real murderer, Adam turns detective. When reminded of the necessity for a detective to spy out information in secret, Adam goes into disguise by coating his very visible metal body with a plastic substance that looks and feels like human skin. In the identity of Pete Larch, a run-down, aging fighter, he haunts the criminal quarter of the city until he picks up the big clue, the name of the man who hired the thugs who actually killed the man for whose murder Eve is held. In "Robot Rescue" and "Human Monster" Adam tracks down the mastermind in his home, overhears plans for a kidnapping, foils that event, and returns for a showdown with Briggs, the culprit, only to have the hired thugs almost incapacitate him with a blow torch. In the tried and true fashion of the melodrama Adam is saved by the fortuitous appearance of Eve who has broken out of jail. Her sudden appearance brings on a confession from the master-criminal and a natural end to Adam's role as detective. In these four brief chapters Eando Binder succeeded in combining elements from robotics, the Sherlock Holmes tradition, the Frankenstein myth, romance, and even the *deus ex machina* convention from Greek tragedy.

A more logical development of the robot-detective lies along the lines of blending machine-like efficiency (à la Daneel Olivaw) more believably with the spiritual elements claimed as human (going beyond

Adam Link). Baker St. Cyr, the cyberdetective created by Dean Koontz in *A Werewolf Among Us* (1973), exemplifies this blending of machine ego and human superego into one smoothly functioning entity. St. Cyr, hired to investigate the murder of one of the children of the wealthy Alderban family, travels to their palatial home on a resort planet, carrying with him his bio-computer. This turtle-shell-shaped appliance he connects by wires to terminals embedded in his chest. Physically the shell fits tightly becoming one with his own body; functionally it augments his mental and rational powers while detracting not a whit from the human "perception of emotions and emotional motivations."[8] The symbiotic relationship of man and machine intensifies the logical capabilities with no interference with ethical sensitivity or sensibility inherent in the human psyche. As St. Cyr patiently and simply explains to an official as he takes the shell through customs, "A cyberdetective is part man and part computer."[9]

As a detective story *A Werewolf Among Us* uses the classical formula so well delineated by W. H. Auden in "The Guilty Vicarage."[10] Here is the small, closed society (the wealthy Alderban family) composed of eccentric individuals (all "hypno-keyed" to intensify their unique creative bent). Not only are they isolated by the diversity of their individual talents, they are isolated geographically (in the remoteness of the planet) and also socially within the group (the house is completely computerized allowing complete privacy to any or all). Their only human contacts outside the family are gypsies living nearby, remnants of the race indigenous to the planet, and possessing a cultural background reminiscent of medieval life. The natural environment contributes both an innocent beauty with the high mountains and lush green fields and a lowering sense of evil in the roughness of the terrain dotted with dead-colored trees.

When murder strikes not once but four times, St. Cyr brings all the power of the man-machine symbiosis to bear on the solution of the crimes. As the computer sorts out the logical threads of the problem, the human mind battles superstitions as old as human history. Both work simultaneously, thus reinforcing each other. At the crucial moment St. Cyr brings all the suspects together for the climactic moment of revelation. Koontz has his cyberdetective follow the accustomed formula: naming of the criminal; presentation of proof (means, motive, and opportunity); the last-ditch effort at evasion by the criminal; the final denouement in a violent scene. Koontz, however, does put a unique twist on the classical situation. The detective faces an unexpected element in the situation when the computer part of him unwittingly betrays the human part of him. The criminal turns out to be the master robot-computer of the Alderban house, one which in some way slipped the leash of its robot training never to harm a human being. The turtle-shell computer, likewise conditioned, failed logically to consider this possibility, therefore rejected important data. Only when human sensibility reasserts primacy in St. Cyr's mind can the detective be saved and the case come to a successful conclusion.

Later writers find the robot-detective a natural object for parody and farce, allowing the human reader to share a sense of superiority over the seemingly infallible machine. Ron Goulart whose stories abound in farcical situations invites us in *The Emperor of the Last Days* (1977) to a parody of the Nero Wolfe-Archie Goodwin formula. Dan Fairleigh, a computer programmer, works for FaxCentral, an information-gathering company. When his work becomes boring, he begins playing armchair detective with the aid of Barney, the computer with which he works. Barney, possessing an all-too-human sentience, urges Dan to become involved in solving the murders of important persons in government. Using the infinite connections with his "cousin" computers, Barney can tap into all sources of stored information. In turn, Dan's mobility allows him to do the requisite leg-work involving recruitment of such worthies as Professor Supermind, who can control machines by his mind; Tin Lizzie, a bionic woman; Deadend, a telekinetic Chicago hoodlum whose thoughts can maim, even kill. Posing as the representative of a philanthropist Bernard Maze (Barney's human *persona*), Dan locates a reporter who in turn helps them uncover a plot by the Millenium gang to overthrow the elected government and establish its own Emperor.

Even with all its "cousins" and its ability to feed the necessary information to the team of corporate detectives Barney remains an object of amusement, a parody of the omniscient machine which threatens the human sense of supremacy. How can anyone feel threatened by a block-shaped mechanism with a sense of humor honed sharply enough to take the pseudonym "Bernard Maze, philanthropist"? When the chips are down, the "cousins" and their accumulated data must yield precedence to the Goulart version of the Baker Street Irregulars, those human specialists such as Tin Lizzie, Professor Supermind, and Deadend.

Parody turns into farce in Isidore Haiblum's *Outerworld* (1979). In an Afterword Ron Goulart says of Haiblum that here he has "blended the hardboiled, the screwball and science fiction" in a "highly entertaining yarn." [11] The action takes place in a parallel world in which the country consists of autonomous city-states with names such as Labor City, Hatesville, Puritan City, Strumpetsville and divided by treacherous areas such as Timewarp Valley. The Board Chairman of Security Plus, largest private protection agency in Happy City, assigns private-eye Ron Dunjer, his Executive Director, to investigate a murder committed on the Chairman's estate. With sophisticated aides at his command, Dunjer's first official act is to activate XX-42 and XX-43, tagged as "two of the best sleuthing mechs on the market." [12] When the murder turns out to be a frame job on Dunjer, the sleuthing mechs and the master contol unit (a Barney without the sense of humor) can no longer help Dunjer. He reverts to the Dashiell Hammett tough-guy mode, relying on such humanly weak human vessels as Whispering Smith, Fingers, and Gimpy Kreeg. Making his private hegira through various areas, Dunjer finally establishes his innocence, brings the true criminal to justice, and re-establishes authority over the thirty-eight sleuthing mechs, lined up army-fashion to receive command. Here is the ultimate derogation of the robot-sleuth, *sans* name, individuality, authority, or moral sensibility.

Name, prestige, and ethics find their most comfortable milieu in the career of the classical crime-solver, that man of independence whose reputation rests upon his ratiocinative ability and a unique mode of operation. Freedom from economic necessity, from loyalty to an official crime-solving body, and from family duties shores up this independence. Even so, the classical detective does recognize social responsibility. Social disorder attracts him. Being governed by reason, he feels motivated to understand the human aberration creating the disorder; by so doing he may restore a modicum of the status quo. Not a judge of moral issues, he serves more as orchestrator of social harmony.

Usually this amateur crime-solver commands a mini-stage with a limited cast: guests at a country-house, residents of a small area within a metropolis, a family gathered for an auspicious event. Restricted physical movement affords a foil for the crime-solver's active mental performance, idiosyncratic behavior, or display of esoteric knowledge. If an armchair detective, he may never leave his own quarters or favorite nook. If he does exert himself to visit the scene of the crime, to interview suspects, or to examine police data, he subjects it all to his own intellect. He may draw conclusions from that data based on personal knowledge beyond a reader's ken. Often the author needs a supporting character to serve as the surrogate for the audience. This individual can assume the reader's ignorance and reflect his amazement at the play of wit and logic displayed by the detective. The more contemporary classical detectives, such as Agatha Christie's Hercule Poirot, while in some cases accompanied by the narrator Captain Hastings, often offers enough information to allow the reader to solve the "clue-puzzle," as Stephen Knight labels it. [13]

In the 1940s and the 1950s Jack Vance created the character of Magnus Ridolph in a series of short stories, later collected in *The Many Worlds of Magnus Ridolph* (1966). This crime-solver would seem to deny one major characteristic of the classical detective, for Ridolph works cases anywhere in the far-flung, populated universe. In the epigraph to "The King of the Thieves" Magnus Ridolph identifies some of the unique worlds of his universe as Almanatz, Judith IV, Medellin, Moritaba; in other stories he finds himself in the Kokod world, the planet Archaemandryx, and The Hub, a complex of bubbles hanging in space. [14] Despite these exotic locales Ridolph manages to limit the actual investigation to a small area and a narrow cast of suspects.

Magnus Ridolph does enjoy the traditional individuality and uniqueness of appearance one expects from the classical pattern. In "Coup de Grace" he early expresses his self-esteem as he assesses the vacationers at the space resort, the bubble Hub; he puts them into four categories—barbarians, boors, a few civilized personages—and himself. A sky-car mechanic in "The Kokod Warriors" sees Ridolph through different eyes, characterizing him as a "little schoolteacher guy with a white beard like a nanny-goat." [15] More than by appearance Magnus Ridolph merits notice by his manner of coping with the current problem. Never flustered even when faced with seemingly insurmountable problems, Ridolph remains one position ahead of the opponent in this game of criminal chess. At the conclusion one finds that Jack Vance has shared all clues with the reader but that his protagonist alone has the acuity to use them not only to restore moral order in some small pocket of the universe but also to redress a personal wrong sustained by Ridolph in the past.

"The Kokod Warriors" illustrates the dual restoration of order in a science fiction/fantasy use of R. Austin Freeman's inverted plot pattern. When a representative of the Women's League Committee for the Preservation of Moral Values seeks aid against a betting syndicate on Kokod, Ridolph takes the case, being motivated by a personal grudge. The gambling officials he had known earlier as men who had absconded with assets of an investment company in which Ridolph was a shareholder. Operating on their turf and being well known to the two shady characters, Ridolph has little advantage except his considerable intellect. He researches local culture and discovers that the casino sits atop a traditional site of one of the Kokod "tumbles," castle-like domiciles. The Kokods, humanoids with secondary bee-like characteristics, engage in carefully regulated but ritualized battles of honor. Coupling this data with his personal knowledge of gambling, Ridolph bids the odds and rigs a battle in the immediate vicinity of the casino, thereby both solving his client's problem and gaining his own peculiar revenge. Within this inverted pattern Jack Vance was able to demonstrate his character's ability to plot a course toward a pre-determined end, much as did Jacques Futrelle's The Thinking Machine. Also, he adds elements of the hero of romance to Ridolph's actions in the battle of good against evil.

"Coup de Grace" presents a puzzle to which Ridolph must apply his not inconsiderable ratiocinative ability. While vacationing on The Hub, anthropologist Lester Bonfils requests Ridolph's aid in forestalling his death threatened by a woman who claims Bonfils has besmirched her honor. Ridolph refuses the case, only to be drawn into it upon Bonfils' death the next day. The Hub being under no formal jurisdiction, Ridolph has no official equipment at his disposal, but that is of little moment. Ridolph becomes the classic armchair detective by retiring to the solitude of the library with only the list of passengers on Bonfils' spaceship plus data concerning planets of their origin. Upon the proprietor's insistence that each be interviewed, Ridolph systematically proves that individual cultural mores would prohibit murder, taboos such as killing while wearing the improper color combination, killing in presence of witnesses, killing by instrument instead of rejection, and other curious ethical restraints. Then drawing upon his fund of cultural data he pinpoints the killer, the least likely suspect whose culture prohibits murder but mandates rendering "constructive service" to living things in anguish. Here the author does not play quite fair with the reader, according to the generally accepted "rules of the game,'' but the provocative solution excuses that point in favor of the subtle comment on ethical and social differences.

In 1958 A. E. Murch in *The Development of the Detective Novel* classed Frederic Brown and Isaac Asimov together as the two writers who had enjoyed success in merging detective themes and science fiction, crediting them with the possibility of inspiring ''a vogue for this specialised variation of the *genre*.''[16] Brown's short story ''Crisis, 1999'' (1949) illustrates his claim to such an accolade. Here he bills his amateur detective, Bela Joad, as ''the greatest detective in the world,'' a reputation admittedly privy only to a few top officials of the world's police forces.[17] In the true style of the classical amateur detective Bela Joad has his mark of individuality, especially notable for being especially unnoticeable. Taking no pay from and giving no special loyalty to any official crime-solving organization, Joad devotes his time and energy to combatting crime.

The crisis in this near-future world created by Frederic Brown arises from the fact that even as the crime rate is falling, criminals consistently beat the lie detector, thus cheating police out of any convictions. No armchair detective, Joad initiates action by approaching the Chicago Chief of Police and imposing his assistance on officialdom. Joad's first plan, an elaborate disguise-and-infiltration move, fails. Then, reminiscent of the Adam Link ploy, by passing himself off as a rising crime figure, Willie Ecks, the detective fakes a murder, goes into hiding, and there ferrets out the lie detector ploy. In the process he links the lie detector puzzle to an earlier-remarked case of a missing professor of criminology from Columbia. After engineering his own disappearance this professor has set himself up in the business of hypnotizing his underworld patrons into forgetting all committed crimes. While so doing, he also predisposes them for a future life in which it is unthinkable to them to commit any crime. Brown casts situation to the service of idea when he forces the question: what if crime fell off to the point of depriving police forces of any function in society?

Stanislaw Lem in *The Investigation* (originally published in 1959 in Poland as *Śledztwo*, translated by Adele Milch in 1974) claims attention for his Dr. Harvey Sciss, mathematician, advocate of the ''statistical method of investigation.'' While Dr. Sciss has a tenuous professional connection with the Scotland Yard authorities, his work offers little realistic help to them. He mirrors the classical detective in some points: he is a non-conformist, given to iconoclastic pronouncements such as ''the classical methods of investigation—the collection of evidence and the search for motives—have failed completely."[18] He delivers his views in lengthy pedantic discourses, displaying a verbal virtuosity and a total dedication to statistical mathematics. All phenomena noted at the scene and time of the crime plus phenomena loosely associated with it go into his calculations.

The case under investigation involves corpses in several villages in England reported by inhabitants as moving, walking, or crawling away from local mortuaries. When inspected by the police, some are no longer in the state of rigor mortis. Since Sciss takes all data as his province in the statistical method of investigation, he includes such irrelevant and innocuous items as the weather, the incidence of cancer deaths in the area, domestic animals at the scene. Discounting common-sense possibilities such as body-snatchers or necrophiliacs or pranksters, offered by the official Detective Gregory, Sciss instead suggests supernatural or extraterrestrial causes, forcing authorities to think in terms of phenomena not traditionally thinkable. While the investigation does end in a solution, it opens up more questions than it answers, evolving into an investigation of the nature of reality, an epistemological case *not* to be solved by collection of evidence, by a search for motives or by the statistical analysis of phenomena. Such a conclusion completely destroys the shield of statistical science protecting Sciss' fragile psyche. *The Investigation* again illustrates marriage of idea to situation in the hands of a master ironist.

Avram Davidson's Dr. Engelbert Eszterhazy needs no protective device for his psyche, for he is a true polymath as a Doctor of Medicine, Doctor of Philosophy, Doctor of Jurisprudence, Doctor of Science, and Doctor of Literature, as well as assorted honorary degrees. With that impressive intellectual pedigree Dr. Eszterhazy is the only person living in the Triune Monarchy of Scythia-Pannonia-Transbalkania qualified to have a uniformed guard with a drawn sword. One keeps watch in front of his private domicile at Number 33, Turkling Street, in Bella, the capital city of the Monarchy. Dr. Engelbert Eszterhazy is not a detective per se, even though his vast knowledge and investigative powers are at the service of both official and private persons, be they as diverse as the Bella Commissioner of Police Karrol-Francos Lobats or his aging English landowner-aunt. Indeed, Eszterhazy's own curiosity need be the only spur propelling him into cases more modestly referred to in Davidson's title as *The Enquiries of Doctor Eszterhazy* (1975).

While reading any one of Eszterhazy's "enquiries" one must accommodate to Avram Davidson's parallel world of the nineteenth century. We recognize that century by its use of gaslights, horse-drawn fire engines, typewriting machines, and steam presses. While one is hard-pressed to locate the Triune Monarchy either in conventional history or on a map of the period, Davidson has firmly anchored it in southwestern Europe with multitudinous cultural references and occasional external geographical points such as Prague or Paris or "Bruklín, a provincial city on Great Island in the American province of Nev-jork." [19]

But Davidson's world is also a world of fantasy where ancient lore still stands respectable and functional. In Eszterhazy's world people believe animal fables, practice diabolism and witness satanic manifestations, produce gold by alchemy, search for the elixir of life, and entertain the possibility of the existence of *doppelgängers*. A closer consideration of Dr. Eszterhazy's scholarly qualifications reveals that his medicine includes herbal prescriptions and folk remedies; his philosophy may draw upon "Basil Valentine's XII Keys and Appendix of the Great Stone of the Antient Philosophers"; and his science relies chiefly on alchemy and phrenology. Despite the archaic nature of Doctor Eszterhazy's learned accomplishments, his great fund of information works to anticipated ends.

Whatever the problem, Doctor Eszterhazy investigates and disposes in his own inimitable way. In "The Church of St. Satan and Pandaemons" a cult of diabolism requests official permission to hold a conventicle, a request deeply disturbing to Count Vladeck, Minister of Cults to the Triune Monarch. He turns to the learned Doctor for aid. How is Eszterhazy to save the Monarchy embarrassment and at the same time save the misguided but solid rural citizenry involved in the cult from official action? He infiltrates the cult to find out a secret code phrase they will act upon. Then he passes this phrase on for innocent use by an agent of the Atlantic, Pacific, and Southwestern Nebraska Railroad who is in Europe searching for settlers to take up free land along the railroad in the newly opened Nebraska area. Eszterhazy's complete knowledge of phrenology enables him to track down a thief in "The Crown Jewels of Jerusalem, or, The Tell-Tale Head," the major clue being the suspect's abnormal bump of amativeness. Even as he muses over the report of his phrenological examination, Doctor Eszterhazy admits the probability that "phrenology must give way to newer and younger sciences," among them being psychology and anthropology.[20]

One testimony to the viability and popularity of any character comes when subsequent authors borrow that character either directly in pastiches or indirectly in parody. Science fiction/fantasy writers are not immune to this brand of borrowing. While many of the stories seem to be done out of the pure joy of reviving a well-loved character, others dance with the delight of humor, as evidenced by such tongue-in-cheek titles as Goulart's *Hail Hibbler* (1980) or Fred Saberhagen's *An Old Friend of the Family* (1979) with a disguised Dracula as the Old Friend. Still others play the name games with the old friend of all families, Sherlock Holmes, giving his literary offspring such handles as Solar Pons, Syalock, or Sherk Oms. Still others combine several characters from different books such as Philip José Farmer's combination of Holmes, Watson, and Lord Greystoke. Still more complex is the tale in which all these inimitable characters come together to serve as metaphors of themselves as in Arthur Byron Cover's *An East Wind Coming* (1979). Whatever the method by which an author resurrects the old and well-established characters, the reader is the winner by being able to experience a two-fold pleasure: reminiscence of the original and appreciation of the art of the author of the pastiche or parody.

Mack Reynolds mixes together allusions to Jack the Ripper, Frankenstein's monster, and the Nazi regime in *Once Departed* (1970) posing the questions: What if Martin Bormann and Hitler's physician survived and now in hiding plan to put together a super-being to take over the world? Is Dr. Grete Stahlecker, ex-Nazi surgeon famous for work in organ transplants, doing the Ripper-like murders of Spanish drifters in order to make her Frankenstein's monster? Reynolds casts an American political columnist and an American reporter in the Holmes-Watson relationship and uses the classic ploy of gathering all suspects together at the end for the denouement.

One of the most prolific science fiction/fantasy writers working the fertile field of pastiche and parody is Philip José Farmer. Farmer goes so far as to bill himself on the title page of *The Adventure of the Peerless Peer* (1974) as both editor and the "American Agent for the Estates of Dr. Watson, Lord Greystoke, David Copperfield, Martin Eden, and Don Quixote." In the 1974 adventure Doyle's doughty pair take a government mission to track down a World War I spy, who has stolen the secret formula for a bacillus to be used against the Germans. The caper soon falls into caricature when we discover that the British had developed the bacillus to feed upon sauerkraut only; however, enemy laboratories might modify it to eat other ethnic foods, thus creating international havoc. Holmes' airsickness, a bit of derring-do when the two must transfer midair from their plane to a zeppelin, a fortuitous appearance by Lord Greystoke in darkest Africa to save them after the airship is downed, and the final comeuppance of the villain complete the increasingly farcical tale.

In 1960 when the Council of Four in Denver issued *The Science-Fictional Sherlock Holmes*, they provided both Holmes buffs and science fiction buffs a spate of literary play. In his introduction Anthony Boucher suggests that Holmes himself crossed the line dividing detective fiction from science fiction when he solved the problem of the eminent Professor Presbury who suddenly had not only undergone a personality change but also had taken to walking on all fours and climbing walls like an anthropoid. Clues involving a trip to Prague, strange little boxes coming from an elderly Bohemian with contacts in Austria and the Balkans, the sudden dislike the Professor's faithful dog has taken to him all combine with his abnormal behavior to suggest lycanthropy or vampirism. But Holmes with his usual reliance on fact and logic discovers the truth: the Professor upon falling in love with a much younger lady has succumbed to man's age-old quest, the search for the elixir of youth, and has placed himself as a guinea-pig in an Austrian scientist's experiments.

If the Creeping Man case admits Doyle into the ranks of science fiction/fantasy mystery writers, his Holmes will not find himself remembered for that adventure alone. In *The Science-Fictional Sherlock Holmes* he will find himself in "The Return" (1953) canonized as a dead and returned god as written in The Books, a one-volume collection of the Sherlock Holmes stories that survived an atomic holocaust. The Pittsburgh Enclave in this tale by H. Beam Piper and John J. McGuire is a small pocket of survivors who have re-organized their lives in a frontier pattern with strong military orientation, leavened only by the mystery and honor surrounding The Books. In Anthony Boucher's "The Greatest Tertian" (1952) Holmes would find himself the focus of speculation of Rom Gul, an alien historian, attempting to clear up the identity of this greatest Tertian (*Tertian* referring to inhabitants of the third planet from the sun). Would he be flattered or annoyed to find that in clearing up the confusion historian Gul has decided that Sherk Oms and Sherk Sper are one and the same? One might speculate that annoyance would more likely come upon reading

Anthony Boucher's "The Anomaly of the Empty Man" (1952) wherein a certain Professor Horace Verner claims to have a cousin with some fame as a private detective. More annoying than the anonymity covering him would be the rephrasing of his guiding principle as "Discard the impossible, and whatever remains, no matter how improbable, must be true."

Sherlock Holmes can meet clones of himself in *The Science-Fictional Sherlock Holmes*, clones in method and self-confidence if not, indeed, in physical appearance. It is a far cry from the lean and thoughtful Holmes to the chubby panda-like Hokas of planet Toka from the imagination of Poul Anderson and Gordon Dickson in "The Adventure of the Misplaced Hound" (1953). When Whitcomb Geoffrey of the Interstellar Bureau of Investigation goes to Toka to track down an interstellar dope-smuggling ring, he receives unexpected aid from the Hokas. This alien race is capable of imitating other cultures, depending upon the reading material they receive from that culture. Predictably in the Hoka Victorian London a Hoka Inspector Lestrade refers them to a Hoka Holmes who in turn helps them capture the dope runner, a ppussjans from Ximba who doubles remarkably well as the Hound pursuing a Hoka Sir Henry of Baskerville. Obviously the title can be none other than "The Adventure of the Misplaced Hound" (1953).

There is, also, the ubiquitous Solar Pons with friend Dr. Lyndon Parker, heroes of some ten volumes of collected adventures authored by different persons but all based on a character created by August Derleth. While many of his adventures do not fit into the science fiction/fantasy mystery category, both "The Adventure of the Ball of Nostradamus" (1955) and "The Adventure of the Snitch in Time" (1953) by Mack Reynolds and August Derleth are included in *The Science-Fictional Sherlock Holmes*. In the latter adventure Agent Tobias Athelney of the T.B.I., planet Terra, consults Solar Pons professionally on his assigned case of tracking down and deterring a band of art thieves headed by Moriarty who cross space-time lines to despoil countries of their prized art treasures. Athelney with the advanced knowledge afforded him by living in 2565 A.D. has experienced some difficulty in locating the *real* Pons, since in some of the space-time continua Pons and Parker are only characters of fiction, figments of an author's imagination!

Syaloch, the Martian detective living in The Street of Those Who

Prepare Nourishment in Ovens, is the contribution of Poul Anderson to the canon of Holmesian pastiches. We meet Syaloch, a storklike, two-legged alien who plays a demifiddle and wears a *tirstokr* hat, in Anderson's "The Martian Crown Jewels" (1957). When the Martian crown jewels disappear on the return trip after being on exhibition on Earth, Syaloch is called in to solve the problem, thus preserving interplanetary peace. Syaloch faces a space-age variation of the locked-room mystery. Witnesses saw the box with the jewels being loaded, and they also saw the workman return with no suspicious bulges where he could have hidden the jewels. Syaloch, drawing upon a fund of scientific knowledge comparable to his model, Sherlock's own extensive knowledge, solves the problem by explaining the use of free fall.

"Hercule Poirot in the Year 2010" (1975) announces the title of Jon L. Breen's pastiche featuring the near-future retread of Agatha Christie's famous Belgian detective. Breen's Poirot is truly a retread, being 150 years old or so and leading "the league in transplants," as he boasts to the police official who has called for his aid on a difficult case.[21] When a well-hated businessman joined his co-travelers in a compartment on the New York-London Underground, he let himself in for a twenty-first-century replay of the murder on the Orient Express. The police detectives, now all mind readers only in method, are stymied; even with the thought records from the scene, the 2010 version of bugging, the police cannot pin down the murderer. They suspect an illegal use of the contemporary development of thought therapy, an activity reminiscent of that uncovered by Frederic Brown's Bela Joad in "Crisis, 1999." Luckily for all, Hercule Poirot's little gray cells still operate in prime condition, so he solves the case in a way that extends the scope of the least-likely-suspect convention customarily employed by an old friend of the police official, a "detective novelist." Of course, the official reminds Poirot, that "lovely gracious lady" could not have a character follow the thoughts of a suspect because that would have been "against the rules of fair play," a tactic now realistically possible in 2010.[22]

Arthur Byron Cover in *An East Wind Coming* (1979) has put together the ultimate pastiche in a science fiction/fantasy mystery. Borrowing some techniques from medieval morality plays, Cover identifies his characters only by epithet: the consulting detective, the fat man with orchids, the universal op easily translate into Holmes, Nero Wolfe, and the Continental Op. Then there are those characters who are more plainly named: the ripper, the wolfman, and the thinking machine. Still others identify twentieth-century social phenomena by their labels: the mature eternal child (a rock star) and the eternal children. In this far-future world inhabited by god-like men, the immortals face a threat of spiritual war; thus intuits the consulting detective. One might well speculate as to how immortals would suffer in a war. Death? Obviously not. The solution ironically comes from the ripper who when cornered by the consulting detective faces him with a philosophical dilemma: what is the purpose of immortality if the potential of evil exists there in the boredom of eternity? Has the consulting detective created his own adversary in the ripper for personal satisfaction to break the tedium? Must people have the tug-of-war between good and evil in order to be complete? Given the parodic situation he has imagined, Arthur Byron Cover has demonstrated with ease how the speculative idea can use situation and challenge the rational pattern of the detective mode at the same time moving the reason to a higher philosophical level.

Just as some science fiction/fantasy writers have found the pattern of the analytical detective usable either as a model to emulate or one to parody, others have adapted the stock character of the hard-boiled private investigator. Working in a mode not particularly lauded for its attention to characterization, science fiction/fantasy writers find the private detective poses another set of problems in translation to the futuristic mode. In some cases he tends to slip into the pattern of the hero of romance; in others, into the comic spirit. Those who have made the translation with success have had to accommodate themselves in various ways.

The private detective, a loner, operates without a group or a friend to support him in failure or commend him in victory. Though solitary, he is not defenseless. Beholden to none, he can take what he needs and use it mercilessly, if so warranted. A non-conformist must train himself to rely on his own resources, anticipate reversals, and act without question on his own intuition. Since he has no family obligations, no demanding love interest, no loyalty to a group liable to threaten as a consequence of his exploits, the private eye enjoys that freedom which protects even as it emboldens its possessor. His situation is paradoxical. While the prototypical P.I. is physically and psychologically tough, able to survive in the gray and seamy areas of human existence, he shields himself with a private code of honor.

Each case has the potential to become a personal crusade with the detective pitted not only against society but possibly against his client. His strong sense of social amorality becomes his personal morality, his major protection.

The character of the private eye has forced a shift from the emphasis on the puzzle with the rational solution to a discovery with moral ramifications. The murderer may well be found, it is true, but what the investigator and the reader find is a reaffirmation of both the limitations and the possibilities of the human being. Through the character of the private eye one plays out the age-old, insoluble puzzle of good versus evil only to reach the equally age-old position of ambivalence. The rational dimension of the local mystery has expanded into the moral dimension of the human mystery.

In the merging of these mystery conventions with science fiction/fantasy, an author must contend with certain problems. If he places his character in a future world or on an unknown planet or in an imaginary society organized by alien forms, the moral criteria operating in these situations may utterly destroy the effectiveness of the investigator's personal code of ethics, that in the more conventional private-eye novel exists mainly by its strength against a known criterion. One solution to this impasse may lie in the old cliché: if you can't lick 'em, join 'em. Jan Darzek, hero of Lloyd Biggle's series of "dark" novels, exemplifies this accommodation of science fiction/fantasy with the private-eye conventions, as Darzek moves from a small-time operator to First Councilor of the Council of the Supreme of the Galactic Synthesis and noted interstellar trader in his own right.

When we first meet Jan Darzek in *All the Colors of Darkness* (1963), he works out of a one-man agency in 1986 New York, assisted by a beauteous but soon-to-be-forgotten ex-model who runs his office. His operation affords him enough money to invest in Universal Transmitting Company, a struggling research company owned by friends. The company has perfected the technology to transmit matter from New York to Brussels or Paris or Rome in the time needed to walk through one transmitter and to come out of another in the second city. The process promises to render other modes of transport obsolete and in time to revolutionize international affairs. That unknown but powerful forces recognize its importance becomes evident when anonymous buyers attempt to corner shares. The company suffers acts of sabotage, mysterious set-backs in testing, and, most seriously, on opening day "loses" two women passengers in transit.

Jan Darzek takes on the investigation. He comports himself in the expected private-eye tradition by physical feats such as jumping over the Universal Trans turnstiles in order to pass over along with a woman suspect. This act of derring-do puts him in touch with a galactic "police force," aliens whose primary job is to patrol space to keep primitive life forms from doing anything disturbing to cosmic harmony. They classify all life forms by the color of darkness within them. Unfortunately human beings have received the sentence of "the wrong color of darkness," their major threat to cosmic harmony now being the matter transmitter. Another move in the traditional private-eye mode is to act in disregard of established rules: Darzek steals oxygen from the Moon Base for the small alien force in sore need of it. This intuitive act so impresses the aliens that they decide to aid rather than destroy the new transmitter.

As the action progresses in this novel, Biggle gradually shifts emphasis from Darzek as sleuth to Darzek as discoverer. He discovers an entirely different moral imperative governing a commanding portion of the universe and in the discovery finds himself in the place of influence. Through his aid earth dwellers can buy time to achieve the right color of darkness. Throughout the remaining four novels of the Darzek series, the main character moves farther and farther from the original detectival context. In *Watchers of the Dark* (1966) Darzek still maintains his New York office of 1988, but ex-model Morris is replaced by a Miss Schlupe, an elderly but spritely assistant investigator. Now independently wealthy, thanks to his original shares in the successful Universal Trans, Darzek takes only cases which command his interest.

Readers of traditional private-eye mysteries feel comfortable with the limited theater of operations of the hard-boiled detective. Travis McGee must not become so socially or professionally mobile as to move far from his Florida boat, the *Busted Flush*. California would not be the same imaginative place without Lew Archer and Philip Marlowe roaming the Los Angeles area from the Valley to the beaches and the many stops in between while Sam Spade keeps the faith in San Francisco. Science fiction, on the other hand, can explode the theater of operations into inner or outer space, future or past time.

Darzek exemplifies this shift in emphasis. In *Watchers of the Dark* a million-dollar retainer lures him and Schluppy into a plot of intergalactic freebooters infiltrating the "certified worlds" by the fatal weapon of the lie. The certified worlds communicate by "small-talk" and "large-talk," neither of which contains the words for *lie* or *liar*.

This particular assignment brings Darzek into contact with Supreme, the computer which maintains the galaxy, much on the same order as does Shalmaneser in John Brunner's *Stand on Zanzibar* (1968). Also, Darzek becomes known to and joins a group of interstellar traders. These two connections lead to his further adventures in *This Darkening Universe* (1975) and *Silence Is Deadly* (1977), adventures which culminate in his position as First Councilor of Council of Supreme. No trace remains of the original lone operator of the private-eye genre; this stock character has been replaced by an even older character, the hero of old romance, the intrepid troubleshooter and restorer of moral order.

Perhaps this paints too serious a picture of the career of the science fictional private investigator. It should balance with reminders of the excitement and high pressure of his existence, that side which keeps a reader anxious to turn the page or go on to the next chapter. In "Public Eye" (1952) Anthony Boucher's detective Fers Brin, living in an unspecified but fairly distant future, gives us a future-eye's view of the twentieth-century private eye. During a video interview the interviewer asks Brin to explain the origin of the "public eyes" now working with the W.F.B.I. (World Federation Bureau of Investigation). Brin explains how Stef Murch, an earlier head of W.F.B.I., originally a teacher of twentieth-century literature, had written a thesis on that specialized mode of literature called *whodunits*. During his research he became especially impressed with the protagonists whom Brin describes as "even wilder than the Mad Scientists and Martians" of other modes of the period. So that his video audience can better understand the twentieth-century private eyes, Brin describes them as able to "outdrink six rocketmen on Terra-leave and outlove an asteroid hermit hitting Venusberg." [23]

Matthew Swain, series detective in Mike McQuay's *Hot Time in Old Town* (1981), *When Trouble Beckons* (1981), and *The Deadliest Show in Town* (1982) along with a projected fourth novel, may not qualify as wilder than a mad scientist or a Martian, but his adventures take him into the human wilderness of a twenty-first-century Texas city. His world is an entropic one in which decay is the most notable condition. Physical decay—cracks in walls, garbage piled up on streets, pitted streets, run-down high rise buildings—provides the gloomy backdrop for the social decay. The town exists as a series of concentric areas radiating from Old Town and Ground Zero outward through the business areas with each store and apartment complex guarded by "fancy Dans," trigger-happy private security forces, and still farther out into the area of wealthy private homes, equally secured against human need and depravation. Ground Zero marks the area of a nuclear plant meltdown, an event precipitating great numbers of mutant humans, all of whom must by law live in Old Town, in the "decay." Here also is located the DMZ, an inner-inner city, center of vice operations controlled by a Maria Hidalgo; the DMZ is a self-controlled unit, organized in a way reminiscent of the old-style crime family setup.

Matthew Swain chooses to live in Old Town. He knows Maria Hidalgo and uses her expertise and connections when needed. Yet the two respect each other's moral code so that her activities do not deter him nor do they frighten him. He is wary of the unknown factor, the irrational behavior able to destroy both his case and his life. With little fear of violence and driven by his internal code, Matthew Swain plays out the formulaic role of the hard-boiled private investigator in three different cases. In *Hot Time in Old Town* Swain searches for the culprit in a locked-room murder, a search which uncovers family hatreds, the classic skeletons in the family closet, and misplaced identities. *When Trouble Beckons* shows a tender side to the hard-boiled detective when he must go on a rescue mission and through the subsequent but fruitless attempt to save his lover's mind. Another locating job in *The Deadliest Show in Town* uncovers a far deadlier case of a plot for political assassination.

In "The Simple Art of Murder" Raymond Chandler, to whom Mike McQuay has dedicated the Matthew Swain series, wrote what has become one of the axioms of the private investigator story: "But down these mean streets a man must go who is not himself mean, who is neither tarnished nor afraid."[24] Matthew Swain fits that brief description. With little trepidation he goes down the mean streets of his twenty-first-century world, wherever they may lead. His work takes him from the depths of the DMZ to the heights of Freefall, a sweatshop town in space; from a well-guarded mansion of an ill and aging man of wealth to the public sex shops. Swain's mean streets test the mettle of the man, and the man survives even though his efforts be unsuccessful. McQuay's success in bringing the near-future, entropic society into a credible existence bids fair to reduce the accomplishments of his protagonist. Swain's mean streets and their intimations of a future that is possible in the light of current events carry an impact far greater than the human activities taking place on them. Here situation intensifies idea to its own loss.

The ancient Greeks still exert definable influence on our esthetic sensibilities: everything in moderation; nothing in excess. As the man who lives in excess excites imagination, he also invites criticism, directly by admonition or indirectly with irony, and satire. Karl Jaeger, the human half of the accidental sleuthing duo of *Nightmare Blue* (1975) by Gardner Dozois and George Alec Effinger, both imitates and derides the conventional image of the hard-boiled private investigator. As Jaeger, Inc., the "only individual private investigator on Earth, as the last of an otherwise vanished breed,"[25] Karl Jaeger has but one thing to offer a client—himself. When Maximilian Schiller, his wealthy but secretive client, disapproves of his performance on the basis of Jaeger's softness under stress, Jaeger demolishes all criticism with a realistic "the tough detective mystique—that's image, it's good for business"[26] and a boast about his own efficiency, a boast which future events prove less than true.

In the discussion of fictional modes in *Anatomy of Criticism* Northrop Frye offers a useful method of classification based on the character of the hero, particularly on his power of action. In his study Frye noted that European fiction steadily moved its focus on the protagonist as the hero of myth to the ironic hero of the twentieth century.[27] While we cannot claim to fit representative detective heroes into all five of Frye's slots, we can notice an abbreviated analogous movement from the now-legendary Sherlock Holmes as hero of romance to the realistic private eyes of the mid-twentieth century and on to the more recent ironic hero-investigator who stumbles more than advances on his way to the solution demanded by the formula.

David Bear in *Keeping Time* (1979) gives us an example of the ironic mode utilized not only in the career of his hero-private investigator Jack Hughes but also in the evocation of the familiar and frightening near-future world in which Jack works. This is 1999 U.S. fraught with problems: energy sources are undependable ever since the fuel rebellion and the sabotage of the southern gas wells some twenty years previously. Tremendous events have shaken the complacency of the citizenry: nuclear plant meltdowns, climatic changes, the loss of part of Southern California in a slide into the ocean. The consequent loss of morale has so marked the populace that it merits a special label,

Apathera or the Era of Apathy. One character describes the situation as producing the "death rattles of civilization." Indeed, it has produced individual death rattles as those who cannot adjust to the pervasive depression commit suicide, euphemistically termed "slipping out the back door."

When his wife and children "slip out the back door," Jack Hughes, Harvard Law School and member of a prestigious law firm, changes his entire life, resigning from the firm to open a one-man detective agency. Jack Hughes is a survivor. To work alone dependent upon his own resources is to retain sanity, but a case from a time-saving and storage business is calculated to destroy that balance. Five tapes contracted by individuals who wish to siphon off segments of present time to store them for future use have been stolen. Hughes discovers strong links between all five persons involved; motives emerge making all five suspect. In the process of the investigation Hughes also discovers a submerged reserve of human emotions when he meets the now grown-up daughter of his former employer. The employer is the husband of one of the suspects. Wheels turn within wheels, cogs within cogs, as the detective fixes on each of the five suspects in turn as logic indicates. Each time, however, reasoning breaks down under unexpected events, such as murders of two suspects, just as he is ready to present his evidence.

Jack Hughes is the true ironic hero. He suffers frustration at each crucial point. In bondage to past memories of his wife and children and to a system of values now rendered inoperable by the Apathera, Hughes works in a truly absurdist world. When he tries to justify his work as "creative interpretation," those imaginative words are belied by a subsequent, more realistic remark: "It's a cut-and-paste job. I have to look for the patterns myself. Sometimes, the patterns I find don't fit right."[28] Even as Hughes solves both crimes, murder and theft, the pieces do not fit right for him, when the culprit turns out to be the same person, the least-suspected one and one whose act undermines his new-found humanity.

Other authors have debunked the image of the detective and have also distorted the basic conventions of the genre itself as a way of testing its durability. Two techniques warrant our consideration: outright burlesque or parody and the attack upon convention by introducing a major irrational element to challenge the cornerstone of the detective mystery genre, ratiocination. Of the two, parody shading toward burlesque invites the reader to humor; the other which tends decidedly toward the occult demands more serious reading in context of the Gothic tradition.

Although he is normally not listed among the science fiction or fantasy writers, Richard Brautigan in *Dreaming of Babylon: A Private Eye Novel 1942* (1977) enjoys romping through the conventions of the private eye novel using fantasy to turn his major character against himself. C. Card, private investigator (or "Eye" to Peg-leg, his friend at the morgue), fits the stereotype of the private investigator. He is at the bottom of his luck with no money in pocket, no credit, no office (he operates out of a phone booth), no cases pending, and most embarrassing of all, no bullets for his gun. Under such circumstances a man might head for the nearest employment office or welfare office. But C. Card heads for Babylon, thanks to a head injury suffered when he was knocked out by a bean ball during a tryout with a professional baseball club some years before. When C. Card finally gets a case, one doomed from the beginning to end, his assignment is to steal a body. Only his fantasy life as a private investigator in Babylon, where he fights the diabolical Dr. Abdul Forsyte and his army of Shadow Robots, saves his, and incidentally the reader's, sanity in the madcap burlesque of the hard-boiled dick.

Ron Goulart also relies on parody and burlesque of conventional characters and plot formula as seen, for example, in *After Things Fell Apart* (1970), *Hail Hibbler* (1980), and *Big Bang* (1982). The worlds of Goulart's novels are ones seen through a glass darkly. In *After Things Fell Apart* the social and political order of California has fallen apart; power such as it exists resides in splinter groups, county-based enclaves, or quasi-official military groups. In this future society each group defends its outré style of life. Androids are so prolific that human beings have to identify themselves as human, and women have an organized movement to kill off the men (Mankill, Inc., more familiarly known as Lady Day movement). Frustrated at the success of the Lady Day killers, the chief of the Intelligence and Investigation office of the San Francisco Enclave calls upon Jim Haley of the Private Inquiry Office for aid in tracking down the key figure in the movement.

Haley is not the lonely private investigator relying on his own wits, although in this unpredictable society he needs them. Instead, he is part of an organization financed by private concerns but for a price available to public groups. When Haley explains that at San Francisco Enclave Free University he had minored in Nostalgia and Pop Culture, Goulart foreshadows what is in store for his detective—a topsy-turvy trip through pop culture gone so wild that the nostalgia is not strong enough to temper its effect. Haley's detective work gets lost in a sea of zither-playing robots, replicas of nineteenth-century western saloons, and a stock shoot-out at the Old G-Man Motel.

The exploits of Jake and Hildy Pace of Odd Jobs, Inc., central characters in *Hail Hibbler* and *Big Bang*, are no less zany. Living in the first decade of the twenty-first century, these two must cope with problems from one-on-one confrontations to others with nationwide implications. In *Hail Hibbler* a patron at Mama Rosa's Mafia Stronghold restaurant watches Jake and Hildy brawl with androids, and he complains that Pace is always on the lookout for trouble. As one follows Jake and Hildy through their trouble-fraught world, Ron Goulart introduces us to Italian androids programmed to be sentimental about motherhood; police forces amalgamated into a Federal Police Agency; a Secretary of Big Business in the President's Cabinet; chimpanzees acting *Hamlet*; and people teleporting to save time. The twenty-first-century technology also breaks down, so these latter folks may well find most of themselves in Berkeley but with one foot still in Ft. Lauderdale.

Goulart's novels do not exist solely on the level of burlesque; they contain some none-too-subtle satire of political intrigue. In *Hail Hibbler* when Jake is invited to be a guest star on the Blab show, his co-star is a senator who is sponsoring a bill authorizing the catching and banding of all private investigators. The show turns out to be an elaborate plot to eliminate Pace's meddling in a plan for the emergence of a Hitler look-alike who has been in cryonic suspension since World War II. In *Big Bang* several big bangs have systematically killed important persons throughout the world. When official bodies fail to turn up the required evidence of a plot, the Paces take over at the request of the twin Presidents of the United States. While the Goulart novels use the private-eye formula to inveigle the reader into laughter at what fools we mortals may become—if indeed we have not already reached that state—they also invite serious consideration of contemporary trends and the ridiculous lengths to which people may carry them.

From the beginning paragraph-sentence "I was bored" to the final paragraph-sentence "And proved it" William F. Nolan's *Space for*

Hire (1971) provides a science fiction/fantasy detective story romp through a clutch of clichés from both members of the symbiotic relationship. In the Author's Preface William Nolan (better known for his collaboration with George Johnson in *Logan's Run*) acknowledges that his detective, Sam Space, is "deliberately cast in the Warner Brothers mold of the 1930's, out of Bogart by Chandler, a Hammettized op thrown gun-first into the future."[29] From the science fiction pulp tradition come Venusian tripleheads, birdfish from Pluto, Loonies from the Moon, and other non-human characters taking quite casually teleportation, cryogenics, gravbelts, and vidscreens. From fantasy come candy forests, witches, fire demons and a Jupiter Big Mouse religion with a human, Waltdisney, as the god's human representative. From detective fiction comes Sam Space with a penchant for getting both in and out of violence, a taste for beautiful females, and a talent for being in the right place at the wrong time or vice versa. Nolan's Sam Space is the ultimate parody of the stock character of the tough-guy private investigator, as the pun of his name suggests none too subtly.

Despite the early reservations about the feasibility of merging science fiction/fantasy with the detective story, these authors have proved that such a symbiosis can be effected with varying degrees of success, depending upon the author's purpose in utilizing the older mode. Whenever an attempt is made to balance two disparate patterns, one must anticipate pitfalls, especially when one pattern focuses on situation and character, the other on idea. Science fiction/fantasy detective story writers who like Robert Louis Stevenson have found themselves "attracted by its peculiar interest when done," and have faced "the peculiar difficulties that attend its execution" have found ways to negate his reservations and have added new life to what he termed the mystery story's "airless, elaborate mechanism."[30]

NOTES

1. Robert L. Stevenson, with Lloyd Osbourne, *The Wreckers* (New York: Scribners, 1892), p. 551.

2. Isaac Asimov uses this plot idea in one of his nonscience fiction mysteries, *Murder at the ABA* (1976). ABA here refers to the American Booksellers Association.

3. Robert Scheckley, *Mindswap* (New York: Dell, 1967), p. 142.

4. Gardner Dozois and George Alec Effinger, *Nightmare Blue* (New York: Berkley, 1975), p. 30.

5. S. Marion Tucker, *Twenty-Five Modern Plays* (New York: Harper and Bros., 1931), p. 757. This speech and the succeeding one occur in Act I of *R. U. R.*

6. Ibid., p. 758.

7. Eando Binder, *Adam Link—Robot* (New York: Paperback Library, 1965), p. 11.

8. Dean R. Koontz, *A Werewolf Among Us* (New York: Ballantine, 1973), p. 2.

9. Ibid., p. 2.

10. W. H. Auden, "The Guilty Vicarage," reprinted in Dick Allen and David Chacko, *Detective Fiction: Crime and Compromise* (New York: Harcourt Brace Jovanovich, 1974), pp. 400–410.

11. *Binary Star No. 3* (New York: Dell, 1979), p. 302. This volume contains both Isidore Haiblum's *Outerworld* and Ron Goulart's *Dr. Scofflaw* with two Afterwords, one by each author on the other's novel.

12. Ibid., p. 147.

13. Stephen Knight, *Form and Ideology in Crime Fiction* (Bloomington, Ind.: Indiana University Press, 1980), p. 107.

14. Jack Vance, *The Worlds of Jack Vance* (New York: Ace, 1973). This later collection includes "The King of the Thieves," also "The Kokod Warriors," and "Coup de Grace" mentioned in the next paragraph.

15. Ibid., p. 154.

16. A. E. Murch, *The Development of the Detective Novel* (1958; rpt. Westport, Conn.: Greenwood Press, 1975), p. 233.

17. Frederic Brown, "Crisis, 1999," in *Space, Time & Crime*, ed. Miriam Allen deFord (New York: Paperback Library, 1964), p. 11.

18. Stanislaw Lem, *The Investigation*, trans. Adele Milch (Cracow, 1959; trans. 1974; rpt. New York: Avon, 1976), p. 18.

19. Avram Davidson, *The Enquiries of Doctor Eszterhazy* (New York: Warner Books, 1975), p. 99.

20. Ibid., pp. 55–56.

21. Jon L. Breen, "Hercule Poirot in the Year 2010" in *The Arbor House Treasury of Mystery and Suspense*, comps. Bill Pronzini, Barry N. Malzberg, and Martin H. Greenberg (New York: Arbor House, 1981), p. 468. See also Breen's "On Science Fiction Detective Stories" in June 1979 *Isaac Asimov's Science Fiction Magazine*, p. 75, where he discusses this story.

22. Breen, "Hercule Poirot," pp. 470, 471.

23. Anthony Boucher, "Public Eye," in *Space, Time & Crime*, ed. Miriam Allen deFord (New York: Paperback Library, 1964), p. 100.

24. Raymond Chandler, *The Simple Art of Murder* (1950; rpt. New York: Ballantine Books, 1972), p. 20. Also reprinted in Howard Haycraft, *The Art of the Mystery Story* (New York: Biblo and Tannen, 1975), p. 237.

25. Dozois and Effinger, p. 30.

26. Ibid., p. 71.

27. Northrop Frye, *Anatomy of Criticism* (1957; rpt. New York: Atheneum, 1969), pp. 33–34.

28. David Bear, *Keeping Time* (1979; rpt. New York: Fawcett/Popular Library, 1981), p. 214.

29. William F. Nolan, *Space for Hire* (New York: Lancer Books, 1971), pp. 5–6. In the Preface author Nolan speaks of his foray into writing straight detective thrillers and a biography of Dashiell Hammett for which in 1970 he won the Edgar Allan Poe Special Award, given yearly by the Mystery Writers of America.

30. Stevenson, p. 551.

PART II

THE SCIENCE FICTION/FANTASY MYSTERY OF CRIME

CHAPTER 4

THE POWER, LAW, CRIME AND PUNISHMENT MATRIX

Et crimine ab uno disce omnis [from a single crime come to know the entire race (*Aeneid* II. 65)], so says Aeneas in condemnation of the Greeks' deception with the gift of the Wooden Horse leading to the fall of Troy. In the brief statement the whole nation is judged, "convicted" of a crime, and punished to the extent that the rest of the world shall know them by their perfidy. Aeneas's simple summary serves well the tale of crime in general: a crime does introduce an outsider to the mores of the society. It discovers the weakness as well as the strength of the standards by which a group governs itself. The tale of crime forces consideration of three major factors: the power center defining "right" action, the law or legal machinery for enforcing it, and the deviancy and attendant punishment exacted by it.

As do most vital organisms, the mystery story has adapted itself to different forms, not the least of which is the tale of crime. Differing from its cousin, the detective story, the crime tale shifts the focus from the challenge of puzzle-solving to the problem of reaffirming social, political, and social norms. While the detective story often develops into a study of the detective's personality and individuality of method, the tale of crime, even the more modern development of the police procedural, concerns itself with limitations of social behavior, best illuminated by examples of deviations from the norm. The aberrant acts of individuals will warrant labels of "crime" or "sin" depending upon the ethical orientation of the judging agency. The mystery of the situation resides in the complexity of relationships, motives, and sympathies engendered in the challenge to the law posed by an individual or group. To satisfy a reader, a tale of crime must convince him to accept the criteria of the judging power as inherent in the society. Also, the reader must be convinced to recognize the challenge as worthy of notice.

What is crime? For centuries the question has occupied philosophers, religious thinkers, social psychologists, lawyers, and more recently criminologists. Even a superficial reading in the literature of criminology will disclose that the question elicits a plethora of explanations. To attempt to compress them into a simple answer becomes an exercise in intellectual arrogance and futility, but some working definition is needed here. All definitions do agree in key respects, best summarized as: "crime" refers to that degree of deviant behavior deemed inacceptable by a society or subsocietal group to which the individual involved owes his allegiance. The standard of group behavior and/or deviancy along with the appropriate rewards or penalties is established either in formal or unwritten law by the individuals in power. Even more simply stated, crime exists once law executed by a power group designates behavior as such. Aeneas's "from a single crime know the entire nation" may well be paraphrased today as "from their crimes know the values of the prevailing social and political power structure." Such a distinction places added responsibility upon a science fiction/fantasy tale of crime, particularly if the setting is in a far-future or an alien society. The story will need a clear definition of the all-important triad of power center, law, crime and punishment in that society. A reader can draw upon historical data describing the triad to use as a valuable resource in understanding the fictional, often futuristic, society of the science fiction/fantasy crime story.

Two ancient codes present object lessons in power, law, crime and punishment.[1] The Babylonian Code of Hammurabi of c. 2270 B.C. reveals two major characteristics of that early culture. First, the Code established justice as a function of the organized state, rather than a prerogative of the family unit. In the prologue Hammurabi credits his authority as coming from the gods and underlines his responsibility to sustain the order of the society according to the prescribed pattern. Second, the Code reflects a rigid social hierarchy with penalties keyed to the social status of both victim and perpetrator. The higher the standing of the victim in the community, the more harsh the reprisal on the criminal. Theft of property from a commoner, for example, would exact repayment ten-fold, from a temple or palace, thirty-fold; death is the sentence upon inability to pay. A doctor's malpractice on a gentleman merited loss of the doctor's hands; on a slave, the exchange of one of the doctor's own slaves to replace the one who died. Punishment was severe. Kidnapping the son of a freeman, harboring of runaway slaves, house-breaking, failure to follow the orders of the king, sorcery, incest, all called for death as the penalty, death by drowning, burning, or suicide.

The Mosaic Law of a millennium later mirrored a comparable theocratic origin and pragmatic world-view with regard to the organization of communal behavior. How concisely the original Ten Commandments spell out individual responsibility toward both the Higher Authority and the immediate social unit. "Thou shalt not" murder, steal, perjure, be adulterous, covet property, dishonor elders, or put another god before Him. The detailed and expanded ordinances throughout the books of the Pentateuch direct themselves to affairs religious and social. Here is the more specific naming of transgressions: idolatry, sorcery, severe treatment of servants, murder, kidnapping, bodily injury to an equal, trespass, sodomy, and sundry other reprehensible acts connected with property, chiefly animals, as expected from a nomadic society. Perhaps not again except in Islam would two allegiances, social and secular, be so closely intertwined in societies influencing contemporary Western civilization. During the Western medieval era, indeed, the division was so defined that canon law held the authority to protect churchmen from civil law through the well-known benefit of clergy.

Lester del Rey's *The Eleventh Commandment* (1962) contains reminders of these ancient models of power, law, crime and punishment. While the title alone recalls Mosaic law, a reading of the novel reveals debts to other patterns also, modified in such a way as to introduce mystery, then revelation, and reaffirmation of a sterner justice than humans can pronounce. When Boyd Jensen, deportee from Mars, debarks from a space ship, he enters a quite different American society from the one from which his great-grandfather emigrated. Now dominated by the American Catholic Eclectic Church, America shows the result of two centuries of conditioned behavior in accordance with the Eleventh Commandment espoused by the Church's power structure. "Be fruitful and multiply and replenish the earth." Called the Original Commandment by the Church, this directive became necessary in 1993 after an accident triggered an all-out nuclear war that decimated the population, leaving survivors with radiation aftereffects. In del Rey's 2190 society the country now suffers the ills of uncontrolled reproduction: filth, over-crowding, hunger, disease, unemployment with the attendant beggary, thievery, mugging, looting, all done by a desperate people.

Boyd Jensen is the archetypal Innocent, as he begins his new life among those with diametrically opposed values to his own from Mars. Jensen's expertise in cytology qualifies him to join the Church establishment. He soon notices a double standard at work and at odds with his own. The hierarchy of the Church, most of them scientists, devotes its time to the problems of food supply rather than to the alleviation of human suffering, especially the control or cure of disease. The subordinate civil authority has reverted to the *lex talionis*, as severe as any under Hammurabi: hanging of muggers, cutting off hands of pickpockets, reviving of whipping posts, and like punishments. By contrast, the Church has abandoned a moral stance on acts such as adultery and suicide, pursuing instead alchemy and heresy, each interpreted to apply whenever necessary to make an arrest. Once Jensen makes a batch of cortisone in his laboratory and is immediately arrested on the possible charge of heresy or alchemy. Alchemy here would be equated with the manufacture of proscribed drugs, most of which our society associates with curative uses.

Jensen repeatedly runs afoul of Church-imposed prohibitions. Successive arrests and incarcerations deepen his mystification. He finds no new insight in the philosophy of dissident groups: the "Romish" or remnants of the traditional Catholic Church; the Witchcraft devotees; or the Bleeders. Finally the head of the Eclectic Church explains. The atomic holocaust of 1993 had done great gene damage in the human populations, damage which could show up generations hence in mutations. Since all carry the burden of the damage, all must carry the responsibility of discharging the "iniquities of the fathers" as now being visited upon the succeeding generations. Only by the profligate breeding and the process of natural selection ("God's Will" in the Archbishop's words) will enough normal people be assured to carry on the race. The power is God's Will; the law, be fertile and multiply and the race will survive; the crime, man's careless husbanding of the earth and his own technology; the punishment, bearing the horrors of the long process toward strength through evolution.

Other historical codes of law add to the appreciation of the part crime plays in the science fiction/fantasy mystery tale of crime. Another millennium or so after the above Codes, during the reign of the Emperor Justinian, Roman law became solidified in the Laws of the Twelve Tables, based on three outwardly simple precepts: live honestly, give each individual his just due, refrain from injuring another. In the expanded Tables, however, one sees a more complex and widespread society that must pay attention to detailed organization. The Code has two parts: a Public Law to oversee administrative particulars; and a Private Law to safeguard individual interests, this latter subdivided into Natural Law, the Law of Nations, and the Civil Law. An important section of Justinian's Code emphasized the *Lex Regia*, the law reaffirming transference of popular jurisdiction and authority to the sovereign. Early Germanic law, by contrast, recognized the power of the people or folk, the "oral and customary" law serving small groups with local justice. As nations developed in size and complex organization, such law could not support the burden accompanying the change. In England, for one example, Henry II (1154–1189) brought all common law together in a codified form, thus making the law "common" for all rather than common to local custom.

To follow the history of law-making with special focus on crime and punishment forces awareness of the ever-increasing complexity of both law and daily life. Medicine has lengthened the life span, thus necessitating official responsibility for social services with the consequent regulatory measures. Genetic engineering and use of chemicals for behavior control have raised demands for legal oversight. Modern technology complicates itself almost faster than the mind can understand it. In the late twentieth century, for one case, the rise in computer fraud has necessitated stepped-up legal attention. Work on genetic scanning to detect and treat persons with antisocial or criminal tendencies may institute a new area of law. Studies by psychologists, sociologists, and criminologists on the causes of criminality may effect a shift of responsibility from the province of criminal justice to other official areas, thus necessitating some decriminalization by law. Above all, with the rapidly expanding population served by an equally expanding computerized informational network, a primary problem for the law promises to be the protection of individual privacy. Faced with concerns such as these, the modern citizen finds himself agreeing with the anonymous wag quoted in the February 8, 1775, *Pennsylvania Gazette*:

> Lost is our old simplicity of times,
> The world abounds with laws and teems with crimes.

With its chief tool, extrapolation, science fiction/fantasy mysteries cannot overlook this loss of simplicity, followed by the abundance of laws and teeming crimes, law to define new crimes and punishments as yet but imagined in the late twentieth century. More than a hint warns of one trend in world societies—over-population. As early as the end of the eighteenth century the English economist and moral philosopher Thomas Robert Malthus expressed his doctrine on population growth, proposing that the population would grow geometrically while resources for subsistence would increase arithmetically. He predicted that humanity would need war, disease, even crime to serve as checks on population.[2] In the following century Karl Marx also saw crime as one way of siphoning part of the excess population off the labor market; another way might entail increasing law enforcement numbers.[3] Speculations from writers such as Malthus and Marx presaging historical changes in the law provide a multi-faceted background against which to study the use science fiction/fantasy mystery writers have put such theory and law.

Population explosion is a popular subject in science fiction/fantasy novels. Joining the above-mentioned *The Eleventh Commandment*, these are worthy of mention: Isaac Asimov's *The Caves of Steel* (1954), Harry Harrison's *Make Room! Make Room!* (1966), James Blish and Norman A. Knight's *A Torrent of Faces* (1967), John Brunner's *Stand on Zanzibar* (1968), to list but a few. While over-population creates familiar conditions conducive to crime, as any newspaper headline may testify, the science fiction/fantasist imagination offers some as yet unexperienced. In *Logan's Run* (1967) William F. Nolan and George Clayton Johnson imagine the ultimate method of population control: a legal age for death. In this twenty-second-century world each citizen receives at birth a color disc implanted in his palm. On the anniversary of each seven years' passage, the color changes from yellow to blue to red. On the day the citizen reaches twenty-one, the disc blinks from red to black as a warning of Lastday. When it stabilizes on black, the law-abiding person reports to a Sleepshop where he pays the death penalty for the crime of life.

What was the rationale behind such a drastic legal move? Two centuries before, in 1988, the social planners had reorganized the entire planet so that it could be directed from a central computer based in caverns near the Crazy Horse sculpture in the Black Hills of South Dakota. Thus relieved of relatively minor concerns, the officials turned to a more pressing problem and more grandiose plans for controlling it. The problem was the uncontrolled growth of population; the plan was a Compulsory Birth Control Act. Angered by what they saw as a usurpation of their freedom of choice, the youthful majority had rebelled, killing off the older generation in what the history books of the twenty-second century designate as the Little War of 2000. In the first part of the twenty-first century population continued to increase past the limits the land could sustain in food, the prediction of Thomas Malthus as realized. Even though people opened up the seas for food farming and processing, the worsening situation demanded more stringent measures. The twenty-one-year life span became law.

For the citizen conditioned to respect and obey the law the desire to live past twenty-one became a moral perversion; the presence of the law itself made any effort to do so a crime. In Logan's world the major power for law enforcement rests with the DS corps, the Deep Sleep Men or the Sandmen, as they are more colloquially termed. Especially trained, these men search out and pursue those who elect to make the "Run" for their lives. The "Run" has become so prevalent as to encourage re-institution of a traditional phenomenon common to all times when refugees have fled from oppression. There is a revival of a nineteenth-century phenomenon, the underground railway. In Logan's world the underground apparatus leads to Sanctuary, a destination unknown to authorities but located in an abandoned space station. Here people can await the complete disintegration of their old world, an almost-certain event because the central computer upon which that world depends is breaking down, and none of the older generation who built, understood, and trained for its maintenance are now alive.

On his Lastday Logan, a member of the DS corps, by chance comes into possession of a key to Sanctuary. He takes the "Run," at first motivated by the dictates of his job; he must search out and destroy the operators of Sanctuary. However, as the run proceeds, new insight destroys his original intent; the Run develops into a journey of recognition that at twenty-one the human organism has just reached the point of giving to instead of taking from the society at large. The ultimate crime in Logan's World becomes the ultimate responsible action in Logan's mind.

Not only in overpopulated societies but in all future ones the law must respond to changing circumstances. To know a crime may be to know the nation. An author may use the triad of power, law, crime and punishment also as satire to italicize the follies and foibles of our own time. William Earls's pen of satire jabs uncomfortably close to the twentieth century despite increasing attention to energy conservation, smaller cars, and soaring oil prices. "Traffic Problem," written in 1969 about a then near-future of 1981, still holds wry humor for a modern reader extrapolating that trend into our near future. New York City of "Traffic Problem" suffers from over-population of automobiles. Continual construction of roads, bridges, overpasses fails to keep abreast of the problem. The traffic flow snarls even with the two-hundred-lane roads over Manhattan and the twelve-tiered highways elsewhere. All considerations fall before the need to keep traffic moving. Central Park is covered by a high-rise parking lot and seven lanes of traffic. The City Library has been demolished to give way to an interchange; the Empire State Building must go next.

In this absurd world, what of power, law, crime and punishment? The picture is clear. Put the power completely in the hands of the Traffic Director. The law then becomes the law of his office with the imperative to keep the traffic moving. He can order arrests for all persons driving two-year-old cars or those who drive too slowly. In this era when drivers take corners at 110 miles per hour, coming out of them at 115, the major crime is driving below a "sane 95." Traffic officers in helicopters spot and apprehend culprits by dropping a can of dye on the hoods of the cars, thus marking them for arrest, fining, or banning from the roads. The latter action passes the automatic and dreaded "sentence" of riding the railways for transportation.

The automobile represents but one highly visible aspect of modern technology or the Machine that seems to manipulate rather than serve. The science fiction/fantasist foresees a future in which men have abrogated their control of law and have transferred the power, not to a Higher Authority that had conferred on them the secular control but to a non-human one. When such authority is challenged, the crime ironically is the individual's sense and exercise of his own humanness. In the dystopic world of E. M. Forster's *The Machine Stops*, written prior to 1914 and published in 1928, people live isolated in underground rooms resembling cells in a beehive. Withdrawn by inertia and custom, the individuals exist in total comfort as far as bodily and mental needs are concerned. Fresh air circulates and food is delivered automatically at the proper times. Lights dim to indicate waking or sleeping hours. When mental exercise seems indicated, a televisor and an aural machine offer programmed communication or exchange of "ideas" with anyone anywhere on the globe. *Ideas* in this context means a rehash of known information with no fresh interpretation or creative thought.

In this future society certain moral taboos have arisen: direct experience is to be shunned; touching is obscene. The close family unit of yesteryears is unthinkable as children are separated from mothers soon after birth, becoming then the responsibility of the state. The Machine and its book of instructions have replaced God and Bible. What possible crime under secular law could exist in such a commonalty where nothing is needed and no one has direct contact with another? Yet there is a crime and a punishment. The crime is any indication of atavism, specifically any reversion to a state of imagination or production of original ideas or the resurgence of a sense of the individual personality. The punishment is a dire one—Homelessness or death. In an extreme effort to forestall any incidents of atavistic behavior the powers of this Machine society practice infanticide on any child born with an appreciable show of strength. When Kuno disturbs Vashti, his mother, by calling her, he does it out of loving concern, but he succeeds only in disrupting her accustomed routine, thereby demonstrating the state of atrophy her deepest sensibilities enjoy. When he further defies the law and goes topside, he invites the penalty of Homelessness from which he is saved only by the fortuitous disintegration of the Machine itself. Forster leaves us with mystery and a question: does society need the "crime" of nonconformity to give it energy and redemption from the stasis whose only hope of movement is a drift into entropy?

The people of Ray Bradbury's *Fahrenheit 451* (1953) have traded the stimulus of direct experience and free exchange of thought and ideas for a frenetic secondhand life. Like the young man in Friedrich Duerrenmatt's "The Tunnel" most people in this Bradburyian future society close off their senses to natural stimuli by stuffing thimble radios, called Seashells, in their ears, glutting their eyes and ears with a daylong soap opera television show featuring The Family, and using drugs to dull the other senses. Unlike Duerrenmatt's fat young man they do not insulate themselves completely from the rest of humanity, occasionally preferring to fill the air around them with small talk, nonsensical chatter, and soft noise such as the sound of air swishing by as their autos race at high speeds past two-hundred-foot-long billboards.

In this world the primal sin and most searched-out crime is the possession of books, especially those classics that might stimulate disquieting thoughts in the minds of people now reduced to a herdlike state. Once a book-owner is suspected, he is doomed to a visit from the firemen, the special corps now dedicated not to putting out fires of physical combustion but to destroying the sources of mental flammability. The firemen serve as "custodians of our peace of mind," as the Chief Fireman explains to fireman Montag, as he seeks to allay Montag's doubts with a mini-history of their profession. His explanation establishes the law against books as the natural result of a great increase of population, the demand for action instead of contemplation, and the satisfaction of that demand by a solid growth of attention-absorbing technology. This in turn exploited the baser instincts of the mass of people. Pressure from minorities grew into a blanket censorship of all controversy or debate. The guiding question for the society became how a thing was to be done, not why or whether it should be done. Here the power is mass control; the law, ban all the original ideas or inquisitive, imaginative thinking; the crime, opening the mind to thoughts through books; the punishment, destruction of books, property, even people. The underground that Montag discovers and finally aids warrants sympathy but cannot entirely dispel the mystery of societal self-deception.

Robert Silverberg in *The Time Hoppers* (1974) explores the mystery in another way, extrapolating to 2490 A.D. to give a detailed cultural context designed to eliminate crimes but which unexplicably seems to foster mindless ones. By 2490 the social structure has frozen into a strict hierarchy with all members classified by number. To each level the system gives specific responsibilities and privileges. Over-population has demolished privacy. In an effort to maintain order, the authorities monitor a citizen's every activity, even to the point of placing the Ear on him without his knowledge or consent. Even though traditional controls of human behavior no longer exist, order does operate.

Many anti-social activities have been decriminalized. With want and hunger eliminated, people need no longer to steal to exist. Rape is unnecessary, because legal sex shops cater to that desire. This would seem to be the best of all possible worlds, a utopia of great social maturity. But it is not so. Legal freedom does not insure social amity or happiness.

Joseph Quellen, a high official in the Secretariat of Crime, becomes well aware of that reality as he checks the daily accumulation of crime reports. There is a concomitant curb to which human beings should owe some obedience—self-discipline. If that curb weakens, crime springs from drives deeper than any law or social reform can satisfy or control en masse. Citizens of 2490 have lost that personal curb. A man of today might judge the crimes on the list before Quellen as motiveless, but he notes that the reasons given range from aimless amusement to personal curiosity or sheer error. Here a man commits a "biological crime" by introducing a flesh-eating substance into the body of a fellow worker, just to see what would happen. There a man deprives a girl of all sensory response in order to bolster his masculine pride, which had been bruised by her rejection. These represent the most dramatic acts in a list containing the usual number of rapes, beatings, theft, laserings, and such conventional modes of social rebellion.

Quellen's purpose in checking the lists has little to do with the daily spate of crime. He does so in the line of duty, for he has an assignment to investigate the reported appearance of time hoppers. This assignment should be an all-absorbing one, but Quellen's mind is too full of a personal problem. Quellen himself has committed a criminal act. Disregarding official prohibitions he has acquired a second home, a hideaway in Africa. He has stolen the privilege of privacy not warranted by his function or position. His being a 7 allows him only a private room. A second home assures that precious commodity, privacy, an award reserved for those of great power in the world. But the law does have two faces in Quellen's world, as he discovers when he does succeed in locating the operator of the time mechanism transporting the time hoppers. The man turns out to be a "licensed slyster" but one that a man with a 1 rating wishes to supplant with a government operation to ship "prolets," the poor and unemployable, back to pre-recorded time, another "legal" way to assure order.

Anyone who has traveled in foreign lands can testify to the daily problem of learning the correct social behavior particularly in cultures quite different from one's own. A color may symbolize the diametrically opposite emotion; the language may trip up the unwary with a word carrying the wrong connotation. A gesture misdirected may cause embarrassment, even deep trouble. Knowledge of the taboos and directives of the other culture is mandatory. This is a lesson we may well need to observe more assiduously should our space-craft probes ever discover an alien civilization with whom we begin to consort. The relationship may be as unbelievable as the symbiotic one of Clement's *Needle* where breaking the law of hospitality is a major crime. On the other hand, the alien mores may sanction an action we condemn as a crime.

This problem faces Magnus Ridolph in Jack Vance's "Coup de Grace" (1958). When Magnus finally tracks down the murderer in a space station resort, he finds not one but two possible suspects among the alien guests. Fiamella of Thousand Candles represents a race wherein the honor of a woman is besmirched if she is rejected by the man she chooses as her own. The only way in which she can redeem that honor is to "kill" by seduction and rejection to the point that the man "dies" for love. However, Fiamella's code utterly rejects use of any mechanical weapon such as the fire gun used on the victim. Once she is eliminated from the list of suspects, Magnus has only the Bronze left. Member of a culture that believes in its special brand of reincarnation, the Bonze kills out of altruism to relieve persons of grave trouble, so that they may be reborn into a state of happiness.

The person tossed backward or forward in time faces other problems. Although blameless, he may become a criminal out of sheer ignorance of local law. When Dr. Jim Parsons waves goodbye to his wife one sunny morning, he little expects to be careened into the twenty-fifth century out of his well-patterned, twenty-first-century existence. He becomes at that moment the title character of Philip K. Dick's *Dr. Futurity* (1960). The world to which he has been transferred by a group planning to change the past is one where the average age is fifteen, where mayhem and government-sanctioned killing are common, and where the term "medical knowledge" means little except possibly a tenuous connection with sorcery or alchemy. When he witnesses a vicious and lethal attack upon a young couple who have befriended him, he is able to save the young girl's life. For his effort he is arrested: the charge, "a major crime against the United Tribes.

The Folk.'' Deliberately saving a human life is a capital offense in this era, but ignorance of the law is not an excuse, the official reminds Parsons. He is sentenced to exile on Mars. ''Rescued'' from this fate by the original group engineering his time jump, Parsons becomes a veritable ''time pawn'' in eras where his original values are tested again and again.[4] Before returning to his own time, Parsons throws his efforts into supporting a group fighting for life against the ''ethos of death.''

As mentioned earlier, the mystery of the science fiction/fantasy tale of crime resides in the complexity of motives, relationships, and sympathies engendered in the challenge to the law. In *Dr. Futurity* the challenge posed by the opposing values, sanctity of life versus value of death, represents a continuing concern. Either-or propositions force moral decisions. As one of the inhabitants of the 2405 world of Dick's novel tells Parsons, ''We—they, if you will—have rigid standards. Maybe you can fit in. Unfortunately, no middle ground. Law of the excluded middle, sort of.'' [5] The mystery here lies in the question necessarily faced by all persons at some time in their existence: *maybe* we can fit in. Or can we? When the alternative answer involves the label of *criminal*, the decisions one makes take on greater burden. In such situations as posed by the formula of the mystery story lies great potential for the idea-oriented science fiction/fantasy.

What of the crime born of sheer chance? In *Iceworld* (1953) by Hal Clement the authorities of Sarr must infiltrate a drug-smuggling organization that has introduced an addictive drug into the planet. Sallman Ken, scientist, is drafted to work as an undercover agent with the illegal operation. His high adventure takes him with the smugglers to a planet so cold that his native atmosphere of sulphur freezes solid. He does locate the source of the drug, first obtained quite by chance when the smugglers landed a ''torpedo'' filled with electronic equipment designed to give data on this new planet. To encourage communication they sent ''swap-boxes'' with the two sides joined by hinged lids. Filling the one side with metal samples from their world, they left the other side empty for the material swapped. The torpedo is found by an adult inhabitant of the Iceworld or Earth. Recognizing the message implicit in the construction of the swap-box, he drops into the empty side whatever he can scrounge from his pockets and the nearby terrain: a piece of paper, some lichen, a rock, a cigarette, and other odds and ends. The trade now has continued for some years with the Sarrian smugglers putting platinum in their side, a useless commodity for them, but a valuable one to the earth trader. In return, they request *tofacco*, or what the Sarrian authorities designate as "sniff," a deadly gas instantly addictive to the peculiar Sarrian physical makeup.

Clement's novel illustrates how the crime element of the mystery can easily be overcome by the science fictional elements, in this case the scientific exposition of the chemical problems encountered by the space expedition. To the purpose of characterization the exposition works efficiently, for the focus beams in on the conflict of two priorities: the scientific orientation of the protagonist complete with his own curiosity about the new world per se and, second, the official responsibility he owes to the Sarrian authorities. The former wins out in the plot, the latter serving only to reinforce the mystery of the personal choice.

The problems of ethical choices move consideration away from formalized political law to the less formal but no less demanding "spiritual law," best formalized in the medieval idea of the Seven Deadly Sins: anger, greed, gluttony, pride, sloth, envy, and lust, balanced by the Seven Cardinal Virtues: brotherly love, liberality, temperance, humility, diligence, meekness, and chastity. Obviously, some of the above attributes have moved into the arena of formalized law, for anger can provoke an act of violence demanding penalty, greed can run a person afoul of property rights, lust can lead to rape.

Even gluttony can become part and parcel of formalized law, as Frederick Pohl's "The Midas Plague" (1954) suggests. What if "being poor" meant that one *must* consume by law and social dictate, "being rich" meant relief from that forced consumption and the reward of a simple, unpretentious life? In this future existence technology and its handmaiden, the production line, have flooded the world with things which *must* be used. If no legitimate use can be justified, the consumption is forced. Who better to use in this thankless job than the official poor? The law says "consume," and the reward for obedience is a change in status requiring lower levels of consumption. When Morey Fry, newly married to a child of "rich" parents who need consume very little, finds his marriage threatened by the difference in status, he turns technology to his benefit. Technology with its overproduction of goods lends itself to the bending of the law and to Morey's salvation. Fred Pohl here uses an ironical situation to force notice of a contemporary production trend demanding both our ridicule and attempts at reform.

While no one person is harmed by the above abrogation of the intent of the law, science fiction/fantasy crime mystery centers more on violence, as do its symbiotic partners, the mainstream tales of crime. While many crimes are acts of violence pure and simple, all crimes are acts of violation. To remind us of but a few: burglary and robbery violate privacy and property; rape, psychic and physical integrity; drug traffic, mental and physical health. Each of these do hold some promise of healing, for possessions can be replaced, rape and drug victims can gain long-term counseling and treatment. Murder holds no such promise. True, as a culture we make some exceptions when we label as justifiable homicide a death coming as the result of a policeman killing in the line of duty or a citizen in defense of home or self. Despite this, murder claims the greatest attention and the stiffest penalties in law.

Most societies place strong prohibitions against murder, as witness the unarguable "Thou shalt not kill," and the equally strong taboos and penalties of the *lex talionis*:

Thou shalt give life for life, eye for eye, tooth for tooth, hand for hand, foot for foot, Burning for burning, wound for wound, stripe for stripe. (Exodus 21:23 25)

While many classify the disobedience of Adam and Eve as the archetypal political crime, one against the highest authority, we stand on equally firm ground to classify the killing of Abel as the archetypal murder. It fits the pattern established by many contemporary sociological studies: the murderer is a non-professional; the victim is not a stranger. The act is not carefully planned but results in a great release of anger and aggression built up from physical and/or psychological frustration. Stuart Palmer in *The Psychology of Murder* defines *frustration* in this context as "that condition . . . which results from lack of satisfaction of a need," be that need a desire for security, ego-gratification, recognition, or new experiences. [6] The frustrations of Cain are familiar enough that we need not belabor the analogy here.

Not all murders fit this neat pattern of the non-professional murderer and the non-stranger victim. John Brunner invites a consideration of the active manipulation of frustration to encourage murder as a way of population control. In "Nobody Axed You" (1965) he invites us to watch television along with the citizens of this near-future world, again an over-populated one. As any television viewer knows, everything shown on the screen depends upon ratings for its continuance on the schedule. In Brunner's world the ratings are measured in DOA (dead-on-arrival) figures. Suicide is morally wrong; murder legally so. But a television show aptly titled "Show-to-Kill-Time," with the *S* and the final word programmed to fade out soon after flashing on the screen, serves a social purpose by encouraging murder. The producers portray common, everyday, stress-filled situations; during the show the actors work out detailed video lessons in murder. Predictable is the psychological effect on a suggestible audience caught in similar situations, keyed up by the tension inherent in over-population. Murders according to the plot then follow as a matter of course. When the murderer is apprehended, the society at large benefits by a twofold reduction in numbers—and the show adds to its ratings.

If personal violence claims the award for the biggest threat to society, war must certainly claim a primary place as the most inhumane outlet for that violence. What if a country found a way to divert such energy into more acceptable channels? Robert Sheckley in "The Seventh Victim" (1954), later developed into the novel *The 10th Victim* (1965), proposes that in the future anyone who wants to kill should be allowed that privilege. The answer is organization under the main authority of the ECB or Emotional Catharsis Boards. The ECB arranges special Hunts, matching victim with hunter. After each hunt the victor signs up with the Board for assignment as the next victim. If an individual survives ten successful hunts as either victim or hunter, he becomes part of an exclusive club, the Tens. This legalized murder is nothing new, as Sheckley's narrator assures the reader, merely a natural extension of the practice of hiring mercenaries to do battle for the nation at large, as well as the recognition of the need to provide a way for people to work off the urge to kill.

While the traditional tale of crime as represented by Poe's "The Cask of Amontillado" (1846) or William Godwin's *Caleb Williams* (1794) focuses on the psychological forces moving the criminal to the point of aggressive release, variations on the mode focus also on the administration of justice and the penalty. Ancient law carried as punishment for murder some form of legalized murder such as death by stoning, decapitation, strangulation, or burning. Although less frequently used today, capital punishment is still regarded by many as the strongest form of deterrent. It is of interest to ponder that for the mythic First Family death was not the penalty. Exile for the disobedient parents and homelessness for the murderer-son were the punishments handed down. Imprisonment in an environment less ideal than the one valued becomes the literal counterpart of the "nightmare Life-in-Death" visited upon Samuel Taylor Coleridge's Ancient Mariner or the modern version of non-entity as suffered in the self-imposed sentence of an Oedipus. Whatever the crime or the punishment, the basic dictum is "play by the rules or pay the penalty."

Once a science fiction/fantasy writer has established the ground rules for his future, alternate, or alien society, the reader can easily spot a person not playing by the rules, but often is surprised by the payment exacted. Envision receiving a sentence of twenty years in cryonic suspension. This would seem to be little more than a deferment of living and no great punishment. But then the prisoner awakens to a world peopled by friends and family twenty years more mature and advanced educationally and socially. The prisoner returns to a social group into which he never again can fit. This is the penalty in Miriam deFord's "Prison Break" (1959). Equally exquisite is the lingering punishment in her "Rope's End" (1960). Upon sentencing, a rope is riveted around the prisoner's neck; each year one inch is cut off until the rope is short enough to strangle the wearer—a most graphic example of "life-in-death." Higher on the nightmare scale is the penalty handed out to persons convicted of antisocial behavior in Frederick Pohl's "Third Offense" (1958). In Pohl's future world time travel is possible. The convicted man may find himself sent to serve time in the Roman galleys, or at Belsen, or, as his character Roykin discovers on third offense, in Philadelphia of 1893, a Philadelphia in the grip of a yellow fever plague, a pre-antibiotic-era city.

The penal colony has become a stock convention in science fiction/fantasy crime stories. There are the prison planets as the one in Piers Anthony's *Chthon* (1967) where the "criminally insane, the incorrigible, the perverted" are sentenced to dig for garnets in the darkness of mines. They are sustained by the single hope of finding the Jewel to deliver them from bondage. Other equally dehumanizing places including Limbo, a prison planet in Jerome Bixby's "The Bad Life" in *Space by the Tale* (1964) and the prison in Cordwainer Smith's "A Planet Called Shayol" (1961) where criminals' arms and legs become the product for harvest and export. Societies throughout history have wrestled with the problem of defusing their dissident elements or political activists. In John Boyd's *The Last Starship on Earth* (1968) the government manipulates its populations by using the penal planet Hell as a way station for further deployment. Both in Thomas Disch's *Camp Concentration* (1968) and Robert Silverberg's *Hawksbill Station*, this one a penal colony set in the far distant past, authorities use the isolation to separate revolutionaries or political prisoners from the mainstream of the population.

When Gilbert and Sullivan's Mikado sings the catchy lyric, the audience smiles:

> My object all sublime
> I shall achieve in time
> To make the punishment fit the crime. (*The Mikado*, Act II)

But amusement fades if one remembers the serious original stricture made by Cicero when he reminded his audience that *salus populi suprema est lex* [the weal of the people is the highest law] and later *noxiae poena par esto* [let the punishment fit the crime]. [7] Science fiction/fantasy mysteries face special problems in fitting the punishment to crimes committed in other worlds and times. The speculative solutions they give the problem, however, can contribute to a general understanding of the relationship of crime to punishment even today.

Will there be special consideration accorded that relationship in a post-atomic world? Given the current levels of nuclear proliferation the question has been raised, discussed, and still demands thought. In "After" (1966) Henry Slesar adds to this subject, even though he camouflages the effort in an ironic situation. "After" is a series of four vignettes, brief but telling glimpses of a post-atomic world from the viewpoint of survivors: a doctor, a merchant, a lawyer, and a chief. In the lawyer's episode the Ciceronian precepts are updated: the good of all the people takes precedence over the good of the individual and the punishment must be equal to the crime. A man who killed another man in a brawl is convicted of the murder; the circumstances are such that in our present world he could have been charged with manslaughter and thus received a lesser sentence. In his time, had he killed a *woman* in the brawl, the sentence would have been less severe. But this is post A-day in a world where the ratio of men to women is 1–800. The verdict is murder in the first degree; the sentence, marriage to the victim's eighteen wives, thus raising the culprit's total wives to thirty-one!

Advances in technology promise avenues for expanded knowledge of ourselves and our world. Benefits will follow to assure a better life. Scientific curiosity will be satisfied or intensified, perhaps leading us to the point of searching out other sentient creatures in the universe. We need some other contacts to relieve our sense of species-loneliness. Naturally the philosophical questions arise: benefits for which species or which individuals within the species? Will the scientific curiosity kill or satisfy? How will such activity complicate the task of the law? By what criteria will non-human species be judged in cases of misdemeanors or crimes tallied under human law? What new laws must be made to cover transactions between aliens and humans, between sentient machines and humans? These suggest but a few of the speculative problems faced by the imaginations of the writers of science fiction/fantasy mystery.

Teleportation as a future means of efficient transference of matter from one place to another fascinates readers and futurists alike. The possibilities of moving both men and materiel stir the imagination. How could crime be attendant upon such a practical activity? In George Langelaan's "The Fly" (1957) Andre Delambre's wife confesses to the killing of her scientist-husband whose body has been found in his lab with the head completely smashed by a trip-hammer. As her trial progresses, the wife contributes little sensible information, being absorbed with catching flies only to release them after close examination. The court judges her action as indicative of madness, sentencing her to an asylum. Andre's brother takes up the investigation, sensing there is more to the affair than obvious by the surface evidence. He discovers that Andre in his work on matter transmission had decided to use himself in one experiment. By accident when his body was reintegrated, he found that a stray fly in the machine had combined with him, leaving him with the fly's head and a human body. The brother completes Andre's wish for destruction by locating the fly with the human head and killing it. Murder or mercy killing? Insanity or sanity?

While the transmission of matter over long distances remains very much in the realm of speculation, transfer of matter from one object to another is a matter of record. In medical science organ transplants become daily more common. But, as the narrative voice in Larry Niven's "Death by Ecstasy" (1969) reminds, "new technologies create new customs, new laws, new ethics, new crimes." [8] In his future world the United Nations Police, the ARM, now spend more than half their professional attention on one special crime, organlegging. This crime is the natural outgrowth of centuries of medical study starting with blood transfusions in the early 1900s, to skin grafts and heart by-passes, and on to wholesale organ transplants in this twenty-second century. Transplants have become so routine that anyone able to pay for the operation can have one, but the big drawback is the scarcity of spare parts.

Governmental action, as described in Niven's *The Patchwork Girl* (1980), first solved the problem by adding to the death penalty a direction that the condemned person be executed in a hospital and his organs be sent to the public organ banks. This effectively saved the death penalty from the protests of those who had worked to abolish capital punishment. When scarcity again threatened, the death penalty was extended to lesser crimes, thus becoming at last a strong deterrent to law-breaking of any kind. Still scarcity threatened, so as expected, illegal activity found a use for the situation and the organleggers set up business. As the narrator explains in "Death by Ecstasy," there are three aspects to this illegal business: kidnap-murder, sales, and the technical-medical branch. Organlegging necessitates an overhaul of current attitudes and law as known to this time, one involving the mystery of the fight for survival despite all cultural taboos or legal obstacles.

While transmission of matter or organlegging still lurk ahead of us, the computer is a very real part of modern life. Can its pervasive presence become an instrument of crime? The answer is *yes* in the business arena where computer fraud already is a problem, but what of a computer crime of violence? Perhaps not all computers can be anthropomorphized as is Ron Goulart's Barney Maze. Neither can all computers view the world and their own function with the benevolence of John Brunner's Shalmaneser in *Stand on Zanzibar* as it periodically compliments itself with "Christ, what an imagination I've got." Such machines exude beneficience, a quality not usually emphasized in computer-crime stories, such as Edward Hoch's series about the Computer Investigation Bureau (CIB). In "Computer Cops" (1969) the CIB headed by Carl Crader and Earl Jazine uncovers a plot to send an invasion force to the moon. The "patriot" mastermind erects an elaborate computer brokerage ploy as a smokescreen to divert the authorities. The CIB foils the plot and continues to function through *The*

Transvection Machine (1971), *The Fellowship of the Hand* (1973), and *The Frankenstein Factory* (1975). Unfortunately for the strain of futuristic fancy in stories of computer crime, events in the real contemporary world have rendered the fictional ones less speculative and more realistic.

Computer analysis becomes the tool propelling an innocent person into crime in some cases. When Paul Felder, disabled Viet Nam veteran and now a student, does a computer analysis of the deathbed ravings of one Kraut Schwarz as the research material for his thesis, he ends up serving the dead mobster in the function promised by the title, "'Mouthpiece'" (1974). In Edward Willen's novella his protagonist Felder at first finds these deathbed remarks to be a potpourri of clichés, repetition of advertising mottos, references to Kraut's contemporaries of the 1930s, literary and cultural allusions, as well as personal comments. With the aid of the computer Felder decodes the mishmash of words so successfully that the personality of the mobster gains control and begins to operate the computer as his alter ego. Using voice contact with Felder, he directs him to visit in turn his old enemies. After each visit the Felder-Schwarz relationship changes with Felder becoming the machine and computer/Schwarz, the director. In tandem they seek out and interview the gang associates, who one by one die as if by accident. All the accidents are in some way tied up with a computer network. A similar "accident" planned for Felder is foiled by a counter-computer attack arranged by Kraut's granddaughter, who has fallen in love with Felder. Fantastic as the events may appear, Willen rouses a specter of modern technology with which future law may have to cope.

While Willen's story does not address itself to the new question of the status of the machine under criminal law, Ray Bradbury's "'Punishment Without Crime'" (1950) does. Enraged with his wife's unfaithfulness, George Hill buys an android from Marionette, Inc., to represent her in a surrogate murder. After he has released the buildup of aggression and frustration by shooting the android, he is arrested, along with the manufacturer. Charge: murder. Under a very new law designating robots as living creatures, George is guilty and accepts his punishment. He must suffer an even greater one when his wife and her lover visit him in prison; this final straw tips him into insanity.

While science fiction/fantasy mysteries invite unlimited speculation upon the delicate relationship of power, law, crime and punishment in situations far removed from the twentieth century, it does encourage unlimited speculation upon the delicate relationship. In the years since Hugo Gernsback encouraged scientifiction as a basic element in the stories in *Amazing* or John Campbell, Jr., insisted on the primacy of hard science in the ones he accepted, important elements have been added. Sociology, psychology, and other social sciences have broadened the scope of the word *science*. They have also opened doors for increased social comment and social satire. One of the major contributions that science fiction/fantasy mysteries make is to alert the readership to ramifications of the ethical, moral, political, and social problems in the contemporary world, especially with regard to the laws under which we live.

NOTES

1. References to ancient laws here mentioned are found in most studies of ancient civilizations or historical treatments of the development of the law. C.H.W. Johns translated the Code of Hammurabi in *The Oldest Code of Laws in the World* (Edinburgh, 1903). The Mosaic law is found *passim* in Exodus, Leviticus, Numbers, and Deuteronomy of the Old Testament.

2. Malthus published two works on population. The first is entitled *An Essay on the Principle of Population as It Affects the Future Improvement of Society, with Remarks on the Speculations of Mr. Godwin, M. Condorcet, and Other Writers* (1798). The second essay, an expanded second edition of the above, was published in 1803 under a new title: *An Essay on the Principle of Population, or a View of Its Past and Present Effects on Human Happiness with an Inquiry into Our Prospects Respecting the Future Removal or Mitigation of the Evils Which It Occasions*.

3. Karl Marx, *Selected Writings in Sociology and Social Philosophy*, trans. T. B. Bottomore, eds. T. B. Bottomore and Maximilien Rubel (London, 1956; rpt. New York: McGraw-Hill, 1964), p. 159.

4. Philip K. Dick's *Dr. Futurity* was originally published as "Time Pawn" in 1954, later expanded to the novel length in 1960.

5. Philip K. Dick, *Dr. Futurity* (New York, 1960; rpt. London: Eyre Methuen, 1976), p. 21.

6. Stuart Palmer, *The Psychology of Murder* (New York: Thomas Y. Crowell, 1962), p. 8. (Orig. publ. as *A Study of Murder* in 1960.)

7. Cicero, *De Legibus*, III, 3, 20.

8. Larry Niven, "Death by Ecstasy," in *The Long ARM of Gil Hamilton* (New York: Ballantine, 1976), p. 26. "Death by Ecstasy" was originally published as "The Organleggers" in 1969. This volume also includes "The

Defenseless Dead'' (1973) and "ARM" (1975). ARM in this context refers to the Amalgamation of Regional Militia, later called the United Nations Police.

CHAPTER 5

THE POLICEMAN-HERO

In the centuries since critics in the classical eras spoke of art as the imitation of nature, their remarks have become aphorisms, the applications going beyond original intent.[1] The term *nature* has expanded to cover not only physical and human nature but also the nature of social institutions, an equally vital phenomenon. Under the umbrella of the extended meaning, the police mystery story fits with its imitation of the changing nature of social controls, as well as historical shifts in society's methods of dealing with its outlaws. As crime poses a more serious affront to the society at large, a wider range of expertise has grown to match it for control. This is testified by the organized police unit with its very sophisticated technological tools to aid in analytical work.

The mystery story proper accepted this challenge of social growth to add a third pattern to the established ones of the classical analytical amateur and the action-oriented private investigator. The police detective became a likely candidate for the part of protagonist instead of being relegated to a minor part as a necessary nuisance or as the antagonist of the private detective of the other patterns. One recalls the early appearances of official detectives: Charles Dickens' police detective Bucket in *Bleak House* and the estimable Sergeant Cuff of Wilkie Collins' *The Moonstone*. Nor can one disregard Lecoq, their near-contemporary in the work of Emile Gaboriau, the French author credited with originating the *roman policier* modeled on the *Mémoires* of Vidocq, father of the Sûreté.

Howard Haycraft in *Murder for Pleasure* gives 1918–1930 as a key time when the English-American mystery stories started to feature police detectives and their methods as the central interest. He mentions especially Inspector French in the novels of Freeman Wills Croft.[2] Other official worthies have joined the roster of police heroes: Arthur W. Upfield's Inspector Napoleon Bonaparte of the Queensland Police Department; Inspector Jules Maigret in his five-decade career provided by Georges Simenon; Ngaio Marsh's Chief Inspector Roderick Alleyn; John Creasey's Inspector West; and Hillary Waugh's Chief Fred Fellows in his basement office in the town hall of little Stockton, Connecticut. These police detectives firmly set the policeman in the role of hero, but in more recent years the interest in police procedure and forensic science has threatened to subordinate the man to the methods. Some critics of the mode suggest that the popularity for the police methods story originated with the comic strips such as *Dick Tracy*, *Radio Patrol*, and *Terry Drake*.[3] Still others draw notice to the U.S. radio drama *Dragnet* (later made into a television series) and the British television series *Z-Cars* and *Softly, Softly*.[4] However, most give credit to Lawrence Treat's 1945 *V as in Victim* as the trend-setter for what is now labeled the police procedural.[5] An excellent contemporary version of the police procedural is the Ed McBain series featuring the 87th Precinct Squad.

A brief historical overview of the growth of police organizations in England helps in recognition of modern science fiction/fantasy mystery borrowings. In Anglo-Saxon times law and order were communal responsibilities with the small local populace subject to call in cases of dire trouble. Known as the *posse comitatus*, the citizenry so empowered joined in the well-known "hue and cry" to track down anyone guilty of disturbing the public peace. After 1066 the Norman conquerors placed initial responsibility for order upon parish constables and justices of the peace, officials we maintain in much-changed form today. As the population began to clump more heavily around centers such as London, this density created other problems. Around 1300 two other officers of note joined the forces of order: the aldermen with administrative powers over the wards of the city, holding power under a mayor; and the watchmen who oversaw order on the streets as the "standing watch" or the "marching watch." Some centuries later, these watchmen or bellmen did special duties as night patrols.

With its conventional reliance on speculative situations science fiction/fantasy can utilize such simple police methods in amazing combinations. The speculative may join with the simple, almost primitive procedures of the early English parish constable of centuries-old tradition, as in William F. Temple's "The Green Car" (1957). Police constable George Peters is a countryman, serving four English villages somewhere near the coast in Cornwall. Peters is an English eccentric. Even though acquaintances have known him for years they classify him as "deep," a "queer 'un" with "a scholar's face with quiet eyes." Peters lives alone. One room of his house is stuffed with books, files, albums, records of such esoterica as the license numbers of all vehicles operated in the area since he has been constable. When a small child is run over by a car bearing a license of one that had crashed into the sea some thirty years before, Peters must investigate. Both the description of the driver and that of the car match those of the original owner and wrecked vehicle. Peters calls up the local Aqualung club in "hue and cry" tradition. Their efforts succeed as they trap the driver, only to discover a sea creature whose line of evolution deviated from that of human beings.

To bring our historical look closer to modern times brings us to the eighteenth century when there was increased attention to organization. During his tenure as London's police magistrate in the late 1740s Henry Fielding, the novelist, formed a group of "thief-takers" from a citizen's constabulary. Since these men operated out of the Bow Street office, they acquired the colorful name of Bow Street Runners. About the same time another word, *police*, entered into general usage, later to be followed by *detective*. William Pitt's bill to establish a police force just for London came in 1785. In 1825 Robert Peel as Home Secretary initiated a system of reforms for English criminal law, one result being establishment in 1829 of the Metropolitan Police. A photo of c. 1860 shows a group of these "bobbies" lined up in formation, brass buttons shining in a row from neck to waist and black top hats striking an incongruous note. [6] By 1860 the force had moved from Bow Street to the first location designated as Scotland Yard. In the 1890s a Criminal Investigation Department (the C.I.D.) added other specialized departments to handle fingerprinting, records, photography, as well as a "flying squad" unit added shortly after World War I to deal with sudden outbreaks of violence. The mid-twentieth century saw further accommodations for cases of drug misuse, fraud, motor vehicle theft, criminal intelligence, and other more modern crimes.

Also departments were added to provide training for police detectives and police dogs.

A particularly strong influence on both the early appearances of police protagonists as strong individuals and the subsequent interest in police methods stems in large part from the continuing growth of organized social control. In England this growth culminated in that enduring symbol of police work, England's Scotland Yard. Old Scotland Yard exists now only in the imagination of devotees of early detective stories or police novels. While tourists may leave London unsatisfied by the sight of the multi-floor modern skyscraper of New Scotland Yard, the romance of this London police organization still attracts readers and writers alike, reminding all of a model emulated in the many fictional police activities, including those of science fiction/fantasy police stories.

Stanislaw Lem in *The Investigation* (1959), discussed in another chapter in a different context, also uses the romance of Scotland Yard. Lt. Gregory of Scotland Yard is assigned to a case that proves to have no rational solutions despite all rational applications. As the tradition-molded police detective, Lt. Gregory operates as a narrative foil for the scientist Dr. Sciss. The latter in outlining his "statistical method of investigation" derogates the time-tried and painstaking method of collecting evidence to establish means, motive, and opportunity. However, in this case both the old methodology and the new science fail, leaving a metaphysical question, "what is real?" dominating the case.

Scotland Yard appears a haven for officers in need of touching up their police technique, according to the initial remarks of Arthur C. Clarke's Detective Inspector Rawlings. In "Trouble with Time" (1960), designated by Clarke as "my only detective story," [7] the Inspector sits in the main observation lounge of a spaceport on Phobos with two other passengers bound for Earth after a visit on Mars. The policeman seems a little sad as he remarks that with so little crime on Mars, he would soon be out of practice. So he is returning to the Yard. When he begins to tell a story of a recent and intriguing case, the narrator as well as the reader begins to doubt the original disclaimer about Inspector Rawlings' lack of practice. As he elaborates on the case, an attempted theft of a famous Martian antiquity, he relates in detail the name of the culprit, the plan for the theft, and the small detail in the planning that caused its failure and the subsequent arrest of the thief. All is known to the authorities except the name of the mastermind behind the plan to steal the Siren Goddess. As the Inspector's story unfolds, his words weave a web of suspicion around one of the two fellow-travelers, woven so tightly that at the end the narrator concedes they will have a "very interesting trip."

John Dickson Carr in *Fire, Burn* (1957) and Len Deighton in *SS ·GB* (1978) place their police heroes in more realistic situations even as they operate in speculative frameworks. Both authors utilize common science fiction/fantasy conventions: Carr, time travel; Deighton, alternate time line. Carr had previously used the time shift in his historical fantasies, *The Devil in Velvet* (1951) and *Fear Is the Same* (1956), the latter written as Carter Dickson. Both Carr and Deighton, known for their previous detective stories and spy thrillers respectively, show this early dedication by incorporating some conventions from these genres in the science fiction/fantasy novels. They draw on the mystique of Scotland Yard as their main characters operate according to the code of that institution and draw strength from its sense of mission. Both Carr's Detective Superintendent John Cheviot of C-1, C.I.D., and Deighton's Archer of the Yard, head of the murder squad, must solve a similar crime, a murder. This is the crime a German general in *SS ·GB* describes as "the only crime seldom committed by criminals." [8] While working on their respective cases, Cheviot and Archer cope with a social system vastly different from the ones in which they were trained. Boxed in on three sides by a stern Law, petty rules and regulations, and social dictates, the police detective can develop as a personality in one area only—his individual humanity. Both Cheviot and Archer of the Yard exemplify how science fiction/fantasy can exploit this area of the mystery format.

In *Fire, Burn* when Detective-Superintendent John Cheviot of 1950s Scotland Yard steps into a motor cab enroute to his office, he little expects to step out of a hackney cab, knocking a black top hat off his head in the process. But he does. It is London, 1829, into which he steps, a London of gas lights, public resentment of the Peelers, and Old Scotland Yard. As the reader prepares to match wits with the detective, he also must cope with the authentic setting of nineteenth-century London reached only by time travel. Cheviot enters the world of the Metropolitan Police and Scotland Yard at its historical inception, even to having a realistic meeting with Sir Robert Peel, its founder. As soon as Cheviot adjusts himself to the time shift, he finds himself applying for a position on this newly-organized force. His initial assignment appears a trivial case, some missing birdseed. The case escalates in seriousness, ending with murder.

The murder occurs in circumstances approximating a locked-room mystery, for it happens before three impeccable witnesses, one of whom is Cheviot himself. While not physically locked tight, the room was "locked" in by Cheviot's trained and sharp perception. Deprived of the aid of twentieth-century technology, Cheviot must rely on his mind and wits to solve the problem. Carr in Detective Cheviot has developed a character relatively unflappable while working in the earlier era, yet balanced emotionally enough to retain the memory of his 1950s origin. His active and wholesome curiosity about the 1829 city and people, his pride at participating in forging the reputation of this fledgling police force, and his undeniable detectival ability add to the attraction of the myth of the force of Scotland Yard.

In a less romantic way Len Deighton's Douglas Archer does identical service for the Yard. Archer operates in an era closer in time to our own but in an alternate time line. What if Germany had defeated England before America entered the war? Archer's world presents one possibility. It is 1941. In an occupied Britain striving to maintain some semblance of national dignity Detective Superintendent Archer must not only pull his own shattered life together but also solve a murder as head of Scotland Yard's Murder Squad. Although Archer's distinguished reputation assures success, he must cope with two sources of antagonism: the weight of public opinion and a maze of political intrigue. Some Englishmen, particularly those in the Resistance, condemn him as a collaborator with the Germans. His only defence is a simple statement: "My job is solving crimes. The British public have a right to be protected against murder, robbery and violence." [9]

The murder is that of an atomic scientist. Soon the investigation assumes greater significance than expected. Archer begins to meet unexplainable obstacles, subtle blocks engineered by the very officials overseeing his work. He becomes aware of political activity beyond his ken. He notes an internal power struggle between the German army and the S.S. The Resistance plans to smuggle the sick King out of the country. There are attempts to draw the United States into war with Germany. All of these forces swirl around Archer's case of the dead scientist. Plots and betrayals force Archer toward a momentous choice, one at odds with his image of his own purpose and one which in failure reconfirms only the importance of the man of integrity rather than the ideal whose time is not yet come.

A noteworthy shift in reader-participation occurs in the stories with a police protagonist. In the classical detective story a Holmes with the patronizing "Elementary, my friend" put-down, or a Hercule Poirot reminding all of his "little grey cells," or a Lord Peter Wimsey with the elegant manners can reduce a reader to being an over-the-shoulder watcher, full of marvel at the clever mind at work. At these times the reader may content himself with a Watson role. With the hard-boiled private eye the reader may wholeheartedly support the detective in his quasi-criminal methods of detection, if the author can set up a close identification with that solitary romantic hero battling for good against sometimes well-organized evil. Most people admire the individual who places himself in questionable circumstances out of a personal belief in what he is doing, even though they shrink from doing it themselves.

The official detective in the same situation as either gifted amateur or private investigator can lose the allegiance of the reader. Most readers come to the police mystery with a curious ambivalence. As taxpayers they consider the police as employees. They represent the social conscience. Having accepted the badge as a symbol of public faith and trust, the policeman should merit sympathy and support. The code of his profession is couched in high-sounding phrases: to serve mankind; to safeguard lives and property; to protect the innocent, the weak, and the peaceful; and above all, to acknowledge the constitutional rights of all men to liberty, equality, and justice. However, the public may disagree with the law as interpreted by the fictional society. When Aristotle in Book 4.4 of the *Politics* spoke of law as order and "good law as good order," he tacitly acknowledged the existence of disorder in the world; his comment also tacitly suggests the possibility of bad law. What if the police protagonist serves under a bad law? Then the sympathy of the reader will shift. No longer a willing accomplice in solving the crime, he may come to support the criminal.

An author using a police detective as protagonist walks a tenuous line. He can strengthen it by working in threads of exposition of the daily routine or of the special routine demanded by the current assignment. The novelist may convince us of the need for both the limits and the freedoms built into the many rules and regulations. More important, he must generate a sensitivity to the ever-present conflict of individual idealism and social realism, a conflict that may tear the character apart. The science fiction/fantasy police mystery has the additional task of making the laws seem to be logical and valuable within the parameters of the speculative world presented. Above all, these efforts must be performed with art. As the mystery story erects a verbal structure, it serves several ends. It entertains. It reveals the dark side of life up to a bearable point. Also, it gives hope to the audience that they may better bear that dark side, even as it reflects the threats of terror and violence in real life. While fulfilling these functions the story must maintain suspense.

As one knows, suspense arises from the unknown or the known, depending on the extent of the threat. If the criminal is known, suspense may hinge on the evidence-gathering process or on the excitement of the pursuit. In science fiction/fantasy mysteries this easily translates into romance and adventure rather than crime-solving, as seen in the early Lensman series of E. E. Smith (1948–1954). The seven-novel series traces the eons-long antagonism of two races, Arisian and Eddorian. As they evolve, they develop diametrically opposite ethical viewpoints, thus embodying the archetypal pattern of good versus evil. To act as their physical surrogates, the intelligent but disembodied Arisians foster a strong human race. In *First Lensman* (1950), the second book of the series, the humans organize the Galactic Patrol, the first interplanetary police force. Cosmic super-cops engage only super-criminals. These latter commit super-crimes such as piracy on the commercial high waves of space, interplanetary drug traffic, galactic political machinations, and "peculiar disturbances in the sub-ether," whatever these may be.[10] Smith's galactic police illustrate the ease with which a mystery story can slip into romantic space opera.

A similar metamorphosis can occur in time opera. The fascination that time travel holds for even the most logically oriented individual proves to be too strong for Andre Norton's Blake Walker sequence, *The Crossroads of Time* (1956) and *Quest Crosstime* (1965), also titled *Crosstime Agent*. The former novel does use police procedure as a strong thread of the narrative. The Wardsmen are para-time policemen, law enforcement officers similar in purpose to the contemporary Federal Bureau of Investigation (FBI). The general population has developed the ability to cross time from one time line to another, an ability certain opportunists are quick to use for profit. The Wardsmen, native to a world called Vroom, bring special psi and telepathic talents to the official search for the time buccaneers. When the Wardsmen discover Blake Walker has psi power, they absorb him into their work. Walker, abandoned as a child and found by a Columbus police detective, has been on his own since twenty years of age. The search for the time crossers meddling in the various time lines gradually takes second place to the rite of passage that Walker goes through as he searches also for his true identity and place in the cosmos.

Hillary Waugh in a discussion of the police procedural has remarked that realism is as difficult to come by in that mode as in those of the classical detective and the private investigator. Despite that difficulty the main police character (or characters, if a team or squad) should come across as human beings, not infallible but subject to restrictions both of job and society.[11] One way of assuring that humanness is to link the police hero with family responsibilities, a link not forged by either the analytical amateur or the private eye by convention. George N. Dove listed "the Policeman with Family Problems" as one of the five conventions he assigned to the police procedural.[12]

While the majority of the science fiction/fantasy police stories do not belabor this relationship, Isaac Asimov does use it to good purpose in his characterization of Lije Baley. In *The Caves of Steel* when first asked by Commissioner Enderby to "put up" the Spacer partner with whom he will be working, Baley's initial response is "Jessie won't like it." But Jessie does like some things, such as her recorded name *Jezebel*, the practical request that was Lije's proposal of marriage to her, and Baley himself. It is Jessie who is terrified when in *The Naked Sun* Baley must take a plane in the course of duty. It is Jessie, along with his seventeen-year-old son Bentley, he hopes will understand what he has learned about Earth from his experience in Solaria. Asimov's police detective demonstrates the effectiveness a personal background can add to the main focus of the detective at work.

Science fiction/fantasy has its own brand of realism. It allows the author the freedom to experiment with highly imaginative police procedures that authors of realistic twentieth-century stories must forego. Telepathy, despite the continued controlled scientific testing of this century, remains an untapped talent for us. Not so in the world of science fiction/fantasy police stories. Randall Garrett and Laurence M. Janifer, collaborating under the pseudonym of Mark Phillips, gambol through the field of psionics with light-hearted enjoyment. *Brain Twister* (1962), *Supermind* (1963), and *The Impossibles* (1963) feature F.B.I. agent Kenneth Malone, whose notable contribution has been to ferret out seven persons with psi talent to aid the bureau in criminal investigations. While one might wonder at the usefulness of these people, all of whom were found in asylums, they can contribute much through their remarkable telepathic powers, especially the lovable but eccentric Miss Thompson, who fancies herself Queen Elizabeth I of England and demands treatment commensurate with that status.

With their aid Malone is able to crack a case of theft by teleportation in *The Impossibles*. Later in *Supermind* Malone must track down the cause of computer snafus creating political and social disorder. He lands in the midst of an idealistic group of telepaths using their power to bring government and society to more perfect working order. They hope to weed out inefficiency and opportunism by misdirection. A more important discovery is that Malone himself is both capable of telepathy and of teleportation, a bureau-trained supermind. That the authors are well aware of the literary tradition of the mystery story they are using is evident in the dropped references to Nero Wolfe, Sherlock Holmes, and most especially to "detectives in books" who "always managed to wrap everything up in the last chapter." [13]

On the other hand, imagine a planet inhabited by a race of telepaths. Since everyone knows everything in others' minds, nothing can be hidden. With no secrets there is no mystery, hence no need for a specially trained force to ferret out clues. Such a place is Lee Killough's planet Egar in *Deadly Silents* (1981). When an outbreak of crime catches them unawares, the Iregara have no resources to curtail it. They send for law enforcement officers from Terra to aid in setting up their own organization with special assignment to deal with the Silents in their population. These Silents, a minority group, have lost their telepathic ability. While they visited Terra as part of a trade commission, they were burned out mentally from the onslaught of thoughts beamed to them from the mass of population. Here the police procedure serves as the way to explore a situation where a great difference in cultural norms exists and where communication fails on a large scale. A note of realism creeps in when Devane Brooks, Director of the Police Department, becomes entangled in bureaucratic details, thus adding to the general misunderstanding.

Larry Niven's series about Gil Hamilton, member of ARM or the Amalgamation of Regional Militia, police force of the United Nations in the 2120s, also uses psychic weapons in crime control. The ARM outfit has three major functions in this future world. They enforce the fertility laws, monitor world technology, and hunt down organleggers. The latter outlaws carry on a futuristic traffic in spare human parts, for sale to the highest bidder and easily obtainable through murder or by preying upon the more unfortunate members of the society. Gil Hamilton's cases range from simple organlegging to murder by electrical pleasure machine or by intense fire to burn away the face. He also investigates theft from trusting persons who had themselves frozen to escape the present world in favor of taking their chances in a future era. Gil's chief weapon of both defense and retribution is his "arm," a third imaginary appendage but one he can wield by psychokinesis. Like Malone he parodies the super-police detective, not as a supermind but as a super-arm.

While a novel's length allows a leisurely look at futuristic police methods and the police protagonist, the short story must take as its province the brief but dramatic highlighting of a future technique, perhaps one as yet unexperienced, indeed, unacknowledged even as a possibility. The law admits evidence of a physical nature and of a psychological nature, but what of meta-physical or meta-sensuous evidence, that beyond the ability of the five senses to record? Wilson Tucker in "Time Exposure" (1971) offers the possibility that the emotions of the participants in a murder are so intense that they leave impressions on the immediate environment for a time up to ten to fourteen hours after the event. When a murder occurs in this society where strict gun control laws prohibit anyone but professionals from carrying weapons, the police are stymied. A routine investigation turns up no evidence of a struggle, no tell-tale stains, no fingerprints. As a last resort the police call in the sergeant-photographer whose camera uses film so sensitive it can record past events. Tucker's story focuses on the details of the photographic method and the problems the sergeant encounters before he catches the telltale record of the murderer's act.

Lee Killough in "The Existential Man" (1982) explores an even more futuristic possibility, yet succeeds in making it seem logical. Killough's Detective Sergeant David Amara unlocks the trunk of an abandoned car to find evidence of a grisly murder. The violent final emotions of the dead man grip him with such intensity as to turn him into an instrument of revenge. *Cogito, ergo sum*, "I think, therefore I am," so concluded René Descartes, seventeenth-century French philosopher. In a futuristic exemplum of Descartes' idea Amara "thinks" himself into a peculiar existence as he proceeds with the more practical work of checking fingerprints, dental records, and bone injuries. Amnesia, extra-sensory flashes of knowledge and sight, plus other paranormal experiences draw him into other cases, a rape case and an investigation of drug traffic. The solution to all three culminates in the recognition of his existential being and the non-dying urge to bring the culprits to justice.

Exploration of the para-physical aspects of an investigation is carried to greater lengths in Kenneth Bulmer's *The Doomsday Men* (1965) where Robin Carver, member of the R.I.D., commonly called Ridforce (Resurrection Investigation Detection), uses his special ability. His job is to penetrate the brain and memory of a murdered person, to relive the memory of the last moments, and to gather clues or discover the identity of the murderer, if the victim saw him clearly. He has three minutes for the psychic fusion before the brain deteriorates beyond the point of memory salvage. In one of the symbiotic penetrations he discovers not only the clues to a crime but also clues to a plot to destroy the Shield. This is an electromagnetic force field that effectively insulates the country against thermonuclear attack, but also isolates the populace from outside mental stimulation, ideas that foster growth by intellectual challenge.

Following a general trend in contemporary concerns, science fiction/fantasy police stories have beamed in on subjects for social comment, particularly the major issues of mind control, over-population, and people's relationship to the machine. The ambivalent attitudes of the reading audience must necessarily complicate the task of an author. Does the audience view the police as protectors or enemies, as symbols of social morality or of social control? If as the first in each of these pairs, then George N. Dove's convention of the Overworked Force may come into operation; if the latter view prevails, then another one of his listed conventions, the Hostile Public, applies.[14]

In 1798 when Thomas Robert Malthus formulated the now oft-quoted doctrine concerning the ratio of population growth as compared to that of resources for subsistence, he predicted dire results unless the traditional checks of war, disease, and crime worked. In 1803 he revised his predictions only to the extent that people might help the situation by moral restraint. That the last two hundred years seem determined to prove Malthus only partially correct is only too evident in the statistics available to us today. Science fiction/fantasy has taken close looks at the current situation, paying attention to depletion of natural resources, ravages to the natural environment, and the psychological consequences of overcrowding in the social environment. These issues have informed novels such as John Brunner's *Stand on Zanzibar*, Lester del Rey's *The Eleventh Commandment*, discussed elsewhere, and James Blish and Norman A. Knight's *A Torrent of Faces* (1968).

The science fiction/fantasy police story has not ignored this subject. Isaac Asimov's Lije Baley in the previously discussed *The Caves of Steel* lives in an over-populated world, in one that has accommodated itself somewhat to the problem. By contrast, Harry Harrison in *Make Room! Make Room!* (1966, later filmed in 1973 as *Soylent Green*) attacks the issue in all of its horror. Detective Andy Rusch of the New York City Police works futilely to maintain order in his area. In 1999 people practice little of the moral restraint desired by Malthus. Uncontrolled population growth has necessitated water rationing. Food is in short supply and living places are overcrowded. Violence sets the temper of the times. In this microcosmic dystopia reflecting worldwide conditions, police detective Rusch has little aid from the traditional institutions of order, the family, church, or political party. Rusch's city suffers conduct unthought of in earlier times. Farmers blow up reservoirs in a battle with cities over water rights. Old people mount demonstrations, even as their very vulnerability invites pickpockets, purse-grabbers, and others to prey upon them. Food riots are common.

When a prominent racketeer is murdered in his luxurious apartment, pressure bears upon Rusch to bring the murderer to justice. The reader soon knows the culprit, a desperate young Chinese boy who entered the apartment to steal for his own subsistence. Rusch's official search devolves into a tedious following of small leads, none of which points to the rival racketeer suspected by Rusch's powerful superiors. No high adventure happens here, no romance of a clearcut difference between the bad and good guys. As Detective Rusch tells the murdered man's mistress, police work is "mostly dull stuff, a lot of walking around, making notes, writing reports—and hoping a stoolie will bring you the answer."[15] In the picture of Rusch's community Harry Harrison does not entertain his readers. He reveals a situation in which the policeman cannot serve as protector or as social conscience or even as enemy, for he exists as an anachronism in a society of no restraints except famine, disease, and the drive for survival. The dystopic view of the narrative chills as it predicts, a purpose further emphasized by the non-fictional introduction to the novel by Paul Ehrlich and an appended bibliography of studies on population dynamics.[16]

While the basic need for food and shelter drives *homo sapiens* into action as it does all forms of life, the need for certain psychological satisfactions demand equal force of action. These needs manifest themselves more subtly than through an empty belly or frozen extremities. The subtlety can betray the individual into giving up that which he may most desire such as freedom of choice, privacy, or individuality. Peter Wahlöö's *Murder on the Thirty-First Floor* (1960) and *The Steel Spring* (1970) warn more than warm a reader's mind to this possibility. In these novels Inspector Jensen must unravel shadow crimes that exist primarily as masks for darker transgressions against human freedom. In *The Steel Spring* a series of unexplained deaths stimulates investigation. Jensen uncovers an unconscionable political ploy exercised by certain powerful men. These plot to influence elections by predisposing the voters with a mind-affecting drug mixed with the glue on stamps. In *Murder on the Thirty-First Floor* (later published simply as *The Thirty-First Floor*) the initial case in a near-future society seems mundane enough. Executives of a communications combine receive a letter threatening a bombing "in retaliation for a murder committed by you." Since the executives are men whose reputations do not countenance such an accusation, Jensen must pursue the matter and stop the bomber.

To move his police inspector to this end, Wahlöö generates suspense by two skillfully executed tracks. First, suspense rises in the inexorable countdown of the hours and minutes of the threatened explosion. No explosion occurs. Then there is the detailed description of Jensen's procedure. The mere recital of the police procedure could have a deadening effect, but Wahlöö organizes it also as a countdown, this time of the days and interviews involved in the investigation. Jensen's notebook, beginning with Number One, continuing with Two, Three, and on, becomes a ticking time bomb of data. For seven days Jensen works doggedly, seven days of the "mostly dull stuff," to use the words of Harrison's Detective Rusch. Only when Jensen discovers the thirty-first floor, an area denied by the external appearance of the communications building itself, does he have the vital clue to the "murder" alluded to in the letter. A pattern falls into place, but it is a micro-pattern inviting a closer look at a greater social evil.

Wahlöö has used the minutiae of police procedure to create suspense as he draws the macro-pattern to strike fear into the hearts of all. Jensen lives in a homogenized society where equality is identified with welfare. No one wants for food, shelter, clothing, but to achieve such a laudable end, much standardization must occur. People live in block units, constructed with a definite sameness. Home furnishings are "impersonal"; clothing is "tasteless." No matter where one eats in public, one eats the identical combinations, all menus being planned at a central agency in the Ministry of Health. Crime, notably juvenile delinquency, has declined. Even as one remarks the attainment of this best of all possible worlds, there are the trade-offs. Jensen's plodding work takes us into a country where individualism is discouraged. While magazines, newspapers, television abound, these all pander to human intellectual laziness, presenting by plan a picture of life free from all problems but also pushing a view that cannot include any show of opposition or challenge to the system.

The two executives who control the media and thereby the thought and values of the country are clever. Outwardly they practice anti-individualism by insisting on identification not by name but as "a publisher" and "the managing director." Covered by these functional labels, they escape personal responsibility for their actions. They also discourage the polite address of "sir" and thus escape any claim for noble or moral responsibility. The anonymity cloaks their crimes.

Only when Jensen discovers the physical anomaly in the building does their crime come out. By chance he hears a rumor of a thirty-first floor. Patient and quiet search brings him to an attic in which a coterie of the brightest questioning minds of the city have been sequestered. Gulled into belief that they are working on a thought-provoking publication and trapped into personal debt by their employers, these men live a useless servile existence at the mercy of their intellectual enemies. Even this meager existence is denied in the wake of a second bomb threat and explosion just as the building, except for the thirty-first floor, is evacuated. The crime *is* murder, not only of the men in the attic room, but of the intellectual murder of an entire population deprived of the stimulus of debate.

The fear of people's inability to come to terms with their own inventions is not a new one, as witnessed by an early police story by Jules Verne, *Master of the World*, the 1904 sequel to *Robur the Conqueror* (1886). Verne offers a pessimistic outlook in *Master of the World*, as the title foreshadows. Robur has become an egomaniac, using his scientific inventions to threaten world peace. Completely amoral in his command of the technology, he becomes the embodiment of the fear that people will be incapable of making science and its attendant technology subservient to higher aims. Robur is opposed by Head Inspector John Strock of the federal police department. The Inspector has only personal courage and mental acuity as his weapons. Even as Robur loses the fight, through his own suicidal gesture, the uneven combat emphasizes human psychological immaturity in the face of technological advances.

By contrast, L. Neil Smith's light and humorous *Their Majesties' Bucketeers* (1981) considers the fears born of the soft sciences. Smith's official police force exists in a twenty-third-century society of an alien race of trimorphic creatures. Their culture is in its technological adolescence. Photographers use flash guns but without electricity. Wireless telegraphy exists but telephones and the "internal conflagration engine" remain in the experimental stage. Until a murder disturbs the routine, Mav, the Extraordinary Inquirer for the Bucketeers, works hardest at introducing new techniques such as clue collecting and the wearing of raincoats. These detectives live in a dry world where they extinguish fires with sand and as their harshest expletive say "Damp!"

When his detective turns to the more challenging work of solving the murder, author Smith turns to the more serious subject of science versus traditional beliefs. As Mav solves the locked-room mystery, which he calls a "closed-chamber paradox," he uses the standard convention of gathering the suspects together for the showdown, thereby forcing a move of betrayal by the culprit. The probing of the investigation touches a festering sore within the body social: a fundamentalist point of view at odds with the new theory of Ascensionism. Against this thinly disguised background of the contemporary creationism-evolution conflict, Inquirer Mav untangles the clues to the murder of passion. Both Verne's early novel and Smith's later one demonstrate the yeoman service that science fiction/fantasy police stories do so well. They encourage consideration of contemporary clashes of the traditional values and human frailty within the scientific and technological context.

In a literary mode not noted for its outstanding female characters, much less female police officers, Municipal Police Chief Anna-Louise Bach of New Dresden, Luna, is an exception to the rule. She appears in two of John Varley's short works: "The Barbie Murders" (1978) and "Bagatelle" (1976). In the former she must investigate a murder in an area dominated by a cult dedicated to sameness. Differentness or originality is the ultimate crime or sin; sameness is achieved by appearance imitating the Barbie doll and by language rules such as prohibition of the personal pronoun *I*. Bach solves the murder by the drastic action of undergoing an operation that turns her into a barbie. This "cover" enables her to infiltrate the group and trap the murderer. In "Bagatelle" Police Chief Bach comes up hard against the human-machine problem. Alerted to a threat of a talking nuclear bomb in a business area, she arrives on the scene to find a cyborged human, a man who felt so controlled by machines that he decided to join the ruling class by becoming a machine himself. With the aid of a vacationing bomb disarmer and amateur psychologist the Police Chief is able to give the cyborg the human attention he yearns for. Thus she gains his confidence and aid in leading her to the group using his fear toward their own ends.

Murder, while still the most heinous crime of human history, will certainly move over to share attention with as yet unspeculated harmful activity in future times, some of it associated with the machines proliferating around us. As early as 1982 a newspaper report anticipated such events with a headline proclaiming that a "robot" had killed a foreign auto worker. In science fiction Isaac Asimov had foreseen such contingencies and in the Three Laws of Robotics assured that such inventions could not harm people. But how does one define *harm*? Clifford Simak in "How-2" (1954) poses such a puzzle for future lawmakers and in due time for the enforcers of the law. Simak envisions a future in which people's great problem is filling up hours of leisure time. One way is to learn to do many things for oneself by use of How-2 kits. But what if the hobby results in construction of an advanced robot that in turn produces more robots to release more people to more leisure time? Is the original act a crime? What is the future role of the police in this event? The questions become irrelevant in Simak's story as the original robot creates three dozen lawyer-robots who clear the human tinkerer by the argument that robots are not property but "people" with all the rights and responsibilities endowed by tradition. The robot Albert seeks to soothe the human segment of the population by assuring them that they will have nothing to fear for the rest of their existence. The reader can but add *sotto voce* "but obsolescence."

Perhaps it is by parody that any literary pattern wins its spurs. The science fiction/fantasy police mystery is not an exception to this claim, as Barry Malzberg in "The Twentieth Century Murder Case" (1981) invites us to look at both the literary format and the social scene with irony. The twentieth century, an aged entity, lies in sad straits in the intensive care ward. The investigator-narrator, *I*, takes to the streets to search out the one guilty of the horrors perpetrated upon this hapless victim. He has a list of likely suspects, all with excellent alibis. He interviews three of the most likely candidates: the head of an advertising agency, the vice-president of a television programming company, and the chairman of the board of a fast-food franchising firm. When one of the trio breaks down under the grilling and confesses to the plot to kill the century, one assumes the case closed, but no. Back at headquarters the detective-narrator quits in utter frustration when he hears that even before the old one dies, the new twenty-first century has suffered assaults. Parody? Yes. Fiction or Reality?

A comparison of the science fiction/fantasy police story with the symbiotic amateur detective and private investigator stories indicates that all three can be successful in melding situation with idea. The science fiction/fantasy police procedural faces the general problems faced by the other mixtures. The camera capable of photographing events of the past twelve hours may be no less improbable than the "necromancy of Freud and Jung" or the kymograph and plethysmograph, all used to add interest to a Luther Trant case. The "mostly dull stuff" of the routine work of a Detective Rusch can in the hands of a deft author illuminate by contrast the harbingers of a dire future not at all impossible.

NOTES

1. Aristotle in the *Poetics* spoke of art as imitating men in action, sometimes representing them as better than we are, other times as worse. Horace in *Ars Poetica* advised the Piso brothers to be as true to life as possible in their writing. Seneca in Epistle 65 reemphasized that all art is the imitation of nature.

2. Howard Haycraft, *Murder for Pleasure* (1941; rpt. New York: Biblo and Tannen, 1974), pp. 122–24.

3. K. Arne Blom, "Polis! Polis!" in *Murder Ink*, ed. Dilys Winn (New York: Workman, 1977), p. 335.

4. Julian Symons, *Mortal Consequences* (New York: Schocken, 1973), p. 204.

5. George N. Dove, "Realism, Routine, Stubbornness and System," *The*

Armchair Detective 10 (April 1977), 133. Blom, n. 3 above, also gives credit to Lawrence Treat's novel.

6. One such photograph is reproduced in *Murder Ink*, p. 317.

7. Arthur C. Clarke, *The Nine Billion Names of God* (New York: Harcourt Brace Jovanovich, 1967), headnote, p. 25.

8. Len Deighton, *SS ·GB* (London, 1978; rpt. New York: Ballantine, 1979), p. 72.

9. Ibid., p. 182.

10. E. E. "Doc" Smith, *First Lensman* (1950; rpt. New York: Pyramid Books, 1968), p. 72.

11. Hillary Waugh, "The Police Procedural," in *The Mystery Story*, ed. John Ball (Del Mar, Calif.: Publisher's Inc., 1976), pp. 163–87.

12. Dove, p. 133.

13. Mark Phillips, *Supermind* (1960; rpt. New York: Pyramid Books, 1963), p. 166.

14. Dove, p. 133.

15. Harry Harrison, *Make Room! Make Room!* (1966; rpt. New York: Berkley, 1967), p. 88.

16. This introduction by Paul Ehrlich and the appended list of environmental books and studies are included in the Berkley Medallion Edition, New York: Berkley, 1967.

CHAPTER 6

THE TRANSGRESSOR-HERO

"The individual . . . gets a lot of money . . . and he benefits society by putting large amounts of cash back into circulation. The economy is stimulated, small businessmen prosper, people read about the crime with great interest, and the police have a chance to exercise their various skills."[1] So rationalizes Slippery Jim diGriz in Harry Harrison's *The Stainless Steel Rat Saves the World* (1972) as he goes about robbing a bank, one of the several extralegal activities he indulges in to "save my sanity," as he had remarked earlier in *The Stainless Steel Rat* (1961). Few would argue the social benefit of the rightful exercise of law to protect the innocent from the predator. But what of the balancing benefits of the criminal act, if any? One could debate the point of social catharsis: the exploits of the outlaw allows harmless exorcism of the latent criminal urges any one of us may harbor. Another might opt for the qualitative argument: if good is to triumph over evil, it must conquer something worthy of the effort. Hence a character with perverted yet heroic potentiality is necessary. Since science fiction/fantasy allows speculation and extrapolation, in its symbiotic relationship with tales of crime it also invites consideration of the transgressor-hero.

Literature abounds in outlaws who have attracted interest rather than provoked rejection, have received grudging admiration instead of outright censure. Witness the popularity of the scheming slaves of Roman comedy or Robin Hood as a romantic rather than a criminal figure. Shakespeare felt impelled to kill off Falstaff to assure Prince Hal's predominance as the central character in the history plays. Despite Falstaff's propensity to lie, cheat, belay, and rob worthy pilgrims, the audience feels sympathy for the fat man when Hal as King Henry rejects him. An Othello or a Macbeth in the aftermath of murder rise to become tragic heroes rather than villains. Even John Milton failed to paint Satan other than as a darkly heroic figure in the first two books of *Paradise Lost*.

The picaresque hero made his debut in English literature with Jack Wilson in Thomas Nashe's *The Unfortunate Traveller* (1594) along with others. Wilton and his successors elevated the rascal of low degree to a position of notice along with those of higher degree such as a Falstaff and by so doing shone the spotlight on acts of petty rascality just short of serious crime. Romantic highwayman Captain Macheath in John Gay's *The Beggar's Opera* (1728) adds a touch of class to fence Peachum's Register of the Gang: Crooked-finger'd Jack, Wat Dreary, Slippery Sam, Matt of the Mint, Tom Tipple, Robin of Bagshot, "alias Gorgon, alias Bluff Bob, alias Carbuncle, alias Bob Booty" (Act I, sc. iii). How useful such class is for Gay's satiric purpose is evident in one of the final scenes when the titular author, the Beggar, gives in to the pleas of a player and saves Macheath from the deserved hanging: "Through the whole Piece you may observe such a similitude of Manners in high and low Life, that it is difficult to determine whether (in the fashionable Vices) the fine Gentlemen imitate the Gentlemen of the Road, or the Gentlemen of the Road the fine Gentlemen" (Act III, sc. xvi). Dickens's community of thieves in *Oliver Twist* (1839) may not merit the same consideration, but they do command primary attention and a modicum of admiration for the depths of their villainy. Fagin and the Artful Dodger qualify as villain-heroes.

Late nineteenth- and early twentieth-century genre fiction picked up this popular stock figure, turning it out with many variations. The evil genius of Moriarty commands our acknowledgment as an equal of the commendable genius of Sherlock Holmes. Raffles, E. W. Hornung's gentleman-thief, turns his native cleverness and social breeding to illegal ends without alienating the allegiance of the reader. Melville Davisson Post in *The Strange Schemes of Randolph Mason* (1896) created an unprincipled lawyer who uses his knowledge of the law to defeat the purpose of the law, although in a later novel, *The Corrector of Destinies* (1908) he reformed and reversed his energies to support the law. G. K. Chesterton's Flambeau, the "colossus of crime" in the

Father Brown stories, outdoes even Moriarty in dastardly but clever maneuvering. *The Gentle Grafter*—the very title begs acceptance for the crook as hero in O. Henry's 1908 novel; a similar signal deceives one in meeting The Saint, Leslie Charteris' gentleman-adventurer, a twentieth-century Robin Hood. With increasing emphasis in this century on investigative journalism and social and psychological studies the writers of fiction have found and promoted other extra-legal personages into positions as hero or as protagonist: the gangster, the psychopath, the traitor, and others.

As part of the symbiotic process science fiction/fantasy mysteries have adapted these types for its purpose, much as did the film makers of *Star Wars* make Darth Vader an echo of Milton's Satan. Rebels against authority, thieves, super-crooks, murderers, political deviants, social dissidents, the criminal organization leader, or the professional assassin—these and others find themselves as the unexpected transgressor-hero. Occasionally the criminal receives and accepts the chance to reform and serve society in more acceptable ways; however, he may reject the opportunity in order to follow his own path of action. A few are losers whose careers elicit sympathy that in turn shifts the onus of the situation to society at large. Whatever the pattern of choice exercised by this character, the mystery lies not in the puzzle of a detective story, not in the sensationalism of a thriller, and not in the impersonal international or galactic undertow of a spy story. Rather it lies in the titanic, ethical struggle within the human heart of the transgressor.

That murder signifies villainy to most people bears yet another repetition. With our deeply engrained cultural antipathy toward murder we find it difficult to accept a murderer as a hero. As protagonist, he best serves as a subject for a psychological case study, his perversion or derangement placing him several removes from normal experience. In science fiction/fantasy certain stock conventions provide this necessary distance: time, space, alienness, surrealistic techniques to provide linguistic distance. Jack Vance in the aforementioned "Coup de Grace" uses the alien condition to cope with the anomaly of the transgressor as hero. While detective Magnus Ridolph serves as the central character, interest in the unknown murderer soon eases him from that claim. The situation works a variation on the locked-room formula, when one realizes that the Hub space resort is sealed off from the normal ebb and flow of traffic, its confines containing only the tourists who came in with the murdered man. None of these have any previous connection with or motive for killing him. To solve the murder, the detective must engage in a purely ratiocinative exercise. This leads to the Bonze whose cultural mores direct him to kill when necessary to relieve a man of a troubled life. Such an act is one of exceptional service, hence moral and commendable and heroic.

Charles Eric Maine in *Fire Past the Future* (1959) uses the ten-little-Indians formula made popular by Agatha Christie in *And Then There Were None* (1939). In Maine's near-future a group of scientists gather on Kaluiki atoll (not as evocative a name as Christie's Indian Island) to launch an anti-gravity rocket, the initial step of humankind toward time travel. All specialists in their own field of expertise, the scientists feel no apparent animosity toward each other that would explain the series of murders by strangulation, bludgeoning, and shooting. One by one, the members of the team die. Farrant, the journalist and photographer whose job it is to record the details of the project on film and in word, commits the first murder while suffering possession from a stronger intelligence outside himself. He also is one of the two alive at the end of the story, alive to speculate on the identity of that intelligence. A sentient alien intent on sabotage of the human effort? Temporal police from a future and guarding that time? Which future? Maine successfully transforms here the transgressor of a basic moral law into the vehicle of a philosophical idea. The real murderer remains anonymous but imbued with an aura of goodness fostered by the possible motives for the deaths.

The real murderer in Robert M. Coates' *The Eater of Darkness* (1959) seems obvious. Charles Dograr, living in a state of detachment from the world around him, meets Picrolas, also known as Benjamin Constantin, Thorndyke Smithers, M. Carolo Faudras. Picrolas is a master criminal of international reputation, arrested but acquitted in turn of arson, manslaughter, attempted rape, passing bad checks, forgery, bank robbery, and sundry other crimes. He introduces Dograr to murder. Together they enter the Dead Plane, both a physical location and a state of mind free of ethical constraints. Here awaits a machine designed to send out an x-ray beam of such intensity that one can scan the interior of a person's brain miles away. The two men implement an added feature, a laser-like ability to kill that which the beam can reach. The series of murders galvanizes New York residents and police to action; Charles himself leads the chase by dropping hints and revealing tidbits of information to selected persons. He becomes both hunter and hunted, avid for all experience in a world from which he feels excluded.

Murder and more murder, chase and chance encounters, the intrusion of reality and extrusion of personality—all swirl in a surrealistic montage of events. But did any of it ever happen, or is it merely a creative flow from the mind of the French girl Charles left behind when he went to New York? Or is the only reality Charles' meeting with critic Asa Huddleberry? At that time he had listened to Huddleberry speculate idly about a mystery story he would like to write, a mystery story with an unknown crime and unknowable criminal and other "small, busy important silhouettes against the black shadow of Fate." [2] Coates has created the surrealistic murderer in a de-realized environment, one improbable but possible.

Philip José Farmer tackles a more difficult job with John Carmody in the two-part *Night of Light* (1966). In part 1 Farmer goes out of his way to present Carmody as a completely despicable man: he is a wife-murderer who compounded the intensity of his crime by dismembering both wife and her four-month-old fetus and dumping them in a garbage disposal. He is variously described as "a monster of egotism," "an artist in crime," and "one of the dirty-souled." Under suspicion but not apprehended for his crimes, Carmody escapes earth to accompany two priests to Dante's Joy, an alien planet some 1,500,000 light years distant from earth. While investigating a local religion, they undergo the Night of Light, a period of extreme psychic release accompanying a periodic solar eclipse. With the darkening of the sun comes an enlightenment of the soul, a choosing of good or evil with no compromise. The allusion contained in the name of the planet is too broad to ignore. Like Dante in the *Divine Comedy* Carmody experiences the centrality of evil; unlike Dante he experiences it directly by killing the local god. This act forces a choice: good or evil in support of the successor to the slain god. While his choice directs the plot of part 2 of the novel, it demonstrates forcibly the difficulty in elevating a murderer to serve as hero-protagonist.

In recent years rape has begun to make its own special claim to judgment as villainy. Traditionally science fiction/fantasy has avoided sex as a central issue, but as with most popular genre fiction it has increased its awareness with the more open social attitudes since the

1960s. It is predictable that sexual crimes would follow that lead, even to spawning its own spoofs as in John Boyd's *The Pollinators of Eden* (1969) where a female scientist is raped by an orchid.

In a more serious human vein is Robert Silverberg's *The Second Trip* (1972) which casts convicted rapist Nat Hamlin as the central character. As with each case of the transgressor-hero the author must evoke some area of sympathy where reader and character can meet. In Hamlin's punishment and adjustment we find that area here. Hamlin, an artist producing psychosculptures, exercises little control over his baser instincts, giving way to violent anger, to abuse, and finally to mass rape. When arrested and convicted, he is sentenced to rehabilitation under the Federal Social Rehabilitation Act of 2001. This bureaucratese means death of personality but not of body. In the process of rehabilitation Hamlin is drained of the Hamlin identity; then his physical container is refilled with the personality of Paul Macy, conformist, Mr. Straight-Arrow, one capable of functioning as a holovision commentator but lacking the imaginative power of the original Hamlin. The deletion is not wholly successful. In the ensuing psychological struggle as Macy he strives to maintain some balance and sanity in his existence. Here Silverberg generates the sympathy necessary for the social criminal. Hamlin-Macy becomes Everyman; his struggle, the conventional Freudian one between the id and superego for control of the ego.

A comparable sympathy is hard to bestow upon fifteen-year-old Alex and his three droogs, smashing their ways through their waking hours, wreaking havoc upon the lives of others in a random, thoughtless fashion. But in the violence done to the conventional language Anthony Burgess accomplished a *tour de force* in *A Clockwork Orange* (1962). He created the necessary aesthetic distance to allow thought to enter and augment the initial emotional reaction to Alex's plight. Caught and convicted on the evidence of his antisocial behavior, Alex accepts the proffered Reclamation Treatment, or what he describes as "the beginning of my freedom." Ironically the treatment is the beginning of a brainwashed existence, one deprived of free will, that element which makes him a man. Instead, the social norm is substituted. Alex becomes one "committed to socially acceptable acts, a little machine capable only of good."[3] In the process of the novel Burgess's real hero emerges as the ideal of free will, with both Alex and the society reduced to antagonists in their different ways.

Political dissidents, like the social non-conformist, have become increasingly popular characters in the novels of the last half of the twentieth century. As a focus of official governmental attention they join such traditional group villains of former eras such as the French, the Germans, the "yellow peril," and the Russians. When seen as a worm eating at the heart of the good society, this character serves as the unadulterated villain. But modern perspective has become less polarized, more relative. Dissidents may possess a wisdom denied to the majority. If they note a weakness in the body social or politic, they will illuminate it so that it can be strengthened. Even in losing, they may be gaining, as does the anarchistic Harlequin in Harlan Ellison's " 'Repent, Harlequin!' Said the Ticktockman" (1966). He has won if only one person catches on and carries on the effort.

Ambiguity more often informs the situation: the character is criminal in the eyes of the law, but heroic in the eyes of those with humanitarian concerns. One such hero is Nickie Haflinger in John Brunner's *The Shockwave Rider* (1975). In Nickie's twenty-first-century era everything is so computerized that no fact or personal information is private to anyone who knows how to manipulate the computer codes. The population at large remains ignorant of how they are manipulated, fleeced, and taken advantage of by unscrupulous persons. Nickie is a product of Tarnover, an institution dedicated to detecting genius at an early age and then exploiting it by re-education for specific official use and complete obedience to those in power. In the course of the training all imagination is drilled out of them; logical modes of thought and action dominate entirely. In the public search for wisdom, Tarnover trains for intelligence only. But, as Nickie in one of his many alternative identities recognizes, "intelligence and wisdom aren't the same." [4] When Nickie learns to break the identity code assigned to every person for the convenience of the computer, he is able to escape the intellectual straitjacket Tarnover has put on him. First, he assumes other identities in order to exercise his own imagination and to relearn powers of judgment. Then with the help of others dedicated to individual freedom, Nickie works to break the computer-bound lives of the general public. He introduces a "tapeworm" into the computer net, thus freeing or wiping out large blocks of data. In the process he assures the breakdown of both government and its shadow twin, organized crime. From criminal, deserter, quasi-traitor, Nickie evolves into the category meriting the greatest accolade—wise man.

Jim Barrett of Robert Silverberg's *Hawksbill Station* (1968) possesses a wisdom of a different kind, although he shares with Haflinger the opprobrium of society. Convicted of subversive activity, Barrett exists now as the oldest resident of the station of the title, a penal colony for political dissidents, revolutionaries, nihilists. This station originated when an inventor discovered how to construct a one-way time machine. The government officials appropriated it, recognizing here an ideal solution for disposing of subversive individuals. After due consideration they chose the Cambrian period as the location for the prison. Earth then is a landscape without animals, plants, even soil; the only food is the now-extinct trilobites. Segregated by sex, prisoners are sent to different segments of the era so that there can be no breeding and thus no extension of the human line to interfere with the natural evolution of the world. When a young prisoner comes "down the Hammer" one day, his secretive manner awakens suspicion and marks him as a spy from the new government. The prisoners learn from him that the government is now liberalized politically and in possession of an improved two-way time machine. Here also Silverberg explores the mystery of the human heart as Jim Barrett searches his soul. In the station Barrett has won a place of honor for himself as titular leader of the Hawksbill exiles. In his "old time" of the future he no longer has a place or identity to sustain his ego. Not only has the passage of thirty years rendered him incapable of adjusting to the old life, it also has rendered him incapable of survival without the support of the leadership role.

The murderer and the traitor have never gained firm footholds on the ladder of heroic characters. Even as a mercy-killer, the murderer cannot quite shake off the charge of villainy, despite an author's best efforts to work aesthetic distance to his advantage. The political dissident can receive sympathy when his act reveals the evils of the society he betrays, thereby shifting the onus of accountability, or when his loneliness and alienation transform him into a tragic figure. The rogue, on the other hand, enjoys quite a different reception, often leading to a celebration of his way of life. In the 1907 study, *The Literature of Roguery*, Frank Wadleigh Chandler emphasized that roguery is not villainy, an observation valid even today.[5] When the rogue goes against the dictates of society, he does so with a touch of the comic spirit, pointing at weaknesses needing ridicule and reform. The rogue may highlight pretensions and corruptions in high places or uncover bureaucratic inefficiency and personal incompetency. Neither secular nor religious institutions are privy to exception from his regard.

While the crime most associated with the villain is murder, that most identified with the rogue, according to Chandler, is theft. [6] The thief comes in many guises from the man who cheats at cards to the con-man who attempts to sell the Brooklyn Bridge to a gullible tourist, from the purse-snatcher to the swindler, possibly today the computer expert who can program millions of dollars into his own account. In literature he has belonged to a gang of robbers as the Forty Thieves of the *Arabian Nights* or Fagin's young pickpockets or the men on Peachum's Register. Sometimes chance makes him a thief, as Ali Baba. Or skill and cleverness serve him so that he may live by his thefts as does the Master Thief of European folklore or the clever Trickster of American Indian lore. [7] In the person of Dismas, to use the legendary name given to the penitent thief crucified with Christ, the entire brotherhood of thieves has received a quasi-imprimatur, Dismas being the patron saint of thieves.

Unlike the murderer, the rapist, or the political activist who may act irrationally in the heat of emotion, the thief of myth and literature approaches his craft more objectively. He trains and plans with art. He may cultivate the businessman's habit of keeping books, as does Peachum in *The Beggar's Opera*. If he is a dilettante like Hornung's Raffles, manner and style are important. He recognizes the consequences and can acknowledge along with Brutus Jones in Eugene O'Neill's *The Emperor Jones* that "For de little stealin' dey gits you in jail soon or late. For de big stealin' dey makes you emperor and puts you in de Hall o' Fame when you croaks" (sc. 1). Whatever the motivation or extent of the theft, the rogue always marks his work with his peculiar style. Even when this tell-tale *modus operandi* leads authorities to him, his agile mind and daring imagination may work to let him "steal" himself back from the law.

The Eel, Miriam deFord's title character in a 1958 short story, is such a rogue-thief. The Galactic Police, proud of carrying on the eons-old Royal Canadian Mounted Police tradition of always catching their man, finally catch the Eel. A terrestrial super-crook, the Eel has conned huge sums of money and credits from planets and moons all over the galaxy. He is wanted on Xystil, Artha, Medoris, Ceres, Eb, Ha-Al-mirah, Vairnour, and Agsk. When the bureaucratic dust settles, the

Eel is delivered to Agsk, home of primitive humanoids located at the edge of the galaxy. Their law is simple and direct. Murder is a family affair, necessitating only negotiation between murderer and family members. Grand larceny, the Eel's crime, is much more serious, a societal as well as family affair. The punishment is precise. The thief will live, but the person he loves most will be put to a slow and painful death before his eyes. The Eel, a loner, loves nothing, nobody. But, if Agsk releases him, he will be claimed next by the Medorans who will sentence him to a painful death. To avoid that fate, the Eel, true to his name, slips out of the dilemma by declaring his love for the priestess-judge who will pass sentence upon him.

The four-novel series chronicling the adventures of Harry Harrison's unforgettable Stainless Steel Rat gives a broader look at the rogue-thief in science fiction/fantasy crime stories. In addition, it stands as an example of a complex symbiotic process at work, as Harrison brings in conventions not only from the crime tale but from the detective story, adventure, space opera, spy thriller, fantasy, as well as sly borrowings of conventions as old as the sixteenth-century morality plays. The latter may seem far-fetched until one remembers the Vice acting more as a meddler than as the epitome of Satanic evil. In *The Beggar's Opera* of the eighteenth century let us remind ourselves again of Filch, Crook-finger'd Jack, Nimming Ned, Tom Tipple, Bob Booty. The epithet suggestive of the person's occupation or appearance goes back even further in time if we want to count Homer's use of the epithet to differentiate his gods and heroes, but the epithet descriptive of the thief's practice becomes most noticeable in the above pieces.

Slippery Jim, the Stainless Steel Rat, known in more formal terms as James Bolivar diGriz, is a master-thief. He is a man of many other identities: soldier of fortune, spy, gentleman-adventurer, interstellar agent, interstellar outlaw, detective, depending on which side of the law the exigencies of the moment demand. Living in a world so affluent that no malcontents feel the need to disturb its equanimity, crime is a forgotten art. Only a few persons of strong individuality exist to challenge this comfortable social decay. For diGriz crime becomes a therapeutic activity, serving to keep an imaginative mind from sheer insanity. When Slippery Jim is finally outwitted in *The Stainless Steel Rat* (1961), his nemesis is Harold Peters Inskipp, originally known in the criminal world as Inskipp the Uncatchable, now head of the Special Corps. This law-enforcement body, made up of the most talented criminals available, operates on a supra-level encompassing all nations and planets in the galaxy. Its guiding principle is the old dictum that it takes one to know one, hence in Slippery Jim's case, to catch a thief, send a thief.

His involuntary recruitment into the Special Corps opens the way for a series of interstellar assignments. In *The Stainless Steel Rat* he jaunts off in search of a planet on which a warship is being built in secret; the job raises his morale. As Jim muses in true rogue fashion: "Life was deliciously crooked and worth living again." [8] An important offshoot of the affair is the meeting and eventual recruitment of Angelina, crook, murderess, mastermind of crime, his future wife, and mother of his two boys. Espionage offers opportunity for action in *The Stainless Steel Rat's Revenge* (1970) when he and Angelina team up to infiltrate a planet with a strong militaristic power sructure. More criminal than humanistic, its government is being manipulated by a cadre of "grey men" from an unknown land; they foster evil designs.

Jim continues the fight against primal evil in *The Stainless Steel Rat Saves the World* (1972) when he goes some 32,598 years in the past to a planet called "Dirt or Earth or something like that." This planet Slippery Jim had never heard of since it had "blown up in an atomic war ages ago." [9]

When Angelina is kidnapped in *The Stainless Steel Rat Wants You!* (1979), Jim springs his sons out of the Dorsky Military Boarding School and Penitentiary to aid him in her rescue. The kidnapping turns out to be a plan by Inskipp to get Jim back to work on a ticklish political incident. His assignment takes him into remote nooks of the world, but he finds the enemy, strange life forms eminently qualified to feel comfortable in the most pulpish BEM (bug-eyed monster) stories. Just as he is about to dispose of these creatures by moving them to a parallel universe, he is stopped by the Morality Corps under the direction of one Jay Hovah. A second scheme to dump them in a future time is stopped by order of the Time Police. But a rogue-hero always has possession of wits and imagination. James Bolivar deGriz with aid of the Special Corps inaugurates a brain-twisting program to infuse them with a desire to quit war and depart. The aliens leave but without their material booty that to no one's surprise turns up in Slippery Jim's private possession.

The twists and turns of the various plots in this series create amusement as the rogue-hero works both sides of the legal street. Underlying the humor are opportunities for the reader to count coup upon real or imagined villains in modern situations. For instance, in *The Stainless Steel Rat Wants You!* diGriz takes a passing swipe at taxes as he explains to his sons about the Interstellar Internal and External Revenue Service, the taxmen as enemies. Later, the dust-up on Kekkonshiki forces speculation on conformity and difference. Can superiority exist in a society where new ideas, imagination, intelligence are considered handicaps, with obedience touted as the primary virtue? On war and peace the series forces a question: have we really considered all viable alternatives for peaceful co-existence? The list goes on: militarism, male chauvinism versus femlib, machines as tools or threats, crime in government, bureaucracy-heavy government, the shallowness of contemporary television offerings.

Steven R. Carter has termed the Stainless Steel Rat series as "a study in multiple interfaces."[10] The term is fitting, but Harrison has carried matters further to a point we might call the series a literary melange of formulae and conventions, all swirling around the centrality of the rogue-hero. BEMs, time and space travel, body and memory takeovers, futuristic weaponry, parallel universes and other speculative machinery come from science fiction/fantasy. These mix with detectival clue-gathering, disguises, the techniques of espionage, multiple identities and a James Bond-M relationship in Slippery Jim and Inskipp. All this is seasoned with police procedure and a side glance at bureaucratic inertia and red tape. Holding these all together as catalyst is the rogue imbued with the Comic Spirit that George Meredith said could on human pretensions "look humanely malign, and cast an oblique light on them, followed by volleys of silvery laughter."[11]

Jack of Shadows, Lord of Shadow Guard, Shadowjack the thief of the Darkside or Dr. John Shade, his persona on the Dayside, is a mercurial creature. Rogue when he acknowledges his theft of valuables, he can turn magician as he steals power from his enemies. Whether he be out to steal the Hellflame or to seek the depths of the computer for The Key That Was Lost, Jack exists by virtue of his wits although he is a being who cannot die. He has but one friend who dwells in Twilight, halfway between, a part of both light and dark worlds in this universe where the earth no longer rotates. A creature who has rejected the union with his own soul, Jack must undergo a Dantean-like trip to the underworld, into "the realm of darkness visible" like Milton's Satan and face the Machine at the center of the world in order to set the world aright and to find his own salvation.

In this allegorical novel, *Jack of Shadows* (1971), Roger Zelazny pulls together elements of mystery from high romance, folklore, magic, and the enduring philosophical topic of the two sides of man's science or knowledge: reason and imagination, empirical science and mystical science. From high romance come the medieval trappings of guarded castles, feudal hierarchy, and swords of magic like Excalibur; in the Dayside world these become the guarded computer room with the academic hierarchy and the power of information. From folklore come the symbols of mystery and evil, men turned into bats, stones with magical qualities, vampires, Wise Women with oracular information, and singing statues. There is even a borrowing from ancient myth in the Promethean-like Morningstar, a winged yet human figure partially fused into the harsh side of the mountain on which it keeps watch over the Twilight. It is with Morningstar that Shadowjack plumbs the mystery of the nature of reality, the merits of the mystical Art versus the science of the mind, and the gift of consciousness "which creates its own systems." [12] It is Morningstar who may or may not save this transgressor-hero from his doom.

With its futuristic orientation science fiction/fantasy crime stories can place the criminal-protagonist in highly speculative situations. In "All the Time in the World" (1952) Arthur C. Clarke does this to Robert Ashton, big-time thief who is recruited to steal treasures from the British Museum. The job appears a simple one, especially after his young lady employer gives him a bracelet that alters time so that people around him are frozen in time and therefore unseeing. Ashton should have suspected something when he met up with a crooked art dealer doing the same number on the London art galleries. But greed blinded Ashton. Upon completion of the easy job Ashton decided to con his employer out of the bracelet so to assure safety on his own jobs. Such security became a mixed blessing. After identifying herself as a visitor from the Future here to salvage Earth's treasures from the effects of a superbomb test, the young lady leaves Ashton in possession of the bracelet. He is alone and free to make a choice between two deaths: death by radiation in the destroyed world of the post-bomb blast or the life-in-death of isolation in the time-frozen world.

Science fiction/fantasy crime tales can also speculate on a future in which contemporary concepts of criminal justice are archaic and the words *crime* and *criminal* are redefined. Imagine with Poul Anderson a future in which it is legitimate to join the Criminal Industries Organization. One can sign up with the union boss and get a job for a licensed kidnapping, provided that act is in season. This is the procedure followed by Charles Andrew Rheinbogen, Harvard graduate student in psycho-dynamics, as he searches for a summer job in "License" (1957). In Rheinbogen's time all criminal acts are licensed with the exception of murder and the use of bombs on innocent parties. With licensing the society gains benefit. Upon reaching the status of first-class citizen, one receives legal immunity from murder and physical and criminal assaults. Before a crime is committed, the victim receives fair warning by legal notice allowing him time to take precautionary protective measures. If the person taking the contract fails, he in turn may be subject to full outlawry or be fair game for any other hunter to the death.

As a student of psycho-dynamics Rheinbogen has a more scholarly explanation for the new regulations. When he and his captive Marie Dulac, daughter of a wealthy businessman and target of his competitor, are caught in the wilderness for a time, she tries to find out the reasons for such actions. The ensuing conversation allows author Anderson opportunity for exposition, covering subjects such as the nature of civilization, the benefits and drawbacks of a technological foundation for human life, the definition in human terms of the nature of good and evil. Rheinbogen and Dulac live in a post-Smashup world, one in which people can no longer afford war. Licensed crime affords the release needed for pent-up hatred engendered by the constrictions of their civilized life.

Perhaps the most sad of all the transgressor-heroes are those whose alienation from society's ideal is self-induced. In *Flow My Tears, The Policeman Said* (1974) Philip K. Dick worked with two protagonists, Jason Taverner and Police General Buckman. It is with the second personality that one sees the hero who is also a transgressor. Living in a police state of a near future, Buckman is a man of great power, obsessed with rules yet breaking them at will. Because of his high-handed methods he has lost some rank but still retains power. His private life mirrors the paradox of his professional one. Living incestuously with his sister and fathering a child on her, Felix has flaunted the moral dicta of the society. Yet he hates and fears Alys because of her equally amoral and hedonistic outlook on life, an attitude that disturbs the rule-ridden Buckman. When his sister dies under strange circumstances, his very being is shaken but his professional facade is uncracked. Hiding his weakness behind those rules which have served him well, Buckman uses his power to bring to his own twisted justice another person marshalling less power than he.

From the foregoing description one would see small chance for Buckman's claim to the term *hero*, but Dick bids for reader sympathy by showing the weak human being behind the power shield of office and established rules. Buckman, for example, surrounds himself with objects of beauty but of fragility, like his own psyche. He seeks peace from inner torment by filling his immediate vicinity with the sentimental songs of the sixteenth-century composer John Dowland. These lyrics remind him of lost loves, and misplaced opportunity as in the title's allusion: "Flow, my tears, fall from your springs! Exiled forever let me mourn." When Felix Buckman reduced himself to vengeful action and then to self-pity, he "exiled" himself, losing forever his opportunity to reaffirm what Philip Dick calls authenticity or the innate humanness as opposed to the android response. In failure he bids for sympathy in the midst of transgression.

The transgressor-hero does add a dimension to the science fiction/fantasy symbiotic relationship with the tradition of the mystery story. If a murderer, rogue, subversive character, or self-destructive loner, generally the outlaw is not disposed to work for the general good. Nor is he disposed to defuse a situation threatening the health of his society. We must look elsewhere for his mystery. It lies not in the situation upon which so much mainstream mystery is predicated, but upon the idea which science fiction/fantasy claims as its orientation. The mystery lies within the human heart, the hidden motivations. In the working out of the character's problem an author can offer the opportunity for self-analysis or for social extrapolation to aid in understanding the phenomenon of crime. In the more perverse form of the character, the transgressor-hero may admit the working of the Comic Spirit against human pretensions and error, that Spirit which George Meredith in *An Essay on Comedy* designated as "the genius of thoughtful laughter, which would readily extinguish her [Folly] at the outset."[13]

NOTES

1. Harry Harrison, *The Adventures of the Stainless Steel Rat* (New York: Berkley, 1978), pp. 302–3. See p. 9 for the following "save my sanity" reference. This volume brings under one cover three of the five Stainless Steel

Rat tales: *The Stainless Steel Rat*, pp. 1–126; *The Stainless Steel Rat's Revenge*, pp. 129–273; and *The Stainless Steel Rat Saves the World*, pp. 277–402. The two latest volumes of the series include *The Stainless Steel Rat Wants You* (New York: Bantam, 1979) and *The Stainless Steel Rat for President* (New York: Bantam, 1982).

2. Robert M. Coates, *The Eater of Darkness* (New York: Capricorn Books, 1959), p. 143.

3. Anthony Burgess, *A Clockwork Orange* (1962; rpt. New York: Ballantine, 1974), p. 153.

4. John Brunner, *The Shockwave Rider* (1975; New York: Ballantine, 1978), p. 113.

5. Frank Wadleigh Chandler, *The Literature of Roguery* (Boston: Houghton Mifflin, 1907), I, 1–2.

6. Ibid., p. 4.

7. These two folk-types are classified and discussed in Stith Thompson, *The Folktale* (New York: Holt, Rinehart and Winston, 1946).

8. Harrison, *The Adventures of the Stainless Steel Rat*, p. 63.

9. Ibid., p. 284.

10. Steven R. Carter, "Harry Harrison's *The Adventures of the Stainless Steel Rat*: A Study in Multiple Interfaces," *Extrapolation* 21 (Summer 1980), 139–45.

11. George Meredith, *An Essay on Comedy and the Uses of the Comic Spirit* (New York: Scribners, 1905), p. 84. Originally given as a lecture, this essay was first published in *The New Quarterly Magazine*, April 1877.

12. Roger Zelazny, *Jack of Shadows* (New York: New American Library Signet Book, 1972), p. 65.

13. Meredith, p. 56.

PART III

THE SCIENCE FICTION/FANTASY THRILLER

CHAPTER 7

THE CONTRIBUTION OF THE THRILLER GENRE

"For all books are divisible into two classes: the books of the hour, and the books of all time." So spoke John Ruskin in an 1865 lecture, later printed as the first part of *Sesame and Lilies*. For his nineteenth-century audience Ruskin went on to define his meaning, further categorizing in terms of value: "There are good books for the hour, and good ones for all time; bad books for the hour, and bad ones for all time." [1] Then he stoutly went on record as not speaking of the bad ones in the rest of his lecture.

Had he deigned to do so, he may well have mentioned that fairly recent phenomenon, the mass-marketed fiction for the working classes, variously labeled as penny-issue periodicals, penny dreadfuls, shilling shockers, and in America as dime novels. The very labels testify to their commercial allegiance, one further underlined in an article in the 1845 *London Journal* wherein the author referred to these as "economic literature." Qualifying perhaps more as "books of the minute," these fictions appealed to the reader of little leisure and little learning, relying on melodrama, romance, excitement, violence, mystery, derring-do, horror, seduction, and other sensational appeals. Not penned with any idea of literary permanence, they eventually lost their share of the adult market. Before doing so, they shifted some of their proven appeal to a term less sharp in commercial definition but no less appealing to the reader, the *thriller*, another manifestation of a book of the minute or of the hour or of all time.

To an extent all literature begins as books of the hour, serving an immediate purpose for a designated audience. Sensation is a vital part of that initial impact of any book of the hour. A brief glance at popular fare of early eras confirms this. Imagine the emotional appeal of the ancient Greek bard sitting in a king's *megaron*, singing of Diomedes, Achilles, Hector, and Helen. Indeed, Homer describes Odysseus weeping as he listens to Demodocus sing of the Wooden Horse and the fall of Troy. Centuries later, Shakespeare's theater appealed to the human appetite for sensation. Ever since the novel pushed its way to the forefront of literary forms, it has commanded sensation to the service of its narrative, its presentation of manners, and even of its moral stance. By its very designation the thriller proclaims its use of the element of sensation, one most easily adapted by science fiction/fantasy thrillers as well.

As the sensational immediacy of a piece diminishes, more durable qualities may emerge, sounding that universal note requisite for the "books of all time." What is that elusive note? This is a question serious readers and literary critics of all eras have addressed, one still posed by critics of popular literature, especially for the concern here with the thriller. Some students of the thriller find that they can join it to other more accepted modes in a common historical lineage based on form or convention, tracing all to that "common spring" composed of rills from heroic romance, Gothic romance, and crime literature of earlier centuries, a spring also shared by the classical detective story. Through such connections the thriller gains a certain respectability by association with those modes which can claim books of all time. Still others mine the veins which connect it with those nineteenth-century "economic" or commercial fictions and relegate it to a position as the latest case study in the sociology of literature. Still others reduce the thriller to a status of a popular reflection of the general cultural climate, as highlighted by international intrigue and politics, military and economic by nature.[2]

Let us detach the thriller from this matrix of literary origins, sociology, and history to investigate its own peculiar brand of vitality, that vitality which marks it fair game for use in science fiction/fantasy mysteries. In *Mortal Consequences* Julian Symons remarks that " 'thriller' is so loose a word that it should really be abandoned as a form of description."[3] Advertisers and commentators on the mode seem of the same mind, for one notes that in recent years *thriller* has come more and more to carry either *suspense* or *spy* as its prefatory word.

Suspense admits the thriller to traditional formulae used in any narration which prompts the reader to ask: How does it come out in the end? Attached to *thriller* as a descriptive term it promises much more, throwing readers into situations they never expect to experience directly. Their customary security is temporarily obliterated as they enter a world in which intrigue, conspiracy, machinations are the stuff of life, but on a wider scale than even the amateur, police, or private detective have ever confronted. In this new world power wars with power. Institutions, nations, or blocs of nations submerge their sense of common humanity in the sheer exercise of or battle for power. While these forces operate on some Olympian height or Dantean depth, on the mundane level the human entities go about the lesser acts of manipulation for advantages seldom grasped *in toto*. Even as the action ends and suspense relaxes, *end* is the wrong word. There is no real end to such struggles. In the temporary cessation of activity the actors in the larger drama enjoy a false sense of victory tempered by the deeper intuition that renewed struggle is waiting in the wings.

Spy, on the other hand, narrows even as *suspense* enlarges. The term eliminates all protagonists who go about their lives under fiction's "'sunshine law,'" even those whose activities may be temporarily clandestine in the ordinary run of events. This modern meaning eliminates those ancient spies who served their purpose well in classical legend. The secret agent in a modern thriller can be no Diomedes or Odysseus infiltrating a modern Trojan camp. When Agamemnon needed information about the enemy, these two volunteered in full cognizance of their open esteem as heroes. They used only the natural cover of darkness. When they met Dolon, the Trojan spy, there was no question of the necessary action. They killed him. Once in the enemy camp they gathered the pertinent information, killed as they would on the battlefield, and departed to report. The spies sent into Jericho by Joshua of the Old Testament practiced more deception, using a traitor to hide them. However, they made a deal with the harlot, "our life for yours," a deal honored in full by Joshua. The modern spy can little afford such straightforward actions.

Modern history records some facts about the rise of spy organizations and tactics. Sir Francis Walsingham, a member of the Privy Council of Elizabeth I and minister in charge of Irish and foreign affairs, strengthened the intelligence department at that time. G. M. Trevelyan credits Walsingham's rising influence in part to "the system of spies he had organized [that] repeatedly saved the Queen's life from the assassins set on by Philip and the Jesuits, who destroyed William the Silent for want of such a guard.''[4] Joseph Fouché, Duke of Otranto, who served Napoleon as Chief of Police, created an organization known for its terrorist and spy tactics as well as police work, protecting Napoleon against conspiracies such as the Royalist threats. Under Frederick the Great the Prussians organized a military intelligence arm to perform international espionage service for the government.

With the growth of closer international communication and power politics all nations have felt the need in recent years to increase their collection of strategic and combat information and also to set up counterintelligence forces. Most countries have found it necessary to divide the responsibility between internal intelligence agencies and those devoted to international intelligence. From such need have grown the well-known F.B.I. and Central Intelligence Agency (C.I.A.) in the United States, along with the specialized intelligence operations in various other departments of government. In Russia the present KGB derives from the earlier Cheka, the GPU, the NKVD and the MGB, as need dictated reorganization. Great Britain designates its intelligence agencies as MI–6 and MI–7, while the SDECE, the DST, and the Second Division of the National Defense Staff, an outgrowth of the old Deuxième Bureau, serve France. In the light of the secret nature of the agencies this list represents a simplified view of the now-necessarily complex work, but one which forms the background for contemporary spy thrillers.

History also records the names of a few spies whose dramatic exploits caught the attention of the public. United States history of Revolutionary War days remembers traitor Benedict Arnold and his British spy contact Major André; Nathan Hale, hanged by the British as an American spy, contributed the image of the brave patriot with the only regret that he had but one life to give for his country. World War I memoirs still mark the career of one Gertrud Margarete Zelle, better known as the exotic Mata Hari, German spy. These pale beside the 1950s spy scandal involving Kim Philby, Guy Burgess, and Donald Maclean, Englishmen in responsible positions in the British Secret Service who defected to the Soviet Union, taking many high-level secrets with them to add to information previously relayed to that country. Out of such events has come the ''cloak-and-dagger'' image that many spy thrillers promote, one belied by the more contemporary agent stories that attempt to depict the unglamorous side of the intelligence occupation, the tedious job of collecting statistics, data on economic factors, technological advances, population, climate, as well as coveted military secrets.

Despite these later efforts it is the spy as protagonist that has become a convention in genre fiction, a convention absorbed by science fiction/fantasy spy thrillers, therefore one to be studied more carefully. A modern spy in the field lives in a world of constant flux with the only constant being himself. *Non semper ea sunt quae videntur*, first-century A.D. Phaedrus reminds us. "Things are not always what they seem." The spy exists always with that dictum in mind; indeed his own existence becomes the exemplum of the Latin tag. He is not always what he seems; he is a man of many identities or of no identity. Operating in an absurd world, an existential world, he must create his own meaning. As both hunter and hunted, he lives a paradox, misleading others concurrently with sifting their truths from lies. Even that activity is an absurd one, for his world has no absolutes of good and evil. He creates the only reliable substitute for absolutes—self— out of his professional expertise and personal ability.

Considered another way in terms of patterning of plot, characters, and conventions, the thriller of the twentieth century offers this view worth investigation. The protagonist of a thriller is often the situation itself, the crisis moving the human actors against their wills, although it is through human eyes and human decisions that we share its progress. The thriller mirrors the growing awareness of our increased vulnerability in the face of the sophisticated technology that feeds military machines, communications networks, and laboratories. These confer great power on those who can control them. These tools of power make aggression, infiltration, invasion of country, home, and privacy easier, thereby more to be anticipated and feared. In England particularly the thriller flourished as that country shifted its focus of fear from France, its major enemy in the nineteenth century, to Germany until the end of the two World Wars, and now to Russia.

This increasing awareness underlies the plot of Erskine Childers' *The Riddle of the Sands* (1903), generally conceded to be the first spy thriller claiming literary merit (despite James Fenimore Cooper's *The Spy* [1821], better categorized as a historical novel). The surface plot is simple but originates many of the now-stock conventions of the amateur spy story. Carruthers by his own description is a "young man of condition and fashion, who knows the right people, belongs to the right clubs.'' [5] Even with a promising future in the Foreign Office, he finds himself socially bored in a London from which most of his friends have left for the season. With a vacation coming up, Carruthers has no place to go and nothing befitting his social position to do. When Davies, an Oxford acquaintance, sends an invitation for yachting in the Schleswig fiords, Carruthers accepts. Instead of the expected leisurely trip aboard a luxury craft, Davies gives his friend an exacting trip of exploration aboard a two-man boat. He proposes to check out his suspicions that the Germans plan an invasion of England.

While the activity aboard the *Dulcibella* affords the reader an exciting recital of small-boat techniques, the purpose behind it affords insight into the emerging classical pattern of the amateur spy thriller. Childers receives credit for laying the framework of this pattern. Here is the spy hero: a young gentleman who by chance or through boredom finds himself tilted into a situation of international importance. He accepts the challenge out of a sense of personal responsibility mixed with romance but seasoned with a soupçon of reality acknowledging a ridiculous side of the affair. In one of his musings Carruthers recognizes this heady mixture that has impelled him to action: "Close in the train of Humour came Romance, veiling her face, . . . the gay pursuit of a perilous quest.'' [6] Despite his connection with the Foreign Office he has no qualifications for such an escapade; he is the incompetent spy, learning as he delves more deeply into the secret.

Incompetent, yes, but spy, no, would insist both Carruthers and Davies, an insistence that pervades this early twentieth-century thriller. The language proclaims a double standard. *Spy* refers to the other side, the enemy, or the betrayers of country, such as Dollman. The word also evokes the image of "one of those romantic gentlemen that one reads of in sixpenny magazines, with a Kodak in his tie-pin, a sketchbook in the lining of his coat, and a selection of disguises in his hand luggage,'' as Carruthers describes him. [7] Gentlemen heroes must find some moral justification for their secret forays into posted areas, their short sailing trips into forbidden estuaries, indeed, their very pose as duck hunters. They find that justification in the mere fact that they are Englishmen and they have a right to expose Dollman if he is a traitor to his country. They intuit that the Englishman in German service will lead them to more important secrets. While adapting from the adventure tale standard material such as violence, suspense, the chase, danger, excitement, Childers focused on those two important ingredients:

international intrigue, and the idealistic hero acting out of the standards of his class and viewing his actions as morally justified.

"To reduce a romantic ideal to a working plan is a very difficult thing," mused Carruthers to himself as he and Davies planned how to work through Dollman to gain the German secrets they assume exist. [8] A decade later, this seemed to be no problem for John Buchan as he set about recording the exploits of Richard Hannay in *The Thirty-Nine Steps* (1915) and the sequels of *Greenmantle* (1916) and *The Three Hostages* (1924). In the dedicatory letter of the initial Hannay novel Buchan acknowledged affection for the dime novel and the shocker— "the romance where the incidents defy the probabilities, and march just inside the borders of the possible." [9] Moved by such affection, he decided to write one for himself. The result is *The Thirty-Nine Steps*. The novel does exceed the reach of the dime novel and shocker, as it incorporates some of the components found workable by Childers. Hannay, too, is the gentleman hero, a government official newly returned to England from South African service. Disappointed in his expectations of the return, Hannay fights boredom, seemingly a gentleman's worst enemy. After a visit by an American journalist he finds himself in possession of secret information for a political assassination designed to destroy delicate international cooperation. When someone murders the journalist in Hannay's rooms, Hannay becomes the focal point for both a police investigation and the conspirators' attempts to kill him for the small notebook passed on by the dead man.

Buchan makes much of the pursuit over the back roads, through hawthorn hedges, and up and down the glens of the Scottish countryside. There is a plethora of disguises, a subterfuge dismissed so summarily by Childers' young gentlemen. Secret passwords and the whistled "Annie Laurie" serve to move Hannay closer to the center of the conspiracy. Only by chance does he make contact with someone who can put him in touch with the proper officials at the Foreign Office. Even here he finds that things are not what they seem when he detects an imposter infiltrating a high-level conference. From clues in the journalist's notebook Hannay pinpoints the spy's rendezvous point; then, as he summarizes, he does "his best service," service being his moral justification for all decisions and actions.

In 1928 W. Somerset Maugham published *Ashenden or The British Agent*, a novel based upon his personal experiences in British Intelligence during World War I. Maugham's protagonist shifts emphasis from the rank amateur acting completely on his own to the quasi-professional or amateur impressed into service. Again the emphasis is on *service*. Maugham also focuses on the bureaucrat, the man of administration. In the Preface to *Ashenden* Maugham emphasizes that "the success of such an organization as the Intelligence Department depends much on the character of its chief." [10] Unlike Childers' Carruthers and Buchan's Hannay, Ashenden joins the Service upon recruitment by R.; his profession as a writer provides perfect cover. During the interview no talk of remuneration passes between R. and Ashenden, only the suggestion that the work could turn up material valuable to his writing. The omission marks a subtle distinction in the hierarchy of espionage. The common spy works for money, often a pittance; the agent acts under a mission, or as in the case of Gomez, the betrayed agent, from "a passion of romance." Ashenden himself accepts his position in a detached way, stolidly accepting the proviso from R.: "If you do well you'll get no thanks and if you get into trouble you'll get no help." [11]

Maugham does add a new facet to the thriller formula, a note of realism. While R.'s offhand remark above seems cold and ungrateful, it emphasizes a fact of life in the world of espionage. An agent cannot expect to be patted on the head or coddled. He must also suffer fools gladly. This Ashenden does when he listens to the long "confession" told by the Ambassador under the fiction that he is telling of a junior clerk, but one he must protect by anonymity because "he's made a great success of his career. There is always something a little absurd in success." [12] Equal fools in their own way are the romantic adventurers, the poseurs, the traitors turned spies but ripe for double-agentry, the agitators and revolutionaries, all the figures at work *sub rosa*.

Again, in the Preface to *Ashenden* Maugham summed up the general situation:

But there will always be espionage and there will always be counter-espionage. Though conditions may have altered, though difficulties may be greater, when war is raging, there will always be secrets which one side jealously guards and which the other will use every means to discover; there will always be men who from malice or for money will betray their kith and kin and there will always be men who, from love of adventure or a sense of duty, will risk a shameful death to secure information valuable to their country. [13]

What Maugham did in *Ashenden* was to inject that note of realism; what he did not foresee in the above summary made in 1928 was the rise of totalitarian power centers in Europe, the advent of the cold war, and the proliferation of weapons with power to destroy civilization instead of a solitary national enemy. He was too early to witness the expansion of a lucrative international traffic in drugs, arms, and contraband, or the increasing vitality of nationalistic and religious groups fighting for autonomy. These developments have changed the face of espionage and affected the spy thrillers published since Maugham, as well testified by the novels of Eric Ambler, Ian Fleming, John Le Carré, and others.

At first glance the main characters of Ambler's novels seem to differ little from the earlier Childers-Buchan variety. They too are amateurs: the young languages teacher in *Epitaph for a Spy* (1938); an English engineer in *Journey into Fear* (1940); an American lawyer in *The Schirmer Inheritance* (1953); an American tourist in *Passage of Arms* (1959); Charles Latimer in *The Mask of Dimitrios* (1939) (American title, *A Coffin for Dimitrios*). Their motives are different. They enter the game not out of duty or responsibility but out of personal curiosity or need for money or by chance of being in the right place or position of authority at the opportune time. Despite their sophistication they find themselves caught. As Ambler suggests early in *The Mask of Dimitrios*, "The situation in which a person, imagining fondly that he is in the charge of his own destiny, is, in fact, the sport of circumstances beyond his control, is always fascinating." [14]

Charles Latimer exemplifies well this evolving character in the thriller. University professor, historian, and writer of detective novels, Latimer becomes intrigued with the career and reputation of one Dimitrios Makropolos. He starts his own investigation out of professional curiosity, soon to find he is the sport of circumstances beyond his control. Some critics regard the thriller hero as a variation on the detective formula, and Latimer's moves at investigation would appear to bear that out. Like the private investigator, he works alone employing presumably dispassionate persons in peripheral jobs such as translation. He collects bits of data, fits them together like a puzzle, assessing the importance of each bit logically and objectively at first. Unlike the private investigator he does not work within an integrated society; the puzzle he attacks affects a greater population than the one a client represents. The private investigator knows, although he does not call on it except in exigency, that there is a law and a system to which he can turn for support. Latimer has seen the underside of such laws and systems, a side which belies faith in its rightness. While the private investigator returns perhaps a little wiser to his scruffy office to await the next client, Latimer returns to writing his detective fiction, submerging his new awareness of human nature under the cloak of art. In his own novels he can create a situation where he is in charge of the effects of destiny and the sport of circumstance.

In *The Intercom Conspiracy* (1969) Charles Latimer again appears as unwitting agent but also as a victim of forces beyond his control. When he becomes privy to information that two ex-directors of secret intelligence services (and also co-members of a standing joint intelligence committee of NATO) plan to leak some confidential information in a complicated blackmail attempt, Latimer incorporates the situation into a novel. Upon his disappearance and its subsequent investigation the published novel and notes lay out the plot in detail. The amateur as central focus of the novel steps back from center stage in *The Intercom Conspiracy* to yield primary place to the profession, an attention which Ambler's successor polished to greater perfection.

International events since the turn of the century have torn the veil of innocent romance from earlier thrillers or novels of foreign intrigue. One feels uncomfortable labeling the main characters of later thrillers as *heroes*, for there clings to them little of the moral superiority claimed by a Carruthers or Davies. Even when moved by duty to his employer-organization, this new character must transgress the conventional morality too often to evoke admiration or honor. Amazement, yes; admiration, seldom. His ability to use deception, to extricate himself from seemingly impossible situations, or to employ all known "dirty tricks" and more from the author's fertile imagination may spark a sense of wonder. But the wonder all too often lies under a cloud that threatens more violence to established values already under fire.

Protagonist serves as a more neutral term than *hero*. Protagonist implies an antagonist. Who is the authentic antagonist, the real enemy? On the answer to this question hangs the suspense of the modern thriller. When the agent of a suspense thriller enters the modern world of international intrigue or political crises, he may be indistinguishable from his opposite number. Anonymity cloaks both plotter and counter-plotter. Using similar tactics, they practice morality and amorality with interchangeable ease. The agency for which the agent works may disallow all knowledge of his existence. If that existence proves embarrassing, the agent can rely only on himself. In fact, the agency may become the antagonist. This situation forces isolation from and distrust in anyone or anything except the agent himself. Well trained in the skills of subterfuge, attack, defense, and sheer survival, the agent may lose both idealism and dedication to communal values. Working as he does on the edge of civilization breeds loneliness but also a unique sense of being, one matched only by the human enemy counterpart, equally self-reliant, alone, well trained, and amoral.

Despite the awareness that officially he may be disowned by the agency, the special agent does on one level operate with a support group, even though at any given moment it can melt away. There is the agency that trains and renders technological aid. Of more particular importance is the immediate superior or spymaster, such as R. in *Ashenden*, M in Ian Fleming's James Bond adventures, Control in John Le Carré's *The Spy Who Came In From the Cold* (1963), and Dalby of Len Deighton's *The Ipcress File* (1962). In the field identities are not so clear cut, for the person may be working as a double agent or even triple agent. Contacts may be made with a veritable army of specialized persons: researchers, hired killers (especially political assassins), planters of information, keepers of safe houses, caretakers of letter drops, intelligence gatherers from the "peeps" (photographers or camera placers) to the scalp-hunters (specialists in finding high-placed persons ready to defect). While these various people work at gathering intelligence abroad, security forces work to counter any espionage activity from the "moles" or "sleepers," enemy agents infiltrating the home front. While the above we usually associate with political or military espionage, a similar network of operatives work the industrial arena, increasingly important for the jealously guarded technological, bacteriological, and especially computer secrets.

Against this complex backdrop of men and events the central agent does his work, dominating individual events but often overshadowed by the greater situation beyond the control of any one man or combination of men. Were we to ask ten people at random to name the hero of a spy suspense thriller, chances favor the majority as answering "James Bond," that charming amalgam born of the art of Ian Fleming, Sean Connery, Roger Moore, and countless imitators. Charming, yes, but existing as a flat character in the literary meaning of that term. We need know nothing of Bond's childhood, his friends of youth, his off-duty hobbies or responsibilities, his views on the vagaries of the stock market or modern music, or the high cost of gasoline. He exists for us only in the context of the excitement of the mission his creator

Ian Fleming has imagined for him. Bond at work is sensational; Bond bored is boring.

Nonetheless, a flat character has one advantage over a round character or developing character. He comes into memory full blown and unforgettable as a realized person, once his acquaintance is made. Readers (or devotees of Bond films) enjoy the sheer predictability of the unpredictable exploits of the man. In each Bond novel we expect that (1) M will assign him to an impossible, for us, mission; (2) Bond will move onto the enemy's turf with great aplomb and challenge him for position; (3) a female (or more), never to be taken at face value, will share his bed temporarily; (4) forced into a corner by the enemy, Bond will escape after some roughing up to various short-of-fatal degrees; (5) Bond will foil the enemy agent; (6) impeccably dressed, no scars showing, aplomb in place (if indeed it ever slipped), Bond will report to M. However, even as "things come out all right in the end," society cannot be assured that all will "live happily ever afterward."

While Ambler shifted the amateur agent from total romance and idealism to direct confrontation with the bald reality of espionage and Ian Fleming improved on the cold, detached observer/actor role of Ashenden, John Le Carré and Len Deighton give readers the more modern ironic look at the world of the spy. Both writers remind us that even the best trained agent is a human being, and human beings possess the unhappy talent for failure. Perhaps the failure is a personal one; perhaps it is failure of the establishment using him. But these novelists also remind us that human beings possess the equally civilized talent for compassion, an emotion which can only spell disaster in the uncivilized game of espionage.

Leamas in Le Carré's *The Spy Who Came in from the Cold* (1963) affords a piercing look inside the espionage world. He has no illusions: "Intelligence work has one moral law—it is justified by results." [15] He represents the antithesis of Carruthers and Hannay: "a man who was not quite a gentleman." [16] Yet he is not without merit as human commodity for the work he does. When approached by the other side as a potential defector, Leamas recognizes the professionalism of his opposite; by so doing he can play the point-counterpoint game with skill. To his credit he recognizes the dangers in his calling, particularly the danger of living a part, of being convincing in another identity. Knowing deception is his first line of defense, he also is sensitive to his own intrinsic vulnerability: "he must protect himself not only from without but from within, and against the most natural of impulses."[17] In the end Leamas surrenders to that natural impulse, compassion, after he realizes he has been used by his own side. No longer do Humour and Romance beckon the agent. For Leamas and others like the anonymous narrator in Len Deighton's *The Ipcress File* (1962) pathos and irony color their existence. The central character in these novels has moved from romantic hero to ironic hero to anti-hero, one acted upon by forces he does not understand completely despite his professional training.

But in the midst of the ambiguities there is room for the comic spirit with a strong strain of humor. This spirit is at work in Graham Greene's *Our Man in Havana* (1958), one of the novels which Green labeled his "entertainments." When Wormold, English citizen, vacuum cleaner salesman, and worried father of a nubile seventeen-year-old girl, is recruited as the head of a new network of agents in Havana, he little realizes that he becomes the central character in two fictions. The first is the official one, the reports about him, facts which no one will ever read and anyway are "drowned beyond recovery in the tide of the Chief's literary imagination."[18] Then there is the fiction which Wormold weaves himself for his reports to London. If Intelligence is justified morally by results, Wormold strives to please. He fabricates an entire network of agents with the accompanying claims for money. Pushed for information, he passes off a sketch of a dismantled vacuum cleaner as secret installations and invents some enemies, among them a Cuban pilot. As these ludicrous reports gain credence with the bureaucrats who slavishly follow the "drill," Wormold finds himself caught in the toils of his own fantasy, toils which eventually entangle some real people with the inevitable tragedy. While Greene's entertainment does beguile the reader with humor, at the same time it nudges him to consider the folly of the world of espionage. In that folly lies the moral burden we all as either supporters or beneficiaries of its activities must bear.

Novels such as those mentioned above do function as books of the hour but in a more limited sense than suggested by Ruskin's statement. They may seem to echo the headline in the morning paper or the major story of a defection on the evening television news. Cold war, impeccable source, dire international implication—these and other terms run through our daily lives. What is fact and what is fiction? The uncovering of a Maclean-Burgess-Philby conspiracy and its subsequent reverberations into rarefied social circles become the stuff of fiction in thrillers such as those of the exploits of Le Carré's George Smiley, Control, and friends. The exchange of information by code or files or tape or film as described by a novelist of a decade ago easily translates into theft of computer codes and secret information on experimental weaponry or industrial techniques reported as late as the hour's news bulletin. Rather than books of the hour contemporary suspense and spy thrillers rate a description as metaphors of the times. Further translation of the metaphors into future or parallel time lines can prove compatible with the demands of science fiction/fantasy, a mode that has already proved itself capable of absorbing to its advantage conventions and patterns from other variations of the mystery story.

The translation is made easier by the obvious similarity in the development of the protagonist of the detective/crime story and the espionage or suspense thriller. The amateur spy motivated by class consciousness and a personal code of conduct parallels in time the pre-World War I popularity of the classical detective of great intellect and economic independence. The appearance of the private investigator between the two world wars is matched by the appearance of the professional agent, professional by choice or recruitment. Both emerging protagonists provided mass appeal by the violence of their adventures mixed with more realistic detail. One might speculate this appeal came in response to a readership less interested in social or intellectual exclusivity or to the editorial demands for plots with more action. After World War II novelists had to face a tide of scepticism and a readership better informed through the mass media. Local, national, and international events became equally a part of everyone's life. The novelists responded with greater attention to the details of their protagonist's occupation, for example, in the details of police work that form a great attraction in the police procedural. In the world of espionage this called for knowledge of the increasing technology of intelligence gathering and less emphasis on the cloak-and-dagger drama of the fictional spy. A move toward highlighting the methods of the protagonists moved these modes closer to the science of the work without sacrificing the human interest of the character himself.

Periodically both devotees and students of popular literature feel impelled to question the future of their favorite genre. Howard Haycraft in 1945, while summing up the achievements of the detective story in World War II and succeeding years, quoted an unnamed critic as damning with faint praise by labeling the state of the whodunit as "static competence." Haycraft himself did note a "topical trend" worth mention: the espionage theme particularly focused on personal peril a reader might respond to with more awareness.[19] Haycraft's "topical trend" did materialize, but in turn has spawned its own doomsayers. Michael Gilbert in "The Spy in Fact and Fiction" alerted a future writer of the need to study the facts of today's intelligence operations and to adjust his material to fit both the pre-eminence of technology and its attendant work of intelligence-gathering, and the now well-publicized terrorist organizations.[20] Jerry Palmer held no such optimistic brief for the thriller; rather he devoted a chapter to description of the emerging phenomena that he judges to be contributing to the "demise of the thriller," namely "enforcer stories" and "anti-thrillers."[21]

While Palmer's discussion constitutes his "requiem," Donald McCormick agreed with Michael Gilbert on the necessity for spy stories to reflect authentic shifts in political, industrial, and military espionage and equally real shifts in locale, noting the growing importance of areas such as the Far East, especially China, and Africa. In addition to the ultra-realistic technological techniques authors might anticipate future interest in psi powers, astrology, psychometry, the occult phenomena, and "not least, the application of that forecasting work—*I Ching*," reminding us that the *I Ching* has been used in China for a long time. McCormick specifically forecasts that in these techniques the spy tale comes close to science fiction, predicting that "in some areas the two types of story may merge."[22] This is a prediction that a closer look at science fiction/fantasy thrillers will prove to be decades too late. Science fiction/fantasy has pre-empted the movement of spy fiction into its arena by already incorporating many thriller conventions into its own corpus.

NOTES

1. John Ruskin, *Sesame and Lilies* (Boston: Dana Estes, n.d.), p. 36.
2. Nadya Aisenberg in *A Common Spring: Crime Novel and Classic* (Bowling Green, Ohio: Bowling Green Univ. Popular Press, 1979) explores the debt the crime novel and the thriller owe to myth, fairy tale, and fable. Jerry Palmer in *Thrillers: Genesis and Structure of a Popular Genre* (New

York: St. Martin's Press, 1979), pp. 91–206, discusses both the historical perspective and the sociology of the thriller, while Ralph Harper in *The World of the Thriller* (Cleveland, Ohio: Case Western Reserve Univ. Press, 1969) takes a philosophical and psychological approach.

3. Julian Symons, *Mortal Consequences* (New York: Schocken Books, 1973), p. 230.

4. G. M. Trevelyan, *History of England* (Garden City, N.Y.: Doubleday, 1953), II, 115.

5. Erskine Childers, *The Riddle of the Sands* (1903; rpt. New York: Dover, 1976), p. 15.

6. Ibid., pp. 88, 89.

7. Ibid., p. 82.

8. Ibid., p. 182.

9. John Buchan, *The Thirty-Nine Steps* (1915; rpt. Del Mar, Calif.: Publisher's Inc., 1978), p. xv.

10. Somerset Maugham, *Ashenden or the British Agent* (1927; rpt. New York: Avon, 1951), p. 10.

11. Ibid., p. 13.

12. Ibid., p. 140.

13. Ibid., p. 10.

14. Eric Ambler, *A Coffin for Dimitrios* (1939; rpt. Del Mar, Calif.: Publisher's Inc., 1977), p. 47. Original title: *The Mask of Dimitrios*.

15. John Le Carré, *The Spy Who Came in from the Cold* (London, 1963; rpt. London: Pan Books, 1965), p. 13.

16. Ibid., p. 15.

17. Ibid., p. 130.

18. Graham Greene, *Our Man in Havana* (1958; rpt. New York: Bantam Books, 1968), p. 34.

19. Howard Haycraft, "The Whodunit in World War II and After," *The Art of the Mystery Story*, ed. Howard Haycraft (New York: Biblo and Tannen, 1976), pp. 536–42. Orig. publ. in the *New York Times Book Review*, August 12, 1945.

20. Michael Gilbert, "The Spy in Fact and Fiction," *The Mystery Story*, ed. John Ball (Del Mar, Calif.: Publisher's Inc., 1976), pp. 205–21.

21. Jerry Palmer, *Thrillers* (New York: St. Martin's Press, 1979), pp. 207–20.

22. Donald McCormick, "Introduction," *Who's Who in Spy Fiction* (London: Hamish Hamilton, 1977), p. 13.

CHAPTER 8

THE SCIENCE
FICTION/FANTASY SPY
THRILLER

The word *thriller*, as Julian Symons noted in *Mortal Consequences*, may well be a term so loose that it covers a multitude of forms and should be abandoned in favor of more specific descriptions. In science fiction/fantasy it can describe with equal appropriateness the catastrophe stories and tales of monsters and horrors such as those collected by Sam Moskowitz from the "gaslight era" magazines of 1891–1911. *Thriller* can cover the 1930–1940 pulp exploits of Doc Savage, the "Man of Bronze"; Captain Future, the "Man of Tomorrow"; and Clark Kent, Superman, the "Man of Steel"; then go on to admit the many novelizations of *Star Trek*. Under its umbrella-like shelter can rest science fiction/fantasy as different as John W. Campbell's "Who Goes There?" (1938), the 1960s Jason Starr series by Peter Heath, and *Icarus* (1980) by Peter Way. Even if one adds *suspense* to the description, that label does not truly identify the close union that science fiction/fantasy has so well effected. It is on the more specific *spy thriller* that the symbiosis of science fiction and this variation of the mystery mode rests.

Here it is well to recall Somerset Maugham's cold and realistic appraisal of the situation most addressed by the tale of espionage. There will always be secrets a country will guard against those enemies avid to discover them. Of necessity men will risk their all to find and protect that secret data. Plots and counterplots, jealously guarded secrets and equally zealously sought ones, betrayal for malice or money and risk for adventure or duty—the picture that emerges presents the opportunity for suspense that science fiction/fantasy can well exploit.

A symbiotic relationship between the tale of espionage and science fiction/fantasy poses the same basic task that the latter faced in the cases of the detective story and the tale of crime. The situations of the mystery mode must become compatible with the idea-oriented science fiction/fantasy mode. These new situations offered both challenge and opportunity. For one thing the science fiction/fantasy writer could find common ground in the expanded settings the spy thriller offered; international movement has its futuristic analogue in cosmic movement. For the inevitable contact with the foreign enemy of the spy the science fiction/fantasy mode had the inevitable contact with the alien in its stock of conventions. Special elements of the spy thriller such as the intrigue or conspiracy (either within the agency or between two international powers), the pursuit or chase, the "cover" or special disguise demanding more than ever expected of a detective, and the omnipresence of excitement and of violence, all these had found places in science fiction/fantasy mode, one not noted for its skill in characterization.

What Maugham's evaluation did not address directly was the specific categories of people caught up in this moral swirl of cruel war, jealously guarded secrets, greed, duty, adventure, and risk. It is to such specifics that science fiction/fantasy must address itself. Behind his abstract picture of the situation move three major personages: the amateur, the professional, and the administrator (in Maugham's terms the "chief" of the department). With minor but no less important duties the second circle of stock characters includes members of the agent's support group composed of the researchers, monitors of orbiting reconnaissance satellites, photographers, computer experts, various experts in other tactical, economic, or political areas. Then there are the people in the less technical areas such as those watching over safe houses, acting as letter drops, infiltrating the dissident groups, and the like. Still farther from the arena of activity stand the great mass of unknowing people, those innocents whose fate is being determined but whose will is powerless. It is in the utility of such stock characters that the main challenge of symbiosis would come to science fiction/fantasy.

As was mentioned earlier, most people associate the character of the spy with the James Bond created by Ian Fleming. Also known as 007, the British secret service number designating him as one with a license to kill in line of duty, James Bond has his own list of equally capable enemies: Dr. No, Goldfinger, SMERSH, and SPECTRE, none quite able to defeat him. Despite his accomplishments James Bond is a flat character operating within a predictable series of events. Flat characters and patterned plots lend themselves to parody or imitation, just as the Bond stories themselves to an extent parody all spy suspense thrillers.

Isaac Asimov in an *Asimov's Mysteries* headnote labels "I'm in Marsport Without Hilda" (1934) as a "James Bond type of story, written before I had ever heard of James Bond."[1] Max, the Class A agent in the Galactic Service, has little in common with Bond except the yen for women. Normally burdened with a wife and a mother-in-law, he lacks Bond's *savoir-vivre* entirely. As one might expect, he acts like the proverbial kid let out of school when Hilda cannot come to Marsport to share a three-day layover; in this "rowdiest hellhole in the system" lives Flora.[2] Unfortunately for Max the local office of his agency is also located in Marsport. Faced with an interspace emergency, the local agents call upon Max to interview three suspects, two of whom are spaced out on a special drug that eases the rigors of space travel. The third one is an adept at feigning the effect. While Asimov makes a travesty of the agent-villain confrontation, he does redeem it with the broad humor he invests in the free-associative interrogation of the three. The play with language adds a unique turn to an otherwise stock situation.

Harlan Ellison in "Santa Claus vs. S.P.I.D.E.R." (1969) works another Bond parody. When the shrill ring of the red phone awakens Kris in "half-past September," he answers to hear a Secret Service official summoning him to action in an emergency. S.P.I.D.E.R. has taken over the minds of eight key men in the United States, and through their actions it threatens the country with total collapse. Each man works a peculiar havoc: Daley, the smog-maker; Reagan, the insanity-spreader; Johnson, the war-monger; Nixon and Humphrey, the confusion- and dissension-spreaders; and on through Wallace, Maddox, and Agnew. Kris answers the call. One by one he challenges and frees the minds of these men from the small, hairy, multi-legged alien possessing and directing them. After this task is finished, Kris becomes aware that his lovely bed partner also is infested by S.P.I.D.E.R. In the classic Bond fashion he does her in.

In addition to the Bond parody this short story also hits the reader with political satire in the equally classic mode of Jonathan Swift. Ellison has used periphrasis much as did Swift in the "Modest Proposal for Preventing the Children of Poor People from Being a Burthen to Their Parents or Country" (1729). First, both authors present a serious situation in a ridiculous way, posing an outrageous solution. Then in the final statement they emphasize the real problem in not so subtle a fashion. After proposing that the Irish poor aid the economy by exporting year-old children as food for wealthy foreigners, Swift's persona commands, "Let no man talk to me of other expedients."[3] Then he details those very expedients. Ellison's version of this stylistic ploy works to a similar end. After teasing with clues to the identity of S.P.I.D.E.R., he explains that all one has to do is to take out the periods. The first letters do *not* serve as acronyms for such nefarious groups as "Secret Preyers Involved in Demolishing Everything Right-Minded," or "Society for Pollution, Infection and Destruction of Earthmen's Resources," or other sobering phrases.

While the James Bond pattern does have its own dramatic force, the other stock characters that have developed during the course of changes within the tale of espionage have their special strength to offer. As we have seen, the original spy of the Erskine Childers-John Buchan era of the first two decades of the twentieth century was an idealistic amateur, thrown into circumstances or a crisis he did not completely understand but to which by training and personal code he must react. We find persons of this ilk in science fiction/fantasy thrillers. Meric Albano, presidential press secretary in Ben Bova's *The Multiple Man* (1976), for example, is a curious amalgam of political savvy and idealism. After a presidential duplicate is found murdered in an alley near the hall in which the real President is giving a speech, Albano starts a one-man spy operation to discover the threat. Assassination, even by default, screams conspiracy. Albano's loyalty to the man and the office pushes him to pursue the idea of conspiracy to its most hidden and most unlikely center.

In Michael Kurland's *Psi Hunt* (1980) three amateurs team up to investigate the activities of two subversive groups. One is the John Paul Jones Society, motivated by fiery patriotism; the other, a Chinese cult imbued with its own brand of fervor. If these two succeed in their purposes, they will engulf the world in a military and social conflagration. Kurland's future world is one of overcrowding and fear, one receptive to anything promising meaning for life, especially for the

Unpeople of the Unworld or the "officially unemployable." Together the three amateurs defuse the situation. In the process author Kurland draws on conventions of the spy story, mixes them with telepathy, cryptograms, subterranean military bases, classical references, and social comment to produce high adventure. Here idealism overcomes incompetence in the best romantic tradition.

Amateurs recruited for espionage should suspect the offer, but often have no choice. When the Team impresses the Rev. H. Hornswell Hake into service that is unexpected, unwanted, and unexplained, he finds himself in an unreal world. This world abounds in code names, disguises, sealed instructions, the full complement of melodramatic cloak-and-dagger procedures, as being used by this perverted offspring of the earlier but now disbanded C.I.A. Hake finds himself tossed into the title conflict of Frederick Pohl's *The Cool War* (1979). This is a war Hake had not suspected even existed. It is one engineered to disrupt ordered existence wherever possible, short of actual conflict. In *The Cool War* the amateur represents the strong center that holds. The "professional" espionage agents are the incompetents. They have lost all contact with reality and by so doing have created a view of the world where "complexity was cubed, muddle was confounded," as Hake muses to himself at one point.[4] Once he recognizes the state of affairs, Hake can fight the stupidity and incompetence, the lack of insight and loss of reality. Despite his own self-acknowledged limitations he will and does take up the battle.

The amateur spy relying only on his own moral purpose does echo other stock figures of romantic fiction—the lonely western gun-fighter, the knight on the white horse, the single champion standing before the walls of Troy. But the science fiction/fantasy amateur spy has unique technology at his own disposal. Paul Kosloff II in Mack Reynolds's *Computer World* (1970) lives in a world of three major political powers but one dominated by computer data banks. These can easily be linked to encourage free flow of information and the eventual realization of the ideal One World. But this idea is anathema to certain powerful men. When Kosloff, son of a famous espionage-counterespionage agent, suffers forcible recruitment by the Inter-American Bureau of Investigation, he presumably must investigate tapping of two of the three major data banks. In reality the Bureau has set him up as a patsy so he will appear to be the tapper. When Kosloff discovers the intrigue, he uses the only resource at his disposal, a weekly language lesson beamed through the Tri-Vision University of the Air. This lesson acts as the electronic equivalent of the gun, sword, or spear of his predecessors in spy-romance fiction.

In another Mack Reynolds story his protagonist Rex Bader finds himself serving not one but five master plots, as the title, *The Five Way Secret Agent* (1969) proclaims. If Fred Pohl's the Rev. Hornswell Hake saw his escapade lead him into cubed complexity and confounded confusion, Rex Bader could match cube for cube. No dewy-eyed idealist or put-upon amateur, but a down-at-the-heel private investigator living on Negative Income Tax, Bader needs work. He receives offers from the Meritocrats, the Technocrats, the IABI (Inter-American Bureau of Investigation), a remnant of the Syndicate, and the Russian secret organization. This melange of conspiratorial groups invites not just espionage and counter-efforts, but also betrayal of causes by leaders who are themselves spies. Rex Bader blunders along, doing only what he does best—investigating and attempting to sort out the muddle logically. He is not an intelligence agent but rather a foil for the puzzle that counterintelligence operations foster. In addition, the conglomeration of special interests allows author Reynolds to indulge in various discussions of economic theory. Situation thus serves idea.

Since betrayal of causes rates as an act of evil in most minds, the choice to betray one's mission rather than betray one's ethical position must qualify as the choice of the lesser of two evils. The amateur agent suffers in the process, since his original motivation grew out of idealism, an outlook that often renders a situation more simple than it is. The suffering intensifies the more the individual delves into the moral complexities of the choice. But what of the amateur who refuses to choose and by so refusing delivers himself up to total submission? This condition D. G. Compton in both *The Quality of Mercy* (1965) and *The Steel Crocodile* (1970) explores through the framework of the spy story.

Both novels take place in a near-future world; both the protagonists are professionals in other fields now impressed into spy activities. In each case their primary system of professional ethics betrays them into support of activities they should have recognized as total evil. In *The Quality of Mercy* Captain Donald Morrison urged on by his old squadron leader joins a special duty force to fly PP8 (Peace Probe missions or spy flights) over Russian territory using planes camouflaged as transports. Morrison and his wife live on the secluded base, thoroughly insulated by luxurious comfort and remote geography from disturbing social troubles in the outside world. Only by chance do they hear of a worldwide epidemic of a radiation sickness attacking parts of the world's population. When intelligent segments of the populations begin to question and probe, evidence points to the PP8 flights and comparable ones from the enemy side. Instead of flying spy missions they are in reality dropping canisters of radioactive material over the entire world population, possibly in accordance with a high-level decision between all the major heads of state as a means of population control. Faced with the evidence, Morrison refuses to question even the slightest part of the PP8 work. His TT (Total Training) has erased his moral judgment, even to the point that he commits his wife to an asylum as a high-security risk when she too begins to ask questions. Here the human agent has been transformed into a non-thinking entity, one following orders without query under the aegis of loyalty.

The Steel Crocodile reiterates the lesson that a person cannot follow the dictates of two moral criteria. Sociologist Matthew Oliver receives an invitation to join the staff of a prestigious research center, the Colindale, a place dedicated to the collection and dispersal of new scientific work worldwide. However, the center's administrators have become more and more secretive about the research being done on the premises, an action that has attracted the attention of a liberal watchdog group, the Civil Liberties Committee (C.L.C.). A school friend recruits Oliver as a double agent to search out the truth and to report to the C.L.C. In the rarefied atmosphere of the Colindale scientific community Oliver becomes "converted" to the Colindale philosophy that subverts the free exchange of ideas to the autocratic control of the head man. Those scientists in turn have unwittingly relinquished their own freedom of judgment to the government of the Bohn computer familiarly called "Old Boney." Oliver betrays himself by a simplistic response to the situation. He limits his ability to act by a misplaced dedication to a parochial ideal and by the failure to consider the ramifications of his choice, as with respect to the effect on other human beings.

If incompetence, muddle, and confusion mark the spy world as seen from the perspective of the idealistic or ignorant amateur, the more speculative version of the professional spy offers another perspective of this world. Most readers of spy thrillers are well acquainted with those well-trained operators who do the work as their livelihood and are prepared to accept the personal consequences. The science fiction/fantasy novel has an additional responsibility to readers when it places a professional agent in the field in alien surroundings or in far time or space. The training must be specialized; the psychological preparation must be impeccable in the event the agent finds himself marooned in time and space and lacking any support.

Suzette Haden Elgin takes on this authorial responsibility in the Coyote Jones series now collected under the common title of *Communipath Worlds* (1980). In Coyote Jones one finds some traces of the Bond formula. Like James Bond, Coyote Jones is a professional agent, serving in TGIS, the Tri-Galactic Intelligence Service; his immediate superior is the Fish, a futuristic embodiment of Bond's chief, M. But the reader soon notes differences. The agents of the TGIS do not choose the profession; they are chosen by lottery for a service period of ten years with the option to continue if they wish. The Fish is a veteran of many years over the official term. Despite his impressive seniority Coyote Jones treats him with a flippancy never indulged in by Bond and M.

As Coyote takes on several dangerous missions described in *The Communipaths* (1970), *Furthest* (1971), and *At The Seventh Level* (1972), the Bond similarities are more apparent. Coyote attracts danger as he takes inordinate chances in the various alien environments, but he always extricates himself safely despite sundry injuries. He possesses talents beyond those of ordinary men, especially control of mass telepathic projection whereby he can control others not only singly but also in large crowds. He must be able to recognize and render powerless sophisticated weapons such as psi probes. Always he strives to understand and respond properly to local mores and social conventions. Once these are recognized, like Bond Coyote Jones complies gracefully in order to use them to his advantage, as any accomplished professional would do. Like Bond he has the inevitable encounters with the opposite sex, but unlike Bond not all of them are affairs of the moment. Coyote Jones shows a sentimental weakness by loving a woman, siring a child, and then assuming parental responsibility upon the death of the mother.

The greatest challenge an author must meet is allocation of word space. Ian Fleming can assume an amount of commonplace knowledge in his readership; therefore, he has less need to establish the principles by which a society guides its actions. Not so for Suzette Haden Elgin.

The science fiction/fantasy author must build the credible futuristic world with special attention to societal taboos, values, and manners that might trip up the espionage agent. The Bond formula loses the competition in Coyote's first assignment among the Maklunites whose psi-oriented society must be explained before a reader can appreciate the problems faced by the intelligence agent. Coyote's forays into Furthest with its race-protecting secret and the social atavism that is Abba test the agent's ability to the utmost, also an author's ability to balance the spy conventions with the interest necessarily generated in any imaginative future possible for sentient beings.

Once a space federation of any composition is set up, it is bound to become vulnerable to forces dedicated to its destruction. Conventional wisdom dictates a peace-keeping unit of some kind. In Joe Haldeman's *All My Sins Remembered* (1977) TB11 is the undercover unit attached to the trans-space peace-keeping force. Otto McGavin joins TB11 as an undercover agent. An idealistic person, Otto suffers at the end of each mission from contradictory feelings. While he believes in his mission of helping all sentient beings, human and nonhuman, he must engage in activities contradictory to the idea of help. He must kill, lie, and reject all his religious training in the service of TB11. This ever-present contradiction eventually seals his doom. Before that time he combats in five different episodes of his career the depredations of the anti-forces. In conventional cloak-and-dagger tradition he uses different identities, once as a hired assassin and again as a scholar, an identity imposed on him by personality overlay. Behind these dramatic situations lie ones only too common today: the amorality of vested interests, albeit on alien planets; rackets that cheat the innocent; systematic assassinations, here used as crowd control.

To the stock question of "what if we make contact with an alien culture?" often follows "how shall we go about reconciling this culture to cooperation with us?" Space opera with its battles between space ships of alien and terran forces offers one stock answer. Science fiction/fantasy spy thrillers offer a second. If one cannot find a point of cooperation, then find the other's weakness and use that to advantage. If the opponent refuses all contact, then send in a spy to exploit the weakness.

Robert O. Lang of "Second Game" (1958) by Charles DeVet and Katharine MacLean has such an assignment. When the planet Velda disdains to accept any contact with the Ten Thousand Worlds, a loose federation of Earth's colonies, something must be done. Since Veldians are fascinated with a chess-like game, Lang enters in guise of a games player. Through his expertise at a games booth set up at a Veldian fair Lang hopes to attract attention of men in authority, thus opening an avenue for some peaceable interchange of ideas. Before his identity is penetrated, Lang discovers two major weaknesses of the Veldians: one, a sexual discrepancy threatening their very existence. This is accompanied by a widespread male frustration born of sexual starvation and lack of physical challenge through which to prove themselves. Lang's trained observation in noting these weaknesses opens up the opportunity for communication, an optimistic ending not normally found so quickly in modern mainstream spy novels but truer to earlier pulp science fiction tradition.

Not all such encounters proceed so smoothly. Many traditional spy thrillers gain sensational effect by playing upon an anomalous situation of the agent in the field betrayed by his own people, out of stupidity, incompetence, or design. The bureaucrat back at home base simply cannot know all the forces at work in the field, but is unable to admit his ignorance or to rise above it. Even Maugham with his awareness of the importance of the character of the chief in the Intelligence Department has his character Ashenden remark about the usually level R.:

They were all like that. They desired the end, but hesitated at the means. They were willing to take advantage of an accomplished fact, but wanted to shift on to someone else the responsibility of bringing it about. [5]

Science fiction/fantasy spy thrillers use this situation to advantage within their conventional settings.

Jef Forzon in Lloyd Biggle's *The Still Small Voice of Trumpets* (1961) faces not only the difficulty of the assignment, but also internal problems with his own bureau. For four hundred years Team B of the Interplanetary Relations Bureau has attempted to find a weakness in one of the two advanced civilizations on the planet Gurnil. Although Larnor has certification for membership in the Federation of Independent Worlds, Kurr resists all overtures. Kurr is a real puzzle. The populace of Kurr loves beauty in all its forms: music, art, architecture, dance. Yet it tolerates an autocratic king who for the slightest discordant gesture made in his presence will order dismemberment of the victim's left hand and banishment to isolated villages out of sight of all. No one in Team B has noticed this cultural inconsistency, for they have adapted to Kurrian life so well that they "pass" for natives. Faced with betrayal within his own bureau, the ill-conceived plot of a turncoat, and his own capture, Forzon succeeds in exposing the king before his people and also he averts his own fate. As Forzon reports, he "catches the conscience of the king" by forcing him and Kurr at large to recognize the "moral ugliness" tolerated for one man's personal passion for beauty and harmony.[6]

While the science fiction/fantasy spy thriller loses the immediate support of real and contemporary social and political crises enjoyed by the mainstream spy thriller, it does gain in its ability to address moral crises indirectly through the intermediary of the alien-human relationship. "Moral ugliness" or moral anarchy within the human spirit often appears clearer without the distractions of the closer contemporary political and military chaos. Keith Laumer in *The Glory Game* (1973) nudges the conscience of the reader when two opposing parties of his future world (the Hardliners and the Softliners) set up Commodore Tancredi Dalton as an unwilling spy for both sides. He is assigned to feign contact with approaching alien Hukk spacecraft as if they were threatening military force. When Tancredi assesses the situation, he realizes that the Hukks serve merely as a pawn in the game of local power politics. Only his independent action in selecting and acting upon the best points in each spy plan saves the day. By so doing he maneuvers the two parties into a more amicable relationship with the innocent "enemy" and into a necessary working partnership with each other.

The moral ugliness of power politics is augmented by the moral ugliness of individual ambition in Ben Bova's *Voyagers* (1981). When scientists discover an unidentified blip on their scanner screens, they find the politicians blocking efforts to share such important information with scientists from other countries. Through professional and academic contacts they do manage to pass the word worldwide. As all the important scientists from around the world gather at Kwajalein Island to track the craft together, personal Nobel Prize ambitions clash with scientific idealism. On the national level espionage and counterespionage crank up to furious levels in a jealous effort to garner national honor. Agents and double agents, relying not only on standard procedures but also such avant-garde methods as planting electrodes in agents' brains, join the scientific world in a grand display of moral chaos.

Robert Silverberg faces moral ugliness another remove from human society, but nonetheless pointedly at humans. In *The Silent Invaders* (1963) the relative brevity of the novel leads us to expect a book of the minute, let alone a book of the hour, but it offers more substance than anticipated. The silent invaders of the title come to Earth from mutually antagonistic planets; their task is to mold public opinion on this planet to their separate advantages. Within a century or two they anticipate a gigantic confrontation with one another, a struggle necessitating strong allies in the galaxy. Earth is one of the strongest possibilities as an ally. Hence both planets have sent agents to practice "the art of engineering consent," as one of the Darruuian agents justifies his work to himself. The plan is simple: the agents locate each other and proceed to eradicate their opponents. Meanwhile the human population goes about its daily business with no inkling of the alien activity in its midst.

From the beginning Silverberg dwells on the tension of inner crisis for agent Aar Khioom. On his native planet of Darruui he belongs to a special class; as Servant of the Spirit he belongs to a group dedicated to unquestioning service, to sacrifice, to a sense of highest calling. Also, he carries deep within him affection for the physical world of Darruui; this affection betrays him with moments of homesickness and a desire to return. Aar is not a professional spy but an amateur in the Childers-Buchan sense of the word, one risking his life out of a sense of duty. Nevertheless, that sense of duty to homeland does not override a stronger moral sense, one which questions the order to kill someone who may be an innocent. That moral force is strong enough to enable him to perceive the innate amorality of his co-agents and the misdirected energies of his entire race. This moral strength changes him from agent to double agent and finally to traitor in support of a higher moral cause. By so doing he condemns himself to a life of utter alienation from his roots, but one more clearly dedicated to the ideals implicit as Servant of the Spirit, now a universalized Spirit.

Even as a reader is caught up in the complexity of the alien encounter and the *deus ex machina* resolution, Silverberg's novel draws attention to a use of a key convention of spy thrillers—the cover. The cover may be for temporary use, a story to mask the actual event of a passing moment or to supply an excuse for being in a certain area, an alibi, to put it in more colloquial terms. The assignment may call for more elaborate arrangements such as a completely new identity necessitating a completely different background, the proper papers, and a detailed knowledge of the new personality. The agent must be well trained in the mannerism, customs, and idiom of the society he is penetrating. For such training he needs a strong internal discipline. While living the lie of his assumed identity, he must still retain awareness of his functional identity as agent. This also means coming to terms psychologically with the necessary separation from all that has bolstered him in his real identity. The longer the stint, the more intricate the cover may become.

Science fiction/fantasy spy thrillers exploit this convention in both traditional and untraditional ways. The cover may be as "honest" as that of the Nashville private investigator in Wilson Tucker's "The Job Is Ended" (1950) doing his usual business for thirty years as a cover for a spy operation to locate an alien infiltrator in the Oak Ridge area. Or the agent may simply assume a vocation that will fit into the local society with little notice, such as does Coyote Jones in the above-mentioned *Communipath Worlds*. Coyote's usual cover is that of a traveling folk singer playing an antique, non-electronic guitar. Upon special occasions he can double as proprietor of a MESH, a futuristic coffeehouse, or can operate completely without artificial cover under his own right as a mass projective operative with the Tri-Galactic Intelligence Service. Some other agents shift easily from identity to identity with but simple changes of clothing and identification papers, as does Joseph Greene, also known as Joel Abner (commercial traveler), also known as Captain Joseph Gilead (explorer, lecturer, writer) in Robert Heinlein's "Gulf" (1949).

One expects more imaginative covers from science fiction/fantasy, and we are not disappointed. Even with the modern knowledge of cosmetic surgery, the change of Silverberg's Aar Khioom in *The Silent Invaders* into Major Abner Harris of the Interstellar Development Corps is a major miracle. This alien invader must appear as a respected member of the local society so as not to alarm the humans with whom he must deal. Aar Khioom's gold skin, red eyes, and be-tendrilled but otherwise bald head would draw unwonted attention; these features undergo severe surgery. Since closer attention to his body would be made only *in extremis*, his native surgeons do not tamper with his internal composition that includes a single digestive organ, a double heart, and three lungs. Any change here would require services of others and a chance of irreversibility if the subject wished to return to Darruui. By contrast, the Chameleon Corps of the Political Espionage Office in Ron Goulart's *The Sword Swallower* (1967) uses a shape-changing technique known as the "passade." After a very lengthy training and conditioning period the agent gains a direct and instant control over his cover, being able to change shape, age, features at will. In truth, he becomes a chameleon.

While shape-changing or the "passade" may seem a fantastic extension of the art of the contemporary stand-up comic, brain-washing is a serious phenomenon of the times. Can one speculate on the possibility of extending that to personality-washing, a complete change of memory, background, and decision-making powers with those of another? Jack Chalker uses such a cover device in his Four Lords of the Diamond series (1981). When the Confederacy of 6646 worlds is threatened by an alien in human form who penetrates all defenses and taps the central military computer of that federation, the Operational Security Office acts immediately. It summons its youngest and most adaptable Master detective, Assassin's License. Four dispensable men then must undergo the Merton process that drains their original personalities and replaces them with that of the Master detective. In turn, he acts as a receptor at home base while his training directs the host bodies. In the Chalker series the cloned minds in the four different bodies go to the four Warden worlds, prison planets where nonconformists are exiled when they prove too challenging to the Confederacy. The efficacy of such an undetectable cover depends upon the professional ability of the agent control.

Spy thrillers are books of the hour in the sense that they come into full strength at times of intensified international tension, such as the Cold War. Likewise the industrial spy story gains popularity and credence as business and industry appropriate technological benefits from science. Once a theoretical process becomes functional, holding promise of profit, it becomes a secret to be guarded jealously and sought for by all means, to paraphrase Maugham's remarks about the political and military espionage. Before he finds himself thrown into an adventure completely outside his expertise, Dr. John West, chemist and respectable Cambridge don in Fred Hoyle and Geoffrey Hoyle's *The Molecule Man* (1971) explains his activities. In a matter-of-fact fashion he admits to being "an industrial spy, nothing political or military.'' His respectable academic identity assures him entree to the chemical companies worldwide. Then his ability at trained observation garners trade information for the chemical company using him. Dr. West's frank self-interest motivates alertness whenever he finds himself in the right place at the opportune time.

On a smaller and grubbier scale diamond entrepreneur Ballard in Henry Kuttner's "Piggy Bank" (1942) suffers the depredations of a spy quite by accident. Here is a mini-classic situation of no honor existing among thieves occurring under guise of a business opportunity. Wishing to protect a secret formula for artificial diamonds, Ballard openly displays them on a golden robot, one programmed to protect. A simple reprogramming by a double-crossing employee forces Ballard to use the patent identification number to re-set the robot. Being alert to possibilities inherent in the moment, Ballard's arch-rival Ffoulkes jots down the number, thus assuring the secret no longer a secret and Ballard a soon-to-be business failure.

Chain stores are a familiar sight on American Main Street. Everyone knows the cutthroat competition in this arena of business, as evidenced by price wars and frequent closing of one chain when another moves into town. One expects that the affections of the public will be fickle at times, but what causes total disaffection in a large area? To find the answer to this question became the task of Gilbert Dasein in Frank Herbert's *The Santaroga Barrier* (1968). A member of the psychology department of the University of California-Berkeley, Dasein benefits from the sizable grant endowed by the chain's investment corporation. His job is to spy out the cause of the disaffection, but under cover of a euphemistic "market study." Once in Santaroga Valley Dasein finds himself the target of unfriendly acts: baggage searches, a child shooting at him with an arrow, unauthorized perusal of his papers, even poisoned stew. Dasein as a spy for business plays an ambivalent part: he is an amateur in the battle of profit and loss but a professional in psychological inquiry. The latter professionalism uncovers data (augmented by a local consciousness-heightening drug) that turns him around to pronounce the contemporary organization of life as ''a civilization of battlefields'' and consequently to sway him to the support of the Santarogan choice of a life pattern.

This civilization of battlefields seen by Dasein includes only areas where limited skirmishes are fought. What of the field in which the war may be fought, not only an industrial war, but possibly by a combination of industrial, political, and even military engagements? What of secrets held within the confines of an industrial complex that may render the entire civilization void? When Fred Hoyle in *Ossian's Ride* (1959) predicated such an event, he placed it in the near-future of 1970, but today it might well be located in speculation about the near twenty-first century. When the ICE (Industrial Corporation of Eire) started out as a shoestring company dependent on the financial benevolence of the government, people took little note. But when ICE began to prosper beyond all expectations, industry took a second look. Then British Intelligence became involved as other nations of the world began to ask worrisome questions.

As the novel begins, British Intelligence taps Thomas Sherwood, a Cambridge University student well trained in theoretical mathematics, into its service, sending him into the Kerry area that ICE has secured against any non-official intrusion, non-official as far as the company is concerned. Sherwood is the classic amateur spy. He brings to the danger of the job a naiveté soon to be devastated by misadventure. He accepts the job for the most superficial reason: he had always wanted to visit Ireland!

Ossian's Ride can be read as a textbook illustration of the conventions of the spy story. Sherwood takes as a cover his own identity, student traveling on a tight budget. His journey from the beginning reminds us of the chase in *The Thirty-Nine Steps*. Like Richard Hannay he is caught early in a situation that sets him up as a murderer. He comes into possession of a notebook that must be guarded and passed on to the proper hands. He changes his appearance to blend into the environment from British visitor to "typical Irish student." As he makes his way across Ireland in the Buchan pattern, he must elude a cordon of tractor-mounted enemies, escape by cycle down back roads, slip through areas on public busses, walk when all else fails. Double-agentry is rife. Sherwood soon learns the truth of Phaedrus's warning: *Non semper ea sunt quae videntur* (things are not always what they seem). Up to a point when Sherwood penetrates the ICE compound, Hoyle would seem to have written a standard thriller, but in Sherwood's final report to the head of British Intelligence he unfolds the secret of ICE. To the bureaucratic mentality it is mind-boggling: alien intelligences from a planet destroyed by a dying sun have transferred their knowledge and experience to human beings especially selected for their scientific training and their dedication to rational judgment.

Saboteur has become firmly entrenched in the vocabulary of the thriller, coming far from its original meaning of careless work. It now designates anyone whose activity abets the industrial, political, military, or moral discord of the modern world. Since his job is destruction, often prompted by malice or a deliberate intent to harm, the saboteur gains little sympathy, even from those he may aid in the process. Frank Herbert in "The Tactful Saboteur," collected in *The Worlds of Frank Herbert* (1971), *Whipping Star* (1969), and *The Dosadi Experiment* (1977), defines a saboteur and sabotage in quite a different way. His series character, Jorj X. McKie, works as a Saboteur Extraordinary in the Bureau of Sabotage for the ConSentiency. His bureau is unique in the science fictional world, as well as in the world of today.

BuSab was established at a time when the machinery of government had slipped out of the control of the sentient beings who had organized it. First, it was a Corps but, considering its prime reason for being, ironically had grown to the status of a Bureau. Its prime function, as a character reminds himself in *Whipping Star*, is "to slow the processes of government," or in *The Dosadi Experiment*, "to slow that runaway wheel of government." A quotation from "an Elementary Textbook" used as an epigraph for one of the chapters in *Whipping Star* gives a more philosophical basis for the existence of the BuSab activities:

Taken in isolated tandem, Government and Justice are mutually exclusive. There must be a third force at work for any society to achieve both government and justice. This is why the Bureau of Sabotage sometimes is called "The Third Force." [7]

To fulfill its purpose, BuSab agents may bring public notice to individual incompetence or dishonesty, or they may find themselves engaged in activity more associated with police work or detectival clue-gathering to locate a lost citizen.

The more traditional presentation of the saboteur may be of one misdirecting a computer, blowing up a power station, or wrecking a dam. Depending on whose side benefits from such destruction, the saboteur receives either commendation or censure. In the case of Frank Herbert's *The Dragon in the Sea* (1956) the moral issue clouds up when the act of sabotage is placed in the context of the larger operation. In this near-future society (all too near in the 1980s as compared with the original publication date of 1956) oil is a priority. Oil pirating has become standard procedure with Navy subs slipping into offshore oil fields of the Eastern Powers, tapping wells, filling plastic barges or "slugs" with the oil, and then towing them back to the U.S. ports. A nerve-testing operation under the best of conditions, the missions have now the added tension resulting from a rising number of detections. Ensign John Ramsey of BuPsych must join a crew ostensibly as an electronics officer. In reality he is an undercover agent assigned to monitor the other crew members by using on them a new psychological tool, "emotional telemetering."

In this complexly woven tale Herbert juggles several suspenseful questions. Which of the three crew members is the "sleeper" or the saboteur? Will the submarine evade enemy detection? Will Ramsey's real identity come out? If so, will the other crew members accept him or see him as symbol of a betrayal of their close-knit relationship born of the womb-like environment of the vessel? The question of sabotage pales beside the moral problems raised: internal espionage (betrayal or protection?); the psychological effect on a crew of the environment (good or bad?); science as represented by the BuPsych agent versus religion as personified by the submarine commander (man versus God-Father image?). In this novel the unknown saboteur operates as the catalyst forcing the consideration of basic either-or issues. Here is no human protagonist but humanity itself as protagonist; there is no saboteur-antagonist, only the dynamics of civilized life that test the limits of human endurance.

What many science fiction/mystery thrillers offer is the quasi-optimistic ending. The agent makes the moral choice reaffirming the sense of individual human integrity. The obviously "bad guys" are defeated, or what seemed to be the threat turns out to be beneficial, if accepted and put to use. Before this ending the traditional conventions of the thriller fit in well with the science fiction/fantasy requirements for high adventure and suspense, coupled with the omnipresent awareness that things are not what they seem. This awareness spills over the edge of the plot to allow the author to address other interests such as economic theory, the nature of power, incompetence of government, discrimination, and other problems.

While such philosophical interpolations emphasize the Janus-like responsibility of the genre, there are a few voices who sound a softer but no less penetrating note on the self-devouring or self-defeating nature of the practice of espionage itself. Instead of reaffirming the dictum that things are not what they seem, these voices strive instead to alert us to the foolishness of the art of espionage, especially when it works to the detriment of both the agent and the human race at large. They would seek to remind us of the universal truth of Walt Kelly's inimitable Pogo saying, "We have met the enemy and it is us."

In *Stand on Zanzibar* (1968), that complex, multi-layered novel remarkable for its stylistic and visual as well as its narrative impact, John Brunner makes Donald Hogan the center of one of the dual plots. "Donald Hogan is a spy" baldly proclaims one of the schticks in the initial section of "The Happening World." Twenty-four years old, product of an education that has handed him facts but failed to train his mind, Donald Hogan needs a job. When an offer comes from an agency in Washington, the Dilettante Department of the Office of Research Co-ordination, Donald takes it. He is to study the small Asian country of Yakatang. Ten years later when Yakatang announces a breakthrough in "tectogenetics" or what amounts to a breeding program for supermen, Donald is the logical person to go there to investigate. He travels under the cover of a freelance scientific reporter, but only after "eptification" or "education for particular tasks." He is eptified to kill—Brunner's variation of 007—with one major difference. In four days Hogan is depersonalized and remoulded into Donald Hogan Mark II, a killing machine designated for one task. He is to destroy the Yakatang program because it is not economically feasible for the rest of the world. In the face of such pragmatism Hogan departs for Yakatang only to find the governmental blinders of that country narrowing the vision of its scientist. That one fails to see the full implications of his work. Where Hogan's official superiors look at the genetic work in terms of economic expediency, the Yakatang government judges only on the basis of political expediency. Instead of destroying, Hogan succeeds in aiding the Yakatang scientist to defect. But on the brink of success he kills the man, then retreats into insanity, for him the clearest kind of reason.

Insanity and reason—two faces of the Janus phenomenon—depend on the persons in control applying the names. Donald Hogan Mark II had lost control to name his new mental condition, but not so Lucas Martino of Algis Budrys' *Who?* (1958). Lucas Martino, eminent physicist severely injured in a lab explosion, captured by Soviet authorities, and fixed up with mechanical parts, returns to the West. But is this Lucas Martino or a Soviet spy using an unassailable cover, a metal head effectively prohibiting any show of emotion or expression? Upon return he is forbidden to resume work on the super-secret project K-Eighty-Eight. So he retires to his farm, thus depriving society of his contributions forever. *Who?* emphasizes the built-in paranoia of the cold war mentality.

Probably the most pointed satire of this mentality comes in Stanislaw Lem's surrealistic fantasy *Memoirs Found in a Bathtub* (1973). *Absurd, senseless, meaningless, irrelevant*—synonyms for *pointless* could roll on and on to describe this most pointed satire on the bureaucratic mind pushed to the condition of total inanity. The Introduction, a historical report of a scientific excavation made by people of a far future, alerts us to the situation. During the Prechaotic Age "papyralysis" hit the entire world. This phenomenon was caused by some unknown agent that made paper disintegrate. Deprived of its stored intelligence, civilization collapsed. The military organization retreated to Pentagon III, deep in the Rocky Mountains. There, sealed off from any outside contact, it continued to function as if fed verifiable data about the country. As the report concludes, "in time the pretense became belief, the belief a certainty." [8] In the course of the excavation the far-future scientists come across a scroll of "papyr" containing an account of one man's experience.

We know the narrator in the scroll only as *I*, but a name is unnecessary, for he becomes Everyman caught in the toils of a bureaucratic maze. Unlike Theseus, this narrator is not a brave hero searching the tunnels and cul-de-sacs of a Cretan labyrinth to slay a very real Minotaur. He is a young man reporting for a special mission, the nature of which he never discovers. He steps onto a veritable merry-go-round of frustration. In Pentagon III everyone spies on everyone else; the normal way of life is espionage, deceit, cover-ups. But all this goes on in a place where there is nothing to spy out, nothing to cover up, and no real enemy to deceive. Eventually the only sane act in this absurd world is suicide, for it affirms that life exists, since it can be destroyed.

One is tempted like the prophets and doomsayers mentioned earlier to evoke the shape of spies to come in the science fiction/fantasy spy thriller. Perhaps the future does lie straight ahead in the line set by the past, one echoing Maugham's words of secrets guarded and sought, of malice and money, of adventure or duty motivating men to engage in the activity. As past thrillers have reflected their current events to serve as books of the hour, science fiction/fantasy spy thrillers may address themselves more to the "innocent" technological spying that will make *privacy* an archaic word. While Lem's *Memoirs* strikes dire warning of the absurd direction society may be taking, Herbert's BuSab with its built-in entropic direction may hold a serio-comic hope for the future treatment of bureaucracy. Whatever the direction science fiction/fantasy spy thrillers do take, they will continue to match situation to idea, the major idea being the resilience of the human spirit.

NOTES

1. Isaac Asimov, *Asimov's Mysteries* (1968; rpt. New York: Dell, 1974), p. 130.

2. Ibid.

3. Jonathan Swift, *Satires and Personal Writings* (London, 1932; rpt. London: Oxford Univ. Press, 1962), p. 29.

4. Frederick Pohl, *The Cool War* (New York: Ballantine Books, 1982), p. 276.

5. Somerset Maugham, *Ashenden or the British Agent* (1927; rpt. New York: Avon, 1951), p. 156.

6. Lloyd Biggle, Jr., *The Still, Small Voice of Trumpets* (1961; rpt. New York: Modern Literary Editions Publ. Co., 1968), pp. 142, 203–6.

7. Frank Herbert, *Whipping Star* (1969; rpt. New York: Berkley, 1977), p. 167.

8. Stanislaw Lem, *Memoirs Found in a Bathtub*, trans. Michael Kandel and Christine Rose (Cracow, 1971; rpt. New York: Avon, 1976), p. 16. Original title—*Pamietnik znaleziony w wannie*.

PART IV

THE SCIENCE FICTION/FANTASY GOTHIC MYSTERY

CHAPTER 9

CONTRIBUTIONS OF THE GOTHIC TRADITION

At some point attempts at classification run aground on the individual mode whose uniqueness dictates special consideration. It may command attention not on merit alone, but on evidence of a broken mold or betrayal of expectation. Such non-conformity informs a special group of science fiction/fantasy mystery solvers. If one considers their general mode of operation, they may fit into the slots marked amateur detective, private investigator, spy, or police detective; however, they face special obstacles, must accommodate to outré systems of beliefs, and demand special responses from readers. Ratiocination, method, the balance of conspiracy and counter-intelligence are all fraught with sensationalism. This effect can also rise from another well-established set of conventions, those of the Gothic tradition. In the words of Samuel Taylor Coleridge, stories in this tradition demand "a willing suspension of disbelief" in addition to curiosity as to *whodunit* or speculation on *what if*.

In the patterns of ancient folklore and legend one can easily trace the threads of fear, wonder, and awe adding dark tones and a flash of iridescence to plots. While the eighteenth century was earning its proud title of the Age of Reason, it was only partially successful in relegating the imagination to the underside of the weaving of intellect and thought. With their norms of excellence firmly grounded in the classical aesthetic ideals the eighteenth-century neo-classicists defined *Gothic* as barbarous, ungoverned, wild. By extension they applied the term to writings offensive to the ideal of order and dignity based on reason. Never defeated completely by reason, imagination reinstated sensationalism in literature, thereby adding other nuances of meaning to the term *Gothic*. Later years have applied it in still other ways: Gothic romances, Gothic drama, Gothic novels, Gothic fantasy, and even Gothic detective stories, the latter promising a battlefield for the rational and irrational.

The vigor of the imagination during this century is given testimony by work of authors both in England and on the Continent, especially in France and Germany.[1] Cross-fertilization occurred as poems such as Edward Young's *Night Thoughts* were translated into German, adding to the *Ritter-, Räuber-,* and *Schauer-* tradition of the late eighteenth century. The novels in this tradition featured gloomy medieval settings, robber barons and banditti, violence both physical and supernatural, plus other sensational conventions transferred back in time to England. Accompanying them came the collection of elves, goblins, werewolves, vampires, along with diabolism and acts of vengeance from beyond the grave.

France and England enjoyed a similar mutual exchange, notably with the work of writers such as Abbé Prévost and Baculard d'Arnaud. The Abbé Prévost, usually mentioned in connection with his best known work *Manon Lescaut*, contributed more to the Gothic tradition with lesser known novels that were more popular with the English audiences at the time of translation. Of note are *Cleveland (Le Philosophe anglais; ou, histoire de M. Cleveland, fils naturel de Cromwell* in eight volumes) and *The Dean of Coleraine (Le Doyen de Killerine: histoire morale, composée sur les mémoires d'une illustre famille d'Irlande).* Baculard d'Arnaud, whom Ernest Baker names as Prévost's "understudy . . . whose motto was to out-Herod Herod, and who was recognized as the great master of *le tenebreux,*"[2] merited such an accolade in novels such as *Euphémie.* These two with other French writers of the novels of sensation encouraged English novelists to exploit the possibilities of Gothic settings: dark forests full of dangerous outlaws; cave-dwellings, gloomy and forbidding castles, mansions, monasteries; lonely graveyards. They also made popular those situations soon to become conventional: the chase through the tangled forest or the catacombs or the underground passageways of ancient edifices; spectral manifestations; and embattled love struggling against the forces of unimaginable evils.

When Horace Walpole published the first edition of *The Castle of*

Otranto (1764), he felt constrained to pass it off as a translation of an anonymous work printed in 1529 and written during the time of the Crusades. Furthermore, he included an apology in his introduction to the first edition for the presence in the story of "miracles, visions, necromancies, dreams and other preternatural events," asking the reader to excuse the "air of the miraculous." [3] On the other hand, he did add the descriptive sub-title, "A Gothic Story." When his novel found acceptance and popularity, Walpole added his own name as author to the second edition. In the Preface to that edition he wrote that his intent was "to blend the two kinds of romance, the ancient and the modern," the latter being a copy of nature and the former, all "imagination and improbability." [4] Walpole was one of the first English writers to combine the now-familiar Gothic trappings into one package. *The Castle of Otranto* has a medieval castle complete with a tenant of questionable lineage; subterranean areas with dark vaults; strange appearances, both spectral and human; blood; threatening natural phenomena; dark prophecies; and the like. Ann Radcliffe in novels such as *The Mysteries of Udolpho* refined the nightmarish settings and events with agonized flights by innocents from frightening but sometimes unnamed threats.

In the same year that Ann Radcliffe published *The Mysteries of Udolpho* (1794) William Godwin brought out *The Adventures of Caleb Williams*, foreshadowing the detective story, as has been noted earlier. But William Godwin uses elements of the Gothic, too. Here reason battles with emotion. Hand-in-hand with a demand for a rational explanation of Falkland's treatment of his faithful employee goes the effort to understand both the psychology of the criminal and of the loyal servant. A third response is exacted from the reader: fear. This is the fear that the innocent will be punished while the criminal escapes, protected by status, reputation, and social strictures upon the conduct of men of lower standing.

From these few eighteenth-century exemplars of the Gothic novel one can easily trace the movement of the tradition across the Atlantic and pick up its vitality in Poe and his imitators. Along with a reminder that one glories in the moral activity which disentangles, Poe also impressed his readers by the emotional environment in which his characters glory. In "The Murders in the Rue Morgue" (1841) the narrator describes his task of finding and outfitting a residence for Dupin and himself. It had to suit "the rather fantastic gloom of our common

temper''; he found "a time-eaten and grotesque mansion, long de-
serted through superstitions into which we did not inquire, and totter-
ing to its fall in a retired and desolate portion of the Faubourg St.
Germain." [5] Other details add to the Gothic atmosphere. The two prefer only each other's company; they restrict their activities to the night,
even invoking the night during daytime hours by drawing shutters
tightly and using candles for the little light they need. During the day
they wait for the "true Darkness" when they can seek the "infinity of
mental excitement" in the dark shadows of the city.

From such a lineage, incomplete though it be given here, comes the
intrusion of the Gothic pattern into the forerunners of science fic-
tion/fantasy mystery. These are pieces not fully accepted by some
readers as science-fictional in their plots, yet not comfortable completely in either the detective mode or the Gothic mode without some
acknowledgment of the debts to both. These are modern ghost stories,
stories of cases solved by detectives with occult talents, or stories forcing "science" of the Other. They exact a dual effort from a reader,
for they offer both ratiocinative exercise and "the infinity of mental
excitement" that goes beyond reason. One follows a character as he
attempts to organize a mass of clues and inconsistencies at the same
time that he must deal with the twilight side of man's being. All carry
shadows that frighten even the most rational being, if he but give into
their strength. Whether these shadows come from our childhood's
folklore-fraught education or through a more primal avenue such as
Jung's collective unconscious, no one completely escapes that sense
of Otherness. It is to this experience of our nature that these earlier
writers directed their attention.

Critics generally accord Sheridan LeFanu with the creation of the
first amateur psychic detective or, in this case, a psychic doctor. Dr.
Martin Hesselius, German neuropathist, appears in "Green Tea" (*In
a Glass Darkly*, 1872), therein setting a precedent later developed to
greater degree by Algernon Blackwood in the title character of *John
Silence* (1908). [6] The two psychic doctors, although thirty years apart
in conception, work alike with an acceptance and understanding of the
existence of forces explainable more by metaphysical than by physical
reasons. Dr. Silence, for example, in "A Psychical Invasion" accepts
rationally the phenomenon of the title; through acceptance he then can
work more effectively to counter the "invasion." In "Green Tea" Dr.
Hesselius is called upon to treat a Reverend Dr. Jennings who suffers

from demonic harassment. A small ape-like creature haunts his every waking moment, eventually driving him to suicide. While Dr. Hesselius is unable to avert the inevitable tragedy, he does solve the problem besetting the minister, at least to his own satisfaction and in accordance with his own "science" of psychology. He attributes the spectral illusion to the Reverend Jennings' consumption of green tea, a stimulant that releases the illusion from some interior sense.

Midway between the LeFanu and Blackwood novels appeared M. P. Shiel's *Prince Zaleski* (1895). The title character recalls Poe's Dupin in some respects. A recluse, the Prince rises to the challenge of problem-solving only after being sought out by Shiel acting as a character in his own book. The expected sensational details are present, here as thefts of ancient chalices, mysterious family curses, ancient rhymes with clues to modern crimes, oriental drugs, suicides notable mainly for the pictographic messages on bits of papyrus under their tongues. Highly florid in description and focusing on a detective the reader never quite comes to know, Shiel's stories hold little charm for anyone but the true devotee of the sensational detective story. It fell to the lot of later early twentieth-century novelists to infuse a note of realism to counterpoise the overdose of sensationalism.

The early years of the twentieth century saw several authors follow the path of LeFanu and Blackwood. One who provided the well-needed tongue-in-cheek approach was Gelett Burgess who in the anonymous *The Master of Mysteries* (1912) gives us Armenian-born Astrogon Kerby, better known as Astro. In "The Caledon Kidnaping Case" Astro describes himself as "a vegetarian, a Mahatma, an astrologer, a cabalist, a student of Higher Space, and a thorough believer in the doctrine that an ounce of mystery is worth a pound of commonplace." [7] His occupation is anything but commonplace, for Astro works as a palmist and crystal-gazer. With the ever-ready aid of his secretary Valeska he tracks down the thief of a copy of Shakespeare's First Folio in "The Stolen Shakespeare." He works fairly mundane cases such as "The Macdougal Street Affair" where he aids a plainclothesman track down a dynamiter; but he balances that with an exotic one such as exorcising a ghost that threatens to depress property values in "The Fanshawe Ghost."

To the title, *The Master of Mysteries*, one must add a second epithet, The Great Pretender. Astro's method, seeming to be cloaked in paranormal powers, turns out instead to be very practical detecting dependent on concrete facts and clues as well as a shrewd knowledge of human nature in the best Holmesian style. Burgess added a fillip to his effort by playing two small literary tricks on the readers by inserting a secret message to them. While the title page offers no name of author, that identity comes out in the lengthy acronym, a sentence formed by the initial letters of the stories: "The author is Gelett Burgess." Not content with the one message, he added a second formed by the last letters of each story: "False to life and false to art."

Burgess' contemporaries preferred a more traditional route, playing the occult or psychic detective with less humor. Like Astro in "The Fanshawe Ghost" William Hope Hodgson's title character of *Carnacki, The Ghost Finder* (1913) also seeks the rational explanation for irrational events, but unlike Astro, Carnacki finds his explanations resting on irrational bases. Hodgson used the technique of the frame story much as does Joseph Conrad in his Marlowe stories. Carnacki invites a small coterie of friends in for a quiet dinner, after which he regales them with his latest case, one unfolding in a setting quite different from the quiet sitting-room. These cases play themselves out in truly Gothic backgrounds, castles or old family homes. There are weird occurrences, innocent victims, unearthly noises and manifestations, family legends and ancient grudges.

Despite the Gothic trappings Carnacki himself is one not possessed of paranormal powers, although he is knowledgeable of paranormal studies and procedures. He scoffs at no possibility in nature, accepting a dual existence of the empirically based and the intuitively grasped knowledge. In "The Whistling Room" Carnacki regales his friends with an adventure in Iastrae Castle, Ireland. Sid K. Tassoc plans to wed a local beauty and live in the recently purchased castle but finds himself and his future plans plagued by an unearthly whistling, hooting noise emanating from one of its rooms. Tassoc's initial response to the annoyance is to attribute it to local pranksters, a discomfited local suitor of his destined bride, or some local men who have made rather hefty bets with him over the length of time he will be able to live in the castle.

Not discounting the possibility of the less common explanations, Carnacki combines practical and occult methods in his investigation. He first does the obvious search for hidden passageways and mechanical sources of the sound; he tries to make a recording of the sounds, but all to no avail. He then resorts to less practical measures by

stretching seven human hairs over all openings in the room, by wearing a protective circlet of garlic around his neck whenever he enters
the room, and even considering using a pentacle in the time-honored
way of exorcism. The case comes to a startling conclusion when Carnacki through a window witnesses a spiritual manifestation of hid-
eously pursed, whistling lips on the floor of the room. He orders the
room torn down and destroyed by fire, during which activity he comes
upon an old Celtic inscription directing him to a legend describing an
ancient act of horror. This act, Carnacki reasons, generated a virulent
force of vengeful thought. That developed in strength through the in-
tervening centuries to culminate in intensity at this time.

In "The Horse of the Invisible" Hodgson blends a dual explanation
in Carnacki's solution. Again the friends gather in the psychic detective's room to hear of his experiences in East Lancashire. Again there
is a haunting, an innocent bride-to-be, and a family curse. The girl
unfortunate to be born eldest in the family is doomed. The aural manifestation in this case is the sound of a furiously galloping horse; that
is accompanied by visual sights of enormous hooves suspended in the
air, about to descend upon the innocent's head. Again Carnacki attempts to record the phenomena, this time on film. The image comes
out, giving the detective a clue that leads him to a frustrated lover
desperate enough to engineer all the sights and sounds of the legend.
The man confesses, but just when all seems solved, there is a last
manifestation of the spirit Horse. This unexpected event so frightens
the culprit that he dies. Carnacki is left with an alternative explanation
of Thought Induction or Induced Haunting.

The 1920s brought two expert practitioners of the mode of occult
fantasy or occult detection: Sax Rohmer and Seabury Quinn. Sax Rohmer (pseudonym of Arthur Henry Sarsfield Ward) is well known for
his Dr. Fu Manchu adventures but he also is the creator of Moris Klaw
of *The Dream Detective*. In this successful combination of the Gothic
with the detective formula Rohmer introduces his detective's own peculiar "Science of the Mind" based on the notion that thoughts are
things and as such leave discoverable impressions. These in turn can
be photographed on the sensitive plate of his mind. Moris Klaw, erst-
while antique dealer living in a run-down part of London, while an
unlikely candidate for a successful amateur detective, does provide an
intriguing analog for the good Dr. Holmes. There are the three basic
stock figures: the amateur, eccentric detective; the faithful recorder of

the cases, one Searles, who at one point labels himself a Boswell; and the expectedly inept professional, Inspector Grimsby of Scotland Yard. In addition, Moris Klaw has his beautiful daughter Isis whose exotic beauty often smooths Klaw's path of interfering non-believers.

Klaw's cases draw as expected upon the Gothic with hauntings in ancient houses furnished with medieval artifacts ("The Crusader's Axe"), ghostly phenomena ("The Haunting of Grange"); ancient mysteries still working their will through Egyptian mummies, potsherds and other ancient art objects ("The Case of the Headless Mummies," "The Potsherd of Anubis," and others). "The Whispering Poplars" by its title draws upon a well-used Gothic setting. In all of his cases the narrator reviews Klaw's theory of the Cycle of Crime. Throughout centuries valuable objects have been targets for crime, focal points of human greed, and the subsequent violent expression of that greed. Like history in general, the individual criminal histories repeat themselves. In the process the criminal emotions adhere to the gem or relic, whatever the desired object might be. Klaw's technique is to pick up and record the mental and emotional detritus by "odic photography."

No such exotic talent does Jules de Grandin, a French medical doctor, have at his disposal. In 1976 Seabury Quinn, prolific contributor to *Weird Tales* in the 1920s and 1930s, and his major character, Dr. de Grandin, received renewed notice when about half of the de Grandin stories came out in several collections, titled variously as *The Casebook of Jules de Grandin, The Skeleton Closet of Jules de Grandin*, and similar combinations. Quinn's protagonist is much more average in background than Moris Klaw. A medical doctor who served also as an intelligence officer in World War I, de Grandin later traveled to America where he met a Dr. Trowbridge of Harrisonville, later moving to that town to take up residence with Trowbridge.

While de Grandin personally does not represent the Gothic protagonist in personal appearance or living quarters, he does share with Moris Klaw the privilege of living in an environment seeming to be filled with hag-ridden inhabitants and breeding occult manifestations that require his expert aid in quelling. In his long career (over sixty stories in *Weird Tales*) de Grandin must solve problems such as the one instigated by the vengeful undead ("The Jest of Warburg Tantavul"). He investigates the scourge of a family curse involving an eleventh-century pact with a pre-Christian demon ("Bride of Dewer") and a still more complicated mixture of diabolism, imps, incubi, and a six-toed witch ("The Silver Countess"). With Dr. Trowbridge serving as a slightly more obtuse Watson and with the professional aid of Professor Jacoby, curator of medieval literature, de Grandin traces old legends and occult esoterica to solve the problems his adopted town throws his way. Once de Grandin has tapped what he calls "the wellspring of the malediction" (in "The Doom of the House of Phipps"), he turns the curse or the ancient cure against the modern resurgence of the evil. In his special Gallic fashion Jules de Grandin merits in part the promotional claim for him as "the occult Hercule Poirot."

The detective story sometimes serves as the framework of activity in the material world within which the greater struggle takes place. The "real" world then becomes that internal world or preternatural world where good battles evil. In *War in Heaven* (1930) Charles Williams, member of the Oxford group that included such fantasists as J.R.R. Tolkien and C. S. Lewis, combines the detective format with the mystical eternal struggle. Detective Inspector Colquhoun patiently tracks down the murderer of an elderly employee in an old family publishing house. His clue collecting leads him to the head of the publishing concern. More pertinent to the plot is the parallel search for an ancient chalice, deemed to be the Graal. Gregory Persimmons, the publisher, with the aid of two adepts in the Black Arts tracks it down in a small country church, where the archdeacon valiantly defends it. To strengthen the predominance of the story of good and evil, of the men of God versus the men of Satan, Williams limits the effectiveness of his detective inspector. Only after Persimmons has witnessed a manifestation of Prester John (John the Presbyter), the legendary twelfth-century Asian priest-king, are the chalice, the archdeacon, and a four-year-old boy destined for satanic practices saved from Persimmons and his dark designs. In the novel the science of the Other rates stronger than the science of the detective.

Apparitions of various kinds are an integral part of the Gothic tradition, being described variously as a ghost, or a spirit, or at times more material as when a human changes shape. Vampirism is one such manifestation. An enduring subject, vampirism originated in the dim reaches of regional folklore, gradually working itself into a literary tradition and from there into contemporary science fiction/fantasy mystery as well as occult popular literature. Scholars have found mention of the phenomenon in ancient Chaldean, Babylonian, and Greek accounts. Many countries in Europe, Asia, and North America have some reference to vampires in recorded histories. While history may record, anthropology attempts to explain in the light of cultural and popular fears. Occult studies associate the phenomena with what they term negative psychic forces, draining the victim not necessarily of blood in the time-honored fashion but of vital energy. Modern psychology sees vampirism as one manifestation of repressed sexual impulses or erotic feelings fueled by guilt. None of these efforts, however, have stood up under testing. For all practical purposes they remain theory. It is not our purpose here to subject them to testing. They do serve, however, to reinforce the importance of the phenomenon to which literary persons have devoted much attention.

To Dr. John Polidori, Lord Byron's personal physician, goes credit for an initial literary use of the vampire legend. The occasion for its writing is a familiar story worth repeating. It is June 1816. In the Lake Geneva home of the English poet Shelley is gathered a small group of associates: Shelley and his wife Mary, Lord Byron, and Dr. Polidori. To wile the time away, they decide each to write a story of horror for their mutual amusement. As is well known, out of this literary game came one of the most durable ancestors of modern science fiction/fantasy, Mary Shelley's *Frankenstein*. Also came the fragment by Dr. Polidori, *The Vampyre*, anticipating Bram Stoker's *Dracula* (1897) by some eight decades.

Lord Ruthven, Polidori's vampire-villain, is a nobleman of solemn mien yet subtle drawing power. In *Supernatural Horror in Literature* H. P. Lovecraft describes Ruthven as a "suave villain of the true Gothic or Byronic type." [8] While traveling in Greece, Lord Ruthven lives out part of the local vampire lore, that of a living creature who once a year renews his own vitality by draining that of a lovely young girl. When bandits capture Ruthven, he exerts a promise from them that after they kill him, they will leave his body on a high point where the first cold ray of the moon will touch it. This touch revives him; his reappearance in London is inexplicable to his acquaintances there. However, his identity as a vampire is confirmed; he has become one of the living dead, or the Un-Dead.

While Polidori's fragment presents his vampire decorously, not so the nineteenth-century penny dreadfuls, best illustrated by *Varney the Vampyre* (1847), sometimes ascribed to James Malcolm Rymer or to Thomas Peckett Prest. This "blood novel" outstripped Polidori in sensational scenes; its subtitle, "The Feast of Blood," delivers exactly what it promises. *Varney the Vampyre* elaborates in great detail the more gruesome details of the legends: the batlike figure tapping at the window late at night; the beautiful woman fascinated into submission by the glowing eyes; the fang-like teeth and the quick attack at the neck; the drained body later reviving to madness.

Sheridan LeFanu in *Carmilla* (1872) plays the same tune in a different key, emphasizing the demon lover as the *lamia*, the female preying upon youth and beauty, a theme earlier used by Samuel Taylor Coleridge in "Christabel" (1816). LeFanu's heroine, Laura, lives a sheltered life in a lonely but very picturesque castle in a forest; her only associates are her elderly father and still older nurse. No wonder that she responds without fear to the apparition of a young woman at her bedside to comfort her. Only the pain as if two needles had penetrated her breast destroyed the sense of calm. Later a traveler in distress leaves her young daughter at the castle for a while; the woman looks like the apparition. As one might expect, strange things happen; Carmilla, the guest, turns out to be a vampire, the Countess Mircalla of the family of Karnstein, one of infamous reputation going back a century and a half. Together, with the aid of a priest, the father and a friend dispose of the vampire in traditional way by driving a stake through the heart, cutting off the head, and after burning the body tossing the ashes into flowing water, an element that is anathema to vampires.

While Dracula is alive and flourishing today in the many films, television programs, and novels about him, his pattern of behavior was set long before this century. Bram Stoker's *Dracula* (1897) not only picked up the sensational elements of the legend but elaborated on it in such dramatic ways as to establish firmly the literary home of all such creatures as Transylvania, high in the Carpathian mountains. Stoker's story is unique in comparison with its predecessors in that it is presented as a collection of journal entries, letters, and diaries, all detailing the plan of Count Dracula to move to England and there to reproduce his own kind. The Dracula of Stoker's novel has become a paradigm for all vampire stories, a symbol for the submerged fears of mankind. Evil in the figure of the Count merits a capital letter, a dignity not inherent in the lesser evils seen in the broad daylight of empirical science.

Lycanthropy, another staple of Gothic fiction, has not fared so well in science fiction/fantasy mysteries as has vampire lore despite their common psychological linkage. As far afield as first century A.D., Pliny in the Eighth Book of his *Natural History* gave mention to the commonplace belief in werewolves but promptly went on record as naming such belief as a "loud lie." [9] Folklore gives us the story of the Beauty and the Beast, but when the association turns from such gentle relationships to the more aggressive horror of normality perverted into bestiality, the literary uses of the werewolf convention move closer to pure fantasy. True, the subject has attracted established authors and inspired some memorable pieces such as *The Strange Case of Dr. Jekyll and Mr. Hyde* (1886) by Robert Louis Stevenson. Ambrose Bierce in "The Eyes of the Panther" (1891) calls for sympathy for a loving couple cursed with what the wife terms insanity but is really lycanthropy resulting from a panther attack upon her pioneer mother in their log cabin in the primeval wood. To make the theme more acceptable to skeptical readers some authors preferred identifying lycanthropy with possession, as did Rudyard Kipling in "The Mark of the Beast"; still others, the product of a twisted imagination or warped mentality, such as in Geoffrey Household's "Taboo." [10]

Conventions of the Gothic romance, occult powers, apparitions or unnatural manifestations, whatever term one chooses, there is behind them all the sense of magic one associates with fantasy. Magic has contributed a valuable dimension to all of literature, hence by extension to science fiction/fantasy mystery. Indeed, one may claim a greater contribution to all of human culture, if we go back to the influence of the Magi, that priestly caste of the ancient Medes and Persians who, tradition says, possessed great occult powers. Even the most superficial study of the findings of anthropologists acquaint us with pivotal groups or individuals who have acknowledged existence of the world of unseen forces, untested or untestable phenomena. Bronislaw Malinowski reminds us of the pervasiveness of this sense of the other world and its power in beliefs of primitive men. It resided in the *mana* of the Melanesians and the *orenda* and *wakan* of American Indian tribes. [11] In less primitive eras and cultures a Hermes Trismegistus, the *Bardo Thodol*, the *I-Ching*, and other men and sacred books testify to the world-wide existence of this way of thought and belief.

The poets give credence to this other "science." Hamlet turns to his friend with "There are more things in heaven and earth, Horatio,/ Than are dreamt of in your philosophy" (Act I, sc. v., ll. 165–66).

Two centuries later, William Blake will plead the limitations of the five senses with "If the doors of perception were cleansed every thing would appear to man as it is, infinite." [12] Later in the nineteenth century the English Romantics admitted a sense of the mystical power of nature. William Butler Yeats in *A Vision* (1925) attempted to find a linkage between magic, history, and personality. Still more contemporary is the serious attention the scientific and academic community has given to experiments in extra-sensory perception.

Despite all this, to achieve a working symbiosis between science fiction/fantasy with its reliance on extrapolation of scientific facts or currently accepted beliefs and the Gothic tradition with its reliance on "science" unprovable in a testing arena puts a strain on both partners. Nonetheless, science fiction/fantasy writers in the mid- and late twentieth century have found the obstacles not insurmountable; the challenge, worth the effort. The Gothic tradition has given a rich fund of conventions of setting, situation, characters. Here situation comes to the support of ideas with the science fiction/fantasy mystery drawing upon the sensationalism of the Gothic fiction and its occult partner and then putting it to the service of the idea.

NOTES

1. Scholars disagree on the magnitude and/or origin of the influence. Devendra P. Varma in *The Gothic Flame* (New York: Russell & Russell, 1966), p. 32, flatly contradicts Montague Summers's remark about the direct influence of French and German writers on the English, going on to emphasize the "dangerously complicated assembly of cross-currents" to be noted. Summers in *The Gothic Quest* (New York: Russell & Russell, 1964), p. 148, does acknowledge the reciprocal flow of material. For other writers on the Gothic tradition see the Bibliographical Essay at end of book.

2. Ernest A. Baker, *The History of the English Novel: Novel of Sentiment and the Gothic Romance* (London: Witherby, 1929), p. 133.

3. Horace Walpole, *The Castle of Otranto* in *Shorter Novels: Eighteenth Century*, ed. Philip Henderson (London: Dent, 1963), pp. 99–100.

4. Ibid., p. 102.

5. *The Complete Works of Edgar Allan Poe*, ed. James A. Harrison (1902; rpt. New York: AMS, 1965), IV, 151.

6. Howard Phillips Lovecraft in *Supernatural Horror in Literature* (1945; rpt. New York: Dover, 1973), p. 97, characterizes the Dr. Silence stories as "marred only by traces of the popular and conventional detective-story atmosphere."

7. [Gelett Burgess], *The Master of Mysteries Being an Account of the Problems Solved by Astro, Seer of Secrets, and His Love Affair with Valeska Wynne, His Assistant* (Indianapolis, Ind.: Bobbs-Merrill, 1912), p. 135.

8. Lovecraft, p. 39.

9. Pliny, *The History of the World, commonly called The Natural History of C. Plinius Secundus*, trans. Philemon Holland, sel. Paul Turner (Great Britain, 1962; rpt. New York: McGraw-Hill, 1964), p. 95.

10. "The Mark of the Beast" is reprinted in *Kipling: A Selection of His Stories and Poems*, ed. John Beecroft (Garden City, N.Y.: Doubleday, 1956). Reprinted story is not designated with original date of publication. "Taboo" is reprinted in *Alfred Hitchcock's Hold Your Breath* (New York: Dell, 1965) from Household's *The Salvation of Pisco Gabar and Other Stories* (New York: Little, Brown, n.d.).

11. Bronislaw Malinowski, *Magic, Science and Religion and Other Essays* (1948; rpt. Garden City, N.Y.: Doubleday, 1954), pp. 76–79.

12. William Blake, "The Marriage of Heaven and Hell," pl. 14, in *The Complete Writings of William Blake*, ed. Geoffrey Keynes (London: Oxford Univ. Press, 1966), p. 154.

CHAPTER 10

THE GOTHIC INVASION OF SCIENCE FICTION/FANTASY

Omnia exeunt in mysterium—all vanishes in mystery. So goes an old saying. The twentieth-century mind, still closely linked to its eighteenth-century rationalist training, would prefer adding "unless man exercises his reason to explain and understand." Despite the claim that mystery can be cleared by exercise of reason, the Gothic tradition supports the equal claim of the old Latin tag. By so doing as it invades popular literature, it attracts devotees of the mysterious. The tradition affords a legitimate opportunity to wander in the twilight of the spirit or the shadows of the psyche without direct involvement of belief or charge of superstition. It also provides pleasurable fear, one to be appreciated from a safe aesthetic distance. As one of the characters in Dean Koontz's *The Haunted Earth* (1973) says in another context but in words applicable to this context, "The myth requires it." [1] By so doing, the myth establishes reality for the reader.

The most obvious way in which the myth determines reality or makes itself more real is through setting. As was pointed out in the preceding chapter, Gothic settings tend to run to glooming locations evoking an atmosphere of dread or melancholy. There are hidden places fraught with the romance of magic or the passion of terror and horror. There are suggestive movements and evocative sounds that dismay, even alarm, or at least cause hesitation. Be the locale a whispering forest, the vaults of a family tomb, the shadowed corridors of an old public building, or the streets of a strange town in the early hours of morn, here is a place ripe for a gathering of the folkloric personages. Here might come vampires, werewolves, demon lovers, cruel stepmothers, uneasy spirits seeking their eternal rest, witches, all the mental hobgoblins with which the human mind has made the myth guide the reality.

Ray Bradbury illustrates how a science fiction/fantasy writer can pull the Gothic conventions into his mysteries and avoid using them as clichés.[2] *Something Wicked This Way Comes* (1962) demonstrates the art of assimilation. The reader expects gloom, decaying abbeys or castles, underground tunnels cobwebby or dripping. The buildings will either be perched atop a lonely mountain or deep inside a forest of unpruned trees. If a house, it will lour over a dark tarn as in Poe's *The Fall of the House of Usher* or it might be inaccessible as Dracula's abode. Not so in Bradbury. His settings are Small Town, U.S.A. Not only Small Town, but Small Town, Midwestern U.S.A. His towns are not large enough to support castles, even if one could find on the prairies the huge stones to build one. But small towns have ways and places that invite adventure into mystery. Green Town, Illinois, admits the irrational into its confines when one night Cooger & Dark's Pandemonium Shadow Show puts up its tents near the town. Instead of the dark winding path through the forest down which the innocent heroine must traverse, the carnival has the mirror maze that fractures and destroys the fragile egos of those too weak to look at themselves honestly. Green Town, Illinois, also has the Public Library building, an old building in which silence reigns and rows of books in piled stacks provide a darkened maze through which other fragile selves slip searching for support in the words, hopes, and dreams of the dead.

Bradbury's novel also is a homing place for a clutch of abnormal beings out of ancient folk fears. In *Something Wicked This Way Comes* there is Mr. Dark, the carnival manager. An embodiment of all that appears evil and ominous in our fear-life, Mr. Dark reigns over a true Pandemonium, a mini-city of devil-like beings. The freak show ballyhoos a skeleton and a Mephistopheles, a Dangling Man, a Dwarf, a Lava-Drinker, and Mr. Electrico, a human form galvanized into action by an electrical charge. A Dust Witch from the carnival flies high in a mouldy balloon or drifts low to brush the tops of houses in Green Town. The voice of reason finds its avenue of expression in the father of one of the boys. His "science" is that of honest recognition and acceptance of the advance of age and the natural end of all living things. With this science he can dispel the darkness and fear, for some, if not for all of the inhabitants of Green Town. The boys on their part undergo a rite of passage as they come to terms with Mr. Dark and his fearsome crew in their own way.

Peter Penzoldt in *The Supernatural in Fiction* speaks of three ways in which authors start a ghost story.[3] His categories can apply equally well to modern science fiction/fantasy Gothic mystery. The first method involves laying out a clear-cut direction, letting the reader in on the cause of the mystery and suspense early, in order to devote the remainder of the story to the dispelling of that mystery. This method is highly reminiscent of the inverted detective story made popular by R. Austin Freeman in the early 1900s. A second technique, according to Penzoldt, devotes the beginning paragraphs or chapters to descriptive details building up the Gothic atmosphere of terror and awe. These may include the detailed descriptions of both natural and manmade environment or hints of inexplicable events to create an overall mood of suspenseful terror. The final method is to open the story by giving no hint as to the supernatural or abnormal activity to follow.

It is profitable to look at sample science fiction/fantasy mysteries using Penzoldt's three methods. Particularly do his beginnings illuminate those stories using the vampire tradition, a popular one for symbiosis. Here again the science belongs not to the laboratory or computer but to that knowledge some term superstition but others call instinct bred of the deep need to protect one's existence. As early vampire novels depended mainly on sensationalism, later ones have turned to psychology for clues to an understanding of this very real source of fear. This does not imply that twentieth-century novelists forego the effects of awe and wonder. These can become even more intense in such ordinary settings as Grandmother's boarding house or a small Maine village or a southwestern university campus. Vampires cannot exist in the twentieth century in such commonplace locations, a reader may insist, but some science fiction/fantasy authors have adapted the tradition so well that they convince us between the covers of their books.

One short story from the collection *The October Country* (1955) by Ray Bradbury provides an example of Penzoldt's last method of introduction: open the story by giving no hint of the supernormal events to follow. Eleven-year-old Douglas in "The Man Upstairs" (1947) watches his grandmother prepare chickens for stuffing and baking. An alert child would miss none of the magic of this activity: the collection of shiny utensils needed, the fascinating array of innards removed from the birds, the dexterity of the old lady at work, the ritual of stuffing and sewing up the bird. But the magic turns black when later in the story Grandmother acquires a new roomer, a tall, thin man with strange cold grey eyes. From the first Mr. Koberman differs from the other roomers. He dispenses small tips to Douglas in copper coins, never silver. He eats sparingly at table but only with wooden utensils. Working nights, he sleeps days, a sleep so deep that none of those annoying noises Douglas makes will awaken him. The story gains suspense when a series of unexplained deaths occur in the area, initiating rumors of a vampire in the neighborhood. A glimpse "inside Mr. Koberman" by medium of a stained glass window alerts Douglas to the roomer's lack of "innards." He sets his world aright with a unique recitation of Grandmother's earlier lesson in evisceration and stuffing, the latter being a timely investment of his entire savings of silver dimes.

While Bradbury begins his story with an average situation possible even today for anyone to witness, he does plant some subtle verbal clues such as calling Grandmother "a kindly, gentle-faced, white-haired old witch" as she goes through the "ritual" of stuffing the bird. [4] Even so, these do not push too hard for hidden meaning then, for this view comes through the eyes of an alert, imaginative little boy. Only with the entrance of Mr. Koberman and his strangeness, especially the black umbrella folded against the wall like a bat, does the story pick up undertones of mystery, later to become a full symphony.

Cyril Kornbluth's "The Mindworm" (1950) recalls Penzoldt's first pattern of introduction. Kornbluth poses the possibility of some terrible event occurring as the aftermath of an atomic test with its possibility of causing mutations. He prepares the reader in two ways, one obviously the provocative title. The second is the beginning scene as a Navy nurse and a Navy officer assigned to duty on the same ship during the atomic testing witness a test blast. Later the nurse gives birth to their illegitimate son, a singularly unlovely child whose appearance precludes adoption. Left in a foster home, he must serve himself as he matures. His survival depends not upon the traditional blood of another but upon energy, particularly the high-voltage energy generated by anger or passion. The youngster early learns to worm his way into others' minds, feeding upon them and leaving them drained and often dead. But he does the unforgivable by feeding on and killing a virgin he catches in an alley. In turn he is caught and killed by the local inhabitants, emigrants from southeastern Europe, still steeped in the ancient vampire lore and possessed of minds not encased in the prison of logic.

Kornbluth presents the situation that creates an atmosphere of terror, the atomic blast; then he shifts to the stronger atmosphere of horror to destroy any sympathy one might have for the central character. Words such as *child* and *boy* soon give way to the single epithet—The Mind-worm. Aside from the weird elements in the narrative, Kornbluth's story raises more pertinent questions than does Bradbury's story. A reader can wonder: Are the old monsters of ancient folklore really human mutations? Has the rationalist heritage deprived the human mind of the benefits of intuitive science?

The most usual pattern is Penzoldt's second one, the preparation by setting an emotional mood or atmosphere of mystery inherent in the environment. Following closely in the tradition of Walpole and Radcliffe, Stephen King in *'Salem's Lot* (1975) takes the old conventions of setting but like Bradbury he puts them into twentieth-century structures. Here is a large empty house on a hill overlooking a small town.[5] The house has a forbidding history of murder, suicide, and years of brooding over by the townspeople. As Stephen King populates 'Salem's Lot, each introduction plants seeds of grim anticipation. Here a landlady, there a town drifter; here a beautiful girl, there a priest whose church has eroded his metaphysical foundation by its contemporary concern for social issues—each and all of these appear as vulnerable units, open to manipulation or destruction by any strong and selfish amoral force.

When two strangers purchase Marsten House, the menace shifts from self-destruction through personal spiritual fragility to communal destruction by the demonic energies of the new owners. With the advent of Barlow and Straker also begin the clues to their archaic identity: the traditional night-roaming and day-sleeping, Barlow's need for blood, his dignity and fatal fascination coupled with superhuman strength and telltale red, piercing eyes. Barlow and Straker transform static and self-feeding 'Salem's Lot into its metaphoric counterpart—a town of the Un-Dead. The inhabitants have no inner spirit or spiritual basis from which to grow, no vitality except what they drain from others. Stephen King offers the vampire condition as a dramatic metaphor of the modern, self-enclosed way of life.

From 'Salem's Lot of the twentieth century to a near-future of a century away is an easy step for most science fiction/fantasy readers. For readers of Gothic fiction or weird literature the mere title of Colin Wilson's *The Space Vampires* (1976) may give pause. If it is difficult for the mind conditioned to empirical knowledge to accept vampires in a New England village except as metaphor for a stultified human existence, how much more difficult to accept them in outer space. But Wilson sets the Gothic atmosphere to work for him. When a unit from a patrolling space ship enters a derelict ship to explore its interior, the men must traverse areas reminiscent of soaring cathedrals and lacy forests. Finally they enter a crypt holding thirty corpses in perfect condition, looking as if they were sleeping. Against the dictates of his deepest intuition Captain Carlsen takes three of the bodies back to earth for research, as ordered by the Leader of World Unity, Prime Minister of the United European States. There a curious reporter is drawn to one of the beautiful female corpses and suffers a vampirish attack. The alien thus receives new life, escapes, and aids the others to do the same.

In this year of 2082 the study of vampirism has become an accept-able subject for scientific research with the primary scientist in the field, a Dr. Hans Fallada, irreverently labeled as the "Sherlock Holmes of pathology." While Dr. Fallada's research focuses on a variation of the more traditional blood-sucking act, he personally practices a men-tal vampirism, what he calls "benevolent vampirism." This is the mutual interchange of psychic energy for health's sake. All human energy, he believes, comes from the original flow of pure energy.

The Space Vampires is not a philosophical treatise on the nature of cosmic energy. It is a mystery story in which the "detective" works to locate the renegade members of the Nioth-Korghai culture. These sentient yet bodiless aliens dedicate themselves to the protection of weaker races in the universe by infusing them with life-giving infu-sions of the necessary pure energy. The Ubbo-Sathis renegades, ob-sessed with their own ability, have turned into space vampires rather than energizers. After a visit to Dr. Fallada Commander Carlsen dis-covers that he too has the ability to give and receive energy. In other words, he is a benevolent vampire. He alone can serve as the tool for the Nioth-Korghai detective when that alien consciousness possesses Carlsen's body and speaks through him to the three persons likewise possessed by the three alien vampires escaped from the space ship. The crisis threatening the unwitting populace of the United European

States is averted when the detective through Carlsen convinces the renegades to revert to pure energy wherein they can both give and receive in an infinite state as benevolent vampires.

Suzy McKee Charnas in *The Vampire Tapestry* (1980) provides a perfect example of Penzoldt's pattern that allows the reader no relaxation from start to anticipated climax. In the first sentence Charnas presents Katje de Groot, a South African citizen now a campus widow at the Cayslin Center for the Study of Man. As she watches the eminent anthropologist Dr. Weyland walk from his laboratory, in her mind Katje pronounces him a vampire. Applied so firmly, the term whets the appetite of a reader for all the sensational happenings associated with vampires. Anticipation dims when it is revealed that this scientist is doing important research on sleep, a project meriting his colleagues' admiration. Then ironically Charnas erases any burgeoning sympathy for the man by further revealing that this responsible project provides him with a steady flow of "cattle" from which he draws sustenance. He errs in trying to recruit Mrs. de Groot for the project. When she defends herself by shooting at him, his "cover" is weakened. He must disappear. From this point on through the remaining four parts of the five-part novel, Dr. Weyland struggles to cloak his singularity under other acceptable identities to gain social acceptance as well as to afford food.

Within the timeworn framework of the vampire legend Charnas poses a paradox. Can the prey feel sympathy for the predator? More to the point, what of the lonely creature whose survival admits no feelings of kinship or empathy? At one point Dr. Weyland does let down his guard with a female psychiatrist. Their sessions allow an understanding not only of his own condition but of hers as well. As he faces his own weakness, he identifies their special affiliation not as a professional one but rather as a perversion of the unicorn myth with him as the chaste partner. There is attraction. It will become fatal for him at the same time it protects her, for Weyland cannot bring himself to "feed" on her.

While the vampire theme predominates in *The Vampire Tapestry*, Charnas has succeeded in emphasizing the latter word also. The novel is truly a verbal tapestry. Many plot threads give it a psychological complexity more memorable than the sensational appeal of the first major title word, the obvious subject matter. The predator-prey relationship extends into every aspect of personal and social intercourse:

sex, business, politics, friendship, education, wherever overt or open seduction occurs for personal gain. A loving relationship between Dr. Weyland and Floria can do nothing but betray his nature and weaken his defenses. The open warm relationship between one of Weyland's colleagues and his students drains that professor of energy to the point that he turns to Dr. Weyland for aid not possible from Weyland's nature. As a result, a suicide occurs. There is raw predator-prey status between Weyland and the people who harbor him after he is shot. Upon discovering his nature, they plot to use him in cultist rites and to display him for profit as a freak. In one powerful section of the book, "A Musical Interlude," a performance of *Tosca* creates a musical predator as the music stimulates Weyland's emotions and rouses his lust to feed. The predator becomes prey of his own nature. *The Vampire Tapestry* urges psychological attention to the vampire motif.

Vampire lore of the past has both thrilled and repelled readers, but contemporary story tellers make a bid for another reaction with speculations never addressed by tradition. Hal Clement's "A Question of Guilt" (1976) does raise doubts as to the guilt or blame attached to vampirism. He uses the night forays, all-day slumber, blood-draining, and hidden retreats but with a difference. In this story a second-century Roman family seeks in vain for some way of healing a hemophiliac son, if not healing, at least saving him from early death. The father at last resorts to homely logic. Using the analogy of a leaking jug that a family must keep because it has none other, he asks, "What is the only thing left?" The answer is obvious: "You let it leak, and refill it whenever. . . ." [6] Once decided, the father acts. At night he steals peasant children for the necessary refill, taking them to his cave dwelling. There with a homemade snake-fang syringe-cum-hypodermic needle he does primitive blood transfusions for benefit of his beloved son.

"The Detweiler Boy" (1977) by Tom Reamy makes a chilling apologia for vampirism on the basis of sibling responsibility. The story starts out as a detective story. Bertram Mallory of Bert Mallory Criminal Investigations, when summoned to a man's home to receive some information about a peculiar event, finds the informant dead in a particularly bloody killing. On his own Mallory continues the case that soon involves a young hunchback who lived nearby. Other murders occur at regular intervals of three days. In each case Mallory finds that the Detweiler boy, the hunchback, lives nearby but moves after each murder. Nothing would seem to connect the boy to the murders themselves, but his unusual condition draws Mallory's notice. Seeming to suffer from a debilitating disease, the boy undergoes remarkable rejuvenation soon after each murder. Mallory's investigation discloses a strange sibling relationship. The Detweiler boy's hump is a Siamese twin but an immature creature who kills to ingest enough blood to give the fully-formed boy needed transfusions. As the vampire tradition insinuates itself into what promised to be a routine investigation by a hard-boiled private investigator, it turns the plot into the Gothic province. In the end Mallory betrays the adjective *hard-boiled* when out of compassion after the vampire-brother is killed, he gives the surviving Detweiler boy a gun and takes him to a lonely road.

The popularity of the vampire theme in contemporary science fiction/fantasy mystery continues, as a glance at the monthly list of books published testifies. Within the last few years, for example, these representative titles support that continuing trend. In *Hotel Transylvania: A Novel of Forbidden Love* (1978) Chelsea Quinn Yarbro treats the formula with touch of humor not usually associated with such tales. Combining the convention of demonic possession with vampire lore, Tanith Lee's *Sabella* (1980) works out its plot in a far-future on an Earth now colonized by Mars. Several like novels came in 1981 with Jan Jennings' *Vampyr; Blood Country* by Doris Piserchia (writing as Curt Selby); the Nazi versus vampire in *The Keep* by F. Paul Wilson; and the cyborg vampires of *Vampires of Nightworld* by David Bischoff. In 1982 two authors added to their vampire series. Chelsea Quinn Yarbro's fourth book in the St. Germain series, *Path of the Eclipse* (1981), returned to print to accompany *Tempting Fate*, Book V, delineating the exploits of a vampire who returns at dramatic times in history. Thus Yarbro works the vampire tradition in service of historical fiction. A second series started out as a Dracula pastiche with *The Dracula Tape* (1975). Written by Fred Saberhagen, this series in *An Old Friend of the Family* (1979) shifted from pastiche to a novel standing on its own merits in plotting and mystery. *Dominion*, the 1982 addition, carries on the new direction.

As has been noted before, a mode seems to have won its place when it survives a humorous or satiric treatment. In "Blood Brother" in *The Playboy Book of Science Fiction and Fantasy* (1966) Charles Beaumont invites the reader to listen in on a man's session with a psychiatrist. A self-proclaimed vampire, the man complains about the entire routine. He can not keep jobs because he must sleep all day. Coffins are so high-priced these days, and soil is so hard to come by. He really hates biting people and especially dislikes the blood stains he finds on his shirts. He needs help because he is so helpless. Since mirrors do not reflect for him, he can't get a proper shave. The smell of garlic sickens him; running water bothers him. And then there is the trouble finding a dentist to fix his incisors. He begs the psychiatrist to find a cure for his problem; the doctor obliges in a surprising denouement it would be unfair to give away to a new reader.

Josef Nesvadha in "Vampire, Ltd." (1964) speculates on a situation that as metaphor rings all too familiar. England has gone car-mad; everyone tries to outrace everyone else on the roads. A diplomat caught car-less finds he must hitchhike. When the driver of the super-sports car with whom he gets a ride becomes ill and drained of energy, he takes over the wheel. He finds himself caught up in a super-speed race with an English marchioness, but must give up when he too becomes ill and weak. Upon getting out of the car, he notices a bruised and bloody place on the foot he used on the accelerator. Checking under the hood, he discovers the car to be a special vehicle, made by a man long dead. A one-of-a-kind car, this is a mechanical vampire. But all is not lost when the marchioness cannot resist buying the car to enter in Le Mans and win. As the diplomat muses, all the cars he notices are "racing in a great race with unwritten rules, in which death is of secondary importance." [7]

Lycanthropy, or the "man into wolf" theme, fares less well than vampirism, but science fiction/fantasy mystery does draw upon it in some cases. As previously noted, Dean Koontz used werewolf legends and prophecies by tribal seers to share the interest with the cyber-detective and master-unit robot in *A Werewolf Among Us* (1973), but the share is small. Tanith Lee in *Lycanthia* (1981) in the title foreshadows the end of a quest of a twentieth-century pianist to trace family roots. Fred Saberhagen in *The Dracula Tape* (1975) intimates a close connection of werewolves and vampires but does not belabor the point. Two short novels do offer samples of the diversity we can expect in science fiction/fantasy mysteries when the lore is used: Jack Williamson's *Darker Than You Think* (1940) and Ron Goulart's *Hawkshaw* (1972).

Williamson's novel attempts to present lycanthropy in a dual light, as explainable by hard science and also by soft science, namely psychology. Though intriguing in its fantasy, the story is less satisfying in the scientific explanations. Upon return from a two-year dig in a remote Asian area, Dr. Mondrick and his archeological assistants warn the public of a possible resurgence of a master race, descendants of an ancient mixing of genes between *Homo sapiens* and what they term *Homo lycanthropus*. Genes from the latter blood line have survived in a recessive condition for eons, surfacing upon occasions when successive matings brought them to a dominant position. The scientist uses as specific examples the stories of Romulus and Remus, the animal-headed gods of early Egypt, Fenris of Norse myth, and the mythological couplings of Greek gods with human females with the gods in animal forms. The archeological team believe they have found solid evidence of a contemporary resurgence of the phenomenon, evidence gathered from blood tests of Dr. Mondrick's wife and also one of his prize pupils, Will Barbee. In a reversal of the Beauty and the Beast pattern Will Barbee, ex-archeology student, now a reporter, meets the Beauty/Beast who will eventually prepare him for his own transformation into the Child of Night or the Black Messiah.

Williamson sets up a situation that invites contradictory responses. First, the struggle of Barbee to retain a sense of compassion, pity, and the bonds of friendship commands respect. On the other hand, the equally strong and admirable sense of animal strength, sensitivity, and freedom commands equal admiration. In the tug of war between conflicting urges Barbee must receive sympathy. Williamson has produced some dramatic descriptions of the successive stages of the metamorphosis of man into beast and his physical reaction to the newfound keenness of the senses, the play of muscles, and the feeling of power. Only when the author drops into the quasi-scientific exposition of the process on the basis of atomic probability and the laws of uncertainty does he dampen the excitement of his narrative.

By contrast, Ron Goulart in *Hawkshaw* gives another of his travesties, not only of the werewolf legend but of modern society in general. This is a future America, now reformed into the Thirteen Colonies. When the intrepid hero-reporter Kraft receives the assignment to do an In-Depth story on a Connecticut Colony werewolf, he ends up in a verbal, political, and social stewpot. The assignment uncovers a conservative/liberal political battle: the Robin Hood League, headed by an anonymous George Washington II, is at odds with Hawkshaw, undercover agent for the liberals. The werewolf assignment becomes lost in mid-novel while the reporter goes through multiple encounters with groups such as the Cannibal Gourmets, Uncle Kidnapper, and the Mafia That Doesn't Exist (subdivided into the Sicilian Civil Liberties Union, Neapolitan Anti-Defamation Club, Don't Mess with Italian American League), and similar groups. Goulart finally returns his hero to the original assignment when reporter Kraft resolves the werewolf question by dousing the conservative leader with a canister of his own pacifying agent, a gas with the unfortunate side effect of turning men into wolves.

When science fiction/fantasy adopts the Gothic tradition to intensify a puzzle-mystery, it usually adds a surrogate for the human reason to give some counterpoint for the melodramatic backdrop. The purpose can be fulfilled by several types of characters, all occupied with separating the myth from the reality. They fall into categories roughly paralleling those in other mystery fusions. There is the amateur serving either as a knowing aid to the investigation or as the average man caught in a paranormal situation he understands not a whit. Whichever type he is, he finds that his training tells him it cannot happen, but his instinct tells him that he must pit himself against the unknown forces. The amateur may possess some extra-sensory perception that he accepts as natural and can use in service of the investigation.

There is also the private investigator taking the case for his living; he can do no other but set into motion his logical *modus operandi*, buttressed by whatever understanding he has of human nature, and trust that he can out-maneuver the illogical factor working against him. Finally there is the psychic or occult detective who accepts the irrational as part and parcel of his own science. While that science is not the subject one teaches in a school, it is a measurable entity for one possessing or having access to like paranormal abilities. In the responses of these latter characters lies a point where science fiction/fantasy can feel most comfortable working with the Gothic elements. Here is a place wherein facts and known quantities can extrapolate into the realm of the Other.

The amateur in science fiction/fantasy Gothic mystery fares best as an aid to the official investigators. As an amateur strictly on his own, he becomes the Innocent pursued by the personification of Evil, rather than the puzzle-solver. But the science of psychic phenomena can admit the amateur to the ranks of problem solvers, as Dean Koontz in *The Vision* (1977) has Mary Bergen show. A psychic working with the police department on a semi-official basis, Mary Bergen contributes her peculiar talent of being able to foresee crime before it is committed, thereby enabling the police to prevent it. The title vision is of one of a series of brutal stabbings, this one unique in that Mary feels drawn to the unknown murderer. Her vision leads her to an abandoned tower to meet him face to face, even though she intuits that he means to kill her. The murderer is her brother, a self-proclaimed demon and vampire, who has killed his ex-girl friends when they refused to let him drink menstrual blood. During the confrontation at the tower Mary must confront her own private demon, the long-suppressed memory of her brother's sexual assault upon her when she was but six. The attack included his pushing a bat into her vaginal cavity. In a horrifying scene of poetic justice in the best Gothic tradition Mary defends herself from the present murderous attack by stirring the bats in the tower telepathically. In fury they tear the brother to death. *The Vision*, while unpleasant in detail, proves a more sophisticated handling of the psychological price paid to real or imagined hidden fears.

The private investigator tackling a case tinged with occult overtones must accommodate his usual practical approach to the case. The title character in Ron Goulart's "The Return of Max Kearny" (1981) receives an invitation for a visit to Hollow Hills, a well to do area in Connecticut. Kearny, now an advertising man, did work as a "ghost detective," an occult investigator, prior to going into advertising. Although a guest in Hollow Hills, Max is asked to investigate a "haunting." In this development (Max's hosts are real estate agents) the bathtubs wail like banshees, the toilets yodel, and blood flows from the faucets, all occurrences contrived to drive real estate values down. His delving leads him to Nostradamus, a plumber, who wants to be a writer and who speaks in purple prose; Jill Tillman, who is a writer but unpublished; and Boz Snowden, who has stolen Jill's book and published it under his own name. The title of that book, *Curse of the Demon*, hints at the cause of the plummeting real estate prices and at the denouement when Max counsels Jill to use legal, not demon-logical, means to get her fair share of the book's profits. Goulart's play with words, such as evidenced in the naming and the plumber's speech, claim even attention with the occult detectival work in this story.

Poul Anderson's Eric Sherrinford in "The Queen of Air and Darkness" (1971) takes a more objective view of his role in life. He acknowledges the complementary relationship of appearance and reality, illusion and fact, to the point of admitting that he himself is acting out an archetypal pattern, the "rational detective," a far-future version of the old detective of romance. As the sole private investigator on Planet Roland (he recently moved there from Planet Beowulf) Sherrinford receives a case the authorities refuse to follow up. Barbro Cullen, a scientist with an ecological study group, maintains her small son has been kidnapped by the Outlings, remnants of the indigeneous population. To the human settlers huddled in the two cities built on the half of the planet receiving light from the sun, the Outlings are mere myth. One Outway family believes in the Old Folk, as they term them. They leave propitiatory offerings on rocks nearby, honor the sanctity of certain areas by not entering them, and claim to have seen forms flitting by.

Sherrinford acts the part he admits is his. As rational detective he uses not only logical but technological tools at his disposal: heat-detecting devices, weapons, and a jamming device to prevent telepathic transmission if the Outlings can exercise mind reading. His efforts are successful. When he captures an adult Outling, he discovers these people have a highly developed culture, especially advanced in mind reading and mind manipulation. Pushed to the edges of their own planet, they have turned the invaders' weaknesses against them. The Outlings prey upon all the superstitions of the human race, kidnapping their young and then using shapes and shadows suggestive of old haunting myths of legend and folklore. They succeed in keeping the adult humans away. At the same time they give the kidnapped children the illusion of complete freedom from the trials of existence while in reality they have limited freedom to roam as domesticated animals might enjoy. Over and above the solution to the Cullen kidnapping, Sherrinford proves the necessity of some illusion, provided the person recognizes that it serves a deeply embedded need.

James Gunn in *The Magicians* (1976) presents the essential battle of the forces of good and evil in the life of a very unsure private investigator. To emphasize the situation, Gunn heads each chapter with appropriate epigraphs on witchcraft from authorities such as Virgil, Paracelsus, Shakespeare, D. H. Lawrence, and other writers. Kurt Cullen, better known as K. C. or Casey, is no brilliant amateur dabbling in the moral activity which disentangles, nor is he the hard-boiled private investigator ready to tangle with the mean streets. Rather he is an insecure man who spends at least two pages of chapter 2 berating

his own ineptitude both in his chosen work and in his judgment of his fellow man (he has recently been conned out of both his bank account and his girl friend). Life changes for him when he takes a case involving a "covention" of witches and wizards in progress at a local hotel. Despite his self-assuring that he is "another Philip Marlowe" with trouble as his business, Casey is ill-prepared for the intercoven power struggle, one side wanting to use the Art for nefarious purposes, the other to give the Art to the world at large. The predictable ending fulfills the requirements of Gothic romance with a beautiful witch, a Black Mass, lycanthropy, incantations, and other expected manifestations. Counter-magic wins the day.

Even the most fanciful mix of detective, fantasy, and Gothic elements can provide nourishment for the ideas toward which science fiction/fantasy is oriented. Dean Koontz in *The Haunted Earth* (1973) lets the myth determine the reality and reaps an unexpected dividend from the guidance, a not-so-subtle social comment. The titles of the two parts of the novel signal the Gothic contribution: Part I, The Alien Graveyard; Part II, The Beast at Midnight. Science fiction/fantasy provides the near-future world of 2000 in which an alien invasion by the Maseni has not only introduced an alien race into terran civilization but also a new awareness and acceptance of alien beings from human myth. Folklore brings in the werewolves, succubi, vampires, demons, and angels to co-exist with modern stereotypes no less able to give anxiety. These are groups labeled as wop, nigger, the drunken driver, the old-maid school teacher, and other embodiments of modern dreads.

In *The Haunted Earth* two different Maseni hire Jessie Blake of Hell Hound Investigations to ferret out the facts surrounding the death of a blood brother. (A second private eye, Jess Myers, carries on a parallel investigation into a second such death.) Aided by his special associate, the Hellhound Brutus, and his secretary Helena, Blake turns up not a murder but an elaborate cover-up of a planned invasion of the Maseni planet. Koontz sends his hero-detective on an adventure through all the old and new fears of humanity. Blake is attacked by a vampire, turned to stone by Medusa, helped by a Shambler (a Maseni bogeyman), but is rescued in a most commonplace way by the Los Angeles Police Department. While Koontz's novel sounds ridiculous in this brief summary, it does force re-examination of the source of prejudice, often the stuff of which myth is made. Stereotypes often cloak the fear of difference in another or project a personal weakness. Koontz also opens

up another idea; once a myth is taken as fact, it loses its ability to cause fear, for facts can be dealt with and controlled.

Not all fears are hidden. Some are political and as such find a too solid base in our experience, either directly or through media reports. Frank Lauria in *The Seth Papers* (1979) suggests a modern parallel embodied in a search for ancient artifacts with psychic window-dressing. Dr. Owen Orient is hounded from his job by a quasi-governmental organization, the Company. Although a medical doctor, Orient also operates under two aliases, Mark Rider and Pietro Fermi. Since he has done advanced work in psychical training, the Company wants his aid in their work, definitely non-peaceful in its intent. He escapes them but in so doing finds himself being stalked by a neo-fascist group bent on imposing totalitarian rule worldwide. They also wish psychic help and search for the Hand of Seth, a mummified hand presumably imbued with great psychic power. After a series of daring exploits, wild car chases, and a dramatic burning of the Hand of Seth it comes to light that the Company is engaged in Operation Orient Express, playing the fascist group against Orient and vice versa. Orient almost out-Bonds James Bond with the aid of a lovely, defecting female Company agent and resolves to turn his psychic powers to peaceful, not military or totalitarian ends.

In this brief overview of science fiction/fantasy mystery's awareness of things unknown, unknowable but intuited, one factor emerges. The authors all demonstrate the different ways in which human beings try to manage or solve the puzzle of the Other. Customary behavior, words, organized ritual, all are designed to give the characters control. In the course of the battle of control certain words have come to indicate the direction of that control: black magic, white magic, or sympathetic magic. In science fiction/fantasy Gothic mystery a new term has been bred, particularly to merge science to the occult: forensic sorcery.

Randall Garrett in his series character Lord Darcy presents an official investigator who utilizes the resources of forensic sorcery. Lord Darcy, Chief Investigator of H.R.H. Prince Richard, Duke of Normandy, has enjoyed a long history of successful operations beginning with "The Eyes Have It" (1964) and still functioning well in "The Napoli Express" (1979). Lord Darcy possesses a perceptiveness reminiscent of Sherlock Holmes. Garrett makes certain to make a tenuous connection when in *Too Many Magicians* (1966) Darcy reminds an aide, using a close Sherlockian paraphrase: "Once we have eliminated the impossible, we shall be able to concentrate on the merely improb-

able."[8] Darcy's aide, Master Sorcerer Sean, by contrast, is not a Dr. Watson clone, but a Master in all senses of the word. He is Sean O Lochlainn, Master Sorcerer, Fellow of the Royal Thaumaturgical Society, and Chief Forensic Sorcerer to H.R.H. Richard, Duke of Normandy. The exploits of the two are well chronicled in the four 1964–1973 stories collected as *Murder and Magic* (1979), a second 1974–1979 set of four in *Lord Darcy Investigates* (1981), and the full-length novel, *Too Many Magicians* (1966).

These two worthy cohorts live in an alternate world. Medieval in its hierarchical mode of social organization, it startles an observer with certain technological advances. Even though the internal combustion engine has yet to be invented, the people in Lord Darcy's era use a sophisticated mode of communication, the teleson. They have recently perfected a new "confusion projector" to protect military secrets, a device reminiscent of scramblers in use today. On the other hand, magic is a valid tool of governmental control with spells being utilized to preserve privacy. In this alternate world psi powers complement rational thought and conventional logic. Despite the archaic trappings of the Middle Ages and the pervasive influence of arcane science the crimes are familiar ones: murder, suicide, disappearances, political threats, double agentry, and other subversive activities.

The two investigators recapitulate many of the classic conventions of the Gothic tradition, the detective mode, as well as those derived from science fiction and fantasy. In "The Muddle of the Woad" (1965) Garrett draws on Druidic lore. The title object of "The Ipswich Phial" (1976) contains a psychic shield in the tradition of occult lore, but the shield is a development of a research program in magic being carried on at the Ipswich Laboratories, a respectable governmental research center. Even more modern in their implications are the political enemies often placed on the suspect list: the Serka or Polish Secret Police ("The Ipswich Phial"), the Polish provocateur ("A Case of Identity," 1964); the Holy Society of Ancient Albion, a subversive group in "The Muddle of the Woad"; and the high-placed double agent of *Too Many Magicians*. "The Napoli Express" gives the two investigators opportunity to solve a crime highly reminiscent of the well-known murder on the Orient Express. In *Too Many Magicians* a second murder at a sorcerers' convention involves a locked-door situation and closes with the classic gathering of all suspects with subsequent disclosure of the murderer as the least-likely person. Despite the problems of a symbiosis of such disparate modes, Randall Garrett accomplished the task with skill. Once the reader accepts the premise that in an alternate world thaumaturgic science is a viable and effective tool of knowledge and of criminal investigation, the author rewards him with a most imaginative science fiction/fantasy mystery experience in a conventional setting for science fiction/fantasy—the alternate world.

Randall Garrett's duo provide a fitting place to leave the present consideration of the symbiosis of science fiction/fantasy and mystery fiction. He succeeded in merging conventions from all the modes in one product. The detective, the official policeman, the spy, counter-intelligence, method and magic, rational deliberations, empirical science with its technology balanced by intuitive science and its irreducible elements—all find their places and function in the setting of the science fiction/fantasy world. This set of stories can also provide a starting place for more exhaustive considerations of the various combinations used by science fiction/fantasy writers in effecting a symbiosis with mystery fiction. The authors mentioned in this overview have with some success each in his own way wedded the idea-oriented mode with the situation-oriented mystery mode. Other authors not here mentioned have added additional works awaiting further study. In so doing all have produced books of the minute, of the hour, and time alone will tell if they have produced books for all time.

NOTES

1. Dean R. Koontz, *The Haunted Earth* (New York: Lancer, 1973), p. 73.

2. For an extended treatment see Hazel Pierce, "Ray Bradbury and the Gothic Tradition," in *Ray Bradbury*, ed. Martin Harry Greenberg and Joseph D. Olander (New York: Taplinger, 1980), pp. 165–85.

3. Peter Penzoldt, *The Supernatural in Fiction* (1965; rpt. New York: Humanities Press, 1965), pp. 20–22.

4. Ray Bradbury, *The October Country* (1943; rpt. New York: Ballantine, 1975), p. 211.

5. A similar use of setting can be found in Bradbury's *The Halloween Tree* (1972) and Shirley Jackson's *The Haunting of Hill House* (1959).

6. Hal Clement, "A Question of Guilt" in *The Year's Best Horror Stories*, ed. Gerald W. Page (New York: Daw, 1976), IV, 52.

7. Josef Nesvadha, "Vampire, Ltd." in *Car Sinister*, ed. Robert Silverberg, Martin Harry Greenberg, and Joseph D. Olander (New York: Avon, 1979), p. 35.

8. Randall Garrett, *Too Many Magicians* (New York: Modern Literary Editions Publ. Co., 1966), p. 102.

BIBLIOGRAPHICAL ESSAY

A literary overview demands a broad selection of primary sources for exposition and illustration. Even so, given the great number of science fiction/fantasy short stories and novels published yearly, it is impossible to mention all pieces available for consideration. Therefore the choice made here was on the basis of accessibility and the need to assure a balanced representation by decades.

To that end the original publication dates assumed a primary importance. These are given in the text in parentheses behind all titles. Since many of the short stories are reprinted in different anthologies or collections of the individual authors' works, they may be located with the aid of reference works such as William Contento, comp., *Index to Science Fiction Anthologies and Collections* (New York: G. K. Hall, 1978), and Neil Barron, ed., *Anatomy of Wonder*, 2nd ed. (New York: R. R. Bowker, 1979). For short stories, when the original dates were not available, the title of the anthology and its date are provided.

Five special collections of short stories devoted to crime and mystery are worth noting. These include two edited by Isaac Asimov, Charles G. Waugh, and Martin H. Greenberg: *The 7 Deadly Sins of Science Fiction* (New York: Fawcett Crest, 1980), and *The 13 Crimes of Science Fiction* (Garden City, N.Y.: Doubleday, 1979). Two others are Miriam deFord's *Space, Time & Crime* (New York: Paperback Library, 1964), and Hans Stefan Santesson, *Crime Prevention in the 30th Century* (New York: Walker, 1969). Peter Nicholls in *The Science Fiction Encyclopedia* also mentions *Space Police* (1956), edited by Andre Norton.

Recent years have seen much activity in the production of useful reference books for science fiction/fantasy. Of value for this study was *The Science Fiction Encyclopedia*, Peter Nicholls, ed. (Garden City, N.Y.: Doubleday,

1979), with the entry on Crime and Punishment, contributed by Brian Stable-ford and Peter Nicholls, as an excellent starting point for study. The above-mentioned *Anatomy of Wonder*, edited by 1982 Pilgrim Award winner Neil Barron, offers not only short summaries of selected novels and collections but also has a valuable section on Research Aids. Other aids for this research worth noting include Roger C. Schlobin's *The Literature of Fantasy: A Comprehensive, Annotated Bibliography of Modern Fantasy Fiction* (New York: Garland, 1979) with its inclusive introduction of fantasy as a mode; Donald H. Tuck's *The Encyclopedia of Science Fiction and Fantasy Through 1968*, 2 vols. (Chicago: Advent, 1974, 1978); and *A Research Guide to Science Fiction Studies: An Annotated Checklist of Primary and Secondary Sources for Fantasy and Science Fiction*, Marshall Tymn, Roger C. Schlobin, and L. W. Currey, eds. (New York: Garland, 1977).

The general history of both science fiction/fantasy and the mystery mode has been well documented and presented by authors who themselves are or have been practitioners of the mode they record: Brian Aldiss in *Billion Year Spree: The True History of Science Fiction* (New York: Schocken, 1974); Julian Symons, *Mortal Consequences: A History from the Detective Story to the Crime Novel* (New York: Schocken, 1973); and H. P. Lovecraft, *Supernatural Horror in Literature* (1945; rpt. New York: Dover, 1973). Recent years have brought out helpful quick-reference books. As companion volumes to the first two histories above, the following are useful: *A Reader's Guide to Science Fiction*, Baird Searles, Martin Last, Beth Meacham, and Michael Franklin, eds. (New York: Avon, 1979); *Detectionary*, Otto Penzler, Chris Steinbrunner and Marvin Lachman, eds. (New York: Ballantine, 1977); and *Murder Ink: The Mystery Reader's Companion*, Dilys Winn, ed. (New York: Workman, 1977).

To recognize the problems inherent in the symbiotic process with science fiction/fantasy and the various members of the mystery mode, it is helpful to review not only history but the specific contributions of each of the partners. *Science Fiction: History, Science, Vision*, co-authored by Robert Scholes and Eric Rabkin (London: Oxford Univ. Press, 1977) gives a brief introduction to the sciences involved in that mode as well as of form and themes conventional to it. More specialized information about the early scientific detectives is available in Sam Moskowitz's *Science Fiction by Gaslight* (1968; rpt. Westport, Conn.: Hyperion, 1974), and *Under the Moons of Mars* (New York: Holt, Rinehart & Winston, 1970). These companion volumes together cover the years of 1891–1911 and 1912–1920 respectively and contain historical data, expository material, and reprinted stories of the period, several representative of the early merging of science fiction/fantasy and mystery/crime. Sam J. Lundwall's *Science Fiction: What It's All About* (New York: Ace, 1971) presents an informed discussion of the influence of Gernsback and Campbell.

In addition to the Julian Symons history that covers all aspects of the mystery mode there are more specialized treatments, particularly of the detective story, an understandable majority in light of its long period of popularity. Some useful sources are Howard Haycraft's *Murder for Pleasure: The Life and Times of the Detective Story*, Enlarged Ed. (1941; rpt. New York: Biblo and Tannen, 1974); A. E. Murch, *The Development of the Detective Novel* (1958; rpt. Westport, Conn.: Greenwood Press, 1975); and H. Douglas Thomson, *Masters of Mystery: A Study of the Detective Story* (1931; rpt. New York: Dover, 1978). *Queen's Quorum* (New York: Biblo and Tannen, 1969) by Ellery Queen gives a history of the detective-crime story through brief expository introductions followed by a summary list of 125 classic books ranging from 1845 to 1967. Chris Steinbrunner and Otto Penzler's *Encyclopedia of Mystery and Detection* (New York: McGraw-Hill, 1976) is indispensable for factual information.

The detective story is also well documented as to pattern and central character. For a more complete understanding of the detective-figure as established in his early appearance one finds serious attention given to it in Ian Ousby, *Bloodhounds of Heaven: The Detective in English Fiction from Godwin to Doyle* (Cambridge, Mass.: Harvard Univ. Press, 1976). Howard Haycraft's *The Art of the Mystery Story* (1946; rpt. New York: Biblo and Tannen, 1976) brings under one convenient cover a collection of landmark essays on the whodunit, including the introduction by Dorothy Sayers to her *Omnibus of Crime*, the "rules of the game" as promulgated by S. S. Van Dine, Monsignor Knox, and the Detection Club; and Raymond Chandler's "The Simple Art of Murder."

Several scholars have foreshadowed the increasing use of the detective conventions in science fiction/fantasy. J. O. Bailey in *Pilgrims Through Space and Time: Trends and Patterns in Scientific and Utopian Fiction* (1947; rpt. Westport, Conn.: Greenwood Press, 1972) has a section entitled "Crime and Detection," pp. 184–87, noting the "overlapping" of the detective story into science fiction. Frank D. McSherry has long been intrigued by the combinations of the two modes as testified by two articles in the *Armchair Detective*: "A New Category of the Mystery Story" (October 1968) and "Under Two Flags: The Detective Story in Science Fiction" (April 1969). The former, reprinted as "The Janus Resolution" in *The Mystery Writer's Art*, Francis M. Nevins, Jr., ed. (Bowling Green, Ohio: Bowling Green Univ. Popular Press, 1970) suggests a different product is being offered in the fusion of the mystery-detective-police story with occult or fantasy fiction.

Studies combining history and criticism on the other various members of the mystery mode are many and wide-ranging. Of help in understanding the contribution of the thriller genre to science fiction/fantasy are Jerry Palmer, *Thrillers: Genesis of a Popular Genre* (New York: St. Martin's Press, 1979), and Ralph Harper, *The World of the Thriller* (Cleveland, Ohio: Case Western Reserve Univ. Press, 1969). The former works a formal and historical perspective while the latter considers thrillers from a philosophical and psychological point of view. Nadya Aisenberg, *A Common Spring: Crime Novel and Classic* (Bowling Green, Ohio: Bowling Green Univ. Popular Press, 1979) explores the debt the crime novel and the thriller owes to myth and folk tales.

The Gothic tradition, a long-established form, has also been studied at length both in history and criticism. Some standard treatments of the Gothic novel worth consulting are Edith Birkhead, *The Tale of Terror* (1921; rpt. New York: Russell and Russell, 1963); Ernest A. Baker, *The History of the English Novel: The Novel of Sentiment and the Gothic Romance* (London: Witherby, 1929); Montague Summers, *The Gothic Quest: A History of the Gothic Novel* (New York: Russell & Russell, 1938); and Devendra P. Varma, *The Gothic Flame* (New York: Russell & Russell, 1957). Jack Sullivan, *Elegant Nightmares: The English Ghost Story from LeFanu to Blackwood* (Athens, Ohio: Ohio Univ. Press, 1978) offers insight into the character of the psychic detective as used by LeFanu and Blackwood in the context of the ghost story. Peter Penzoldt in *The Supernatural in Fiction* (1952; rpt. New York: Humanities Press, 1965) lists and discusses the creatures of folklore also borrowed by science fiction/fantasy mystery stories.

Commentators on science fiction/fantasy mystery have acknowledged the use of the Gothic traditions by the later mode. Thomas H. Keeling in "Science Fiction and the Gothic" included in *Bridges to Science Fiction* (Carbondale, Ill.: Southern Illinois Univ. Press, 1980) discusses the general ground on which the two meet. Hazel Pierce's "Ray Bradbury and the Gothic Tradition" in *Ray Bradbury* (New York: Taplinger Press, 1980) focuses on the use to which that well-known science fiction/fantasy writer has put the various Gothic conventions. Donald L. Lawler's anthology *Approaches to Science Fiction* (Boston: Houghton Mifflin, 1978) devotes one section to an expository presentation and several short stories illustrating "Mystery and Horror Science Fiction."

The police crime story tends to follow closely the patterns established by the detective story. Indeed, many of the early detectives were police officials. Their stories tended to be classified more as tales of crime. Nadya Aisenberg in the earlier-noted *A Common Spring* devotes part of her study to the debt owed to myth and folklore by the crime story. On the other hand, the police procedural, the latest variation of the detective/crime story, has found only a few scholars viewing it with a critical eye. George N. Dove's five-part discussion in the *Armchair Detective* of April 1977–1978 offers a balanced look at this modification of the crime story. In "The Police Procedural," in *The Mystery Story*, John Ball, ed. (Del Mar, Calif.: Publisher's Inc., 1976) author Hillary Waugh adds the writer's perspective to the subject, bringing in data from his own experience in writing police procedurals.

To bring a richer appreciation to the science fiction/fantasy crime mysteries a reader may need to go outside the field of fiction and delve into the history of crime prevention, crime psychology, history of police organization, especially of Scotland Yard, and outstanding police personalities such as France's Vidocq. The latter's own *Mémoires* being inaccessible to many contemporary readers, Samuel Edwards' biography, *The Vidocq Dossier: The Story of the World's First Detective* (New York: Houghton Mifflin, 1977) is a worthwhile substitute. Sir Ronald Howe's *The Story of Scotland Yard: A History of the C.I.D. from the Earliest Times to the Present Day* (New York: Horizon Press, 1966), and T. A. Critchley's *A History of Police in England and Wales 900 – 1966* (London: Constable, 1967) provide reliable factual information. To add a bit of contemporary flavor, one may wish to read the reflections by Charles Dickens on the Detective Police of his era as published in the July-September 1850 and the April 1851 issues of *Household Words*.

The reader more interested in the psychology of crime than the organizational matters will find it of more than academic interest to compare non-literary treatments with science fiction/fantasy mystery presentations. Stuart Palmer, *The Psychology of Murder* (New York: Crowell, 1960); Richard Quinney, *The Problem of Crime* (New York: Dodd, Mead, 1975); and Herbert A. Block and Gilbert Geis, *Man, Crime, and Society: The Forms of Criminal Behavior* (New York: Random House, 1962) provide intriguing information to compare with the classic study of the literary crime figures in Frank Wadleigh Chandler's two-volume *The Literature of Roguery* (Boston: Houghton Mifflin, 1907). The specialized figure of modern political importance is discussed by Stephen Schaefer in *The Political Criminal: The Problem of Morality and Crime* (New York: The Free Press, Macmillan, 1974).

Once the patterns of contemporary crime are clear, it becomes informative to extrapolate as have some literary men and also some non-fictional critics. Gene Stephens represents the latter group with "Crime in the Year 2000" published in *The Futurist*, April 1981, pp. 49–52. Frank McSherry's "The Shape of Crimes to Come" in *The Mystery Writer's Art*, ed. Francis M. Nevins, Jr. (Bowling Green, Ohio: Bowling Green Univ. Popular Press, 1970), pp. 326–38, offers speculation on contemporary trends that augur different perspectives on crime in the coming years. McSherry buttresses his speculation with references to authors who already have addressed the matter with success.

Any bibliographical treatment of the topic of science fiction/fantasy mystery fiction would be incomplete without due notice accorded to major scholarly magazines and newsletters dedicated to information on the various genres. For up-to-date information on new publications, as well as pertinent articles by authors and critics, these are of value: *Locus: The Newspaper of the Science Fiction Field* (Locus Publications, Oakland, Calif.), *Fantasy Newsletter* (Florida Atlantic University, Boca Raton, Fla.), and the *Science Fiction & Fantasy*

Book Review, a publication of the Science Fiction Research Association.

Even though the specialized subject of this book does not command attention in each issue, the articles in the scholarly magazines do provide valuable background information and diverse critical treatments of relevant subjects. Of special note in the science fiction/fantasy field are *Extrapolation*, a quarterly published by Kent State University Press, Kent, Ohio, and *Science-Fiction Studies* of SFS Publications, Montréal, Québec, Canada. *The Armchair Detective* (Mysterious Press, New York City) offers informative articles on detective stories, thrillers, and police procedurals. In addition, *TAD* periodically includes the "Classic Corner: Rare Tales from the Archives," featuring reprints of early stories from eras such as that of the scientific detective. From Bowling Green University Popular Press, Bowling Green, Ohio, come two additional publications: *Clues: A Journal of Detection* and the *Journal of Popular Culture*.

Even as the books and magazines mentioned in this Bibliographical Essay offer a starting point for the reader interested in science fiction/fantasy mysteries, the increasing interest in the product of the symbiosis promises additional comments in the future. The combined work of authors and scholars can do no less than assure readers of imaginative and intellectually stimulating experiences to come.

INDEX

About the Author

HAZEL BEASLEY PIERCE is Professor of English at Kearney State College in Nebraska. She has contributed to the critical surveys *Asimov, Bradbury,* and *Survey of Science Fiction* and is the author of *A Reader's Guide to Philip K. Dick.*